STALIN'S OUTCASTS

STALIN'S OUTCASTS

Aliens, Citizens, and the Soviet State,
1926–1936

GOLFO ALEXOPOULOS

CORNELL UNIVERSITY PRESS

Ithaca and London

First published 2003 by Cornell University Press

Printed in the United States of America

Library of Congress Cataloging-in-Publication Data

Alexopoulos, Golfo.
    Stalin's outcasts : aliens, citizens, and the Soviet state, 1926–1936
/ Golfo Alexopoulos.
        p. cm.
Includes bibliographical references and index.
    ISBN 0-8014-4029-7 (cloth : alk. paper)
    1. Citizenship—Soviet Union.   2. Political rights—Soviet Union.   3.
Marginality, Social—Soviet Union.   4. Class consciousness—Soviet
Union.   5. Soviet Union—Politics and government—1917–1936.   I. Title.
    JN6583 .A64 2003
    323.3'222'0947—dc21   2002012223

Cornell University Press strives to use environmentally responsible
suppliers and materials to the fullest extent possible in the publishing
of its books. Such materials include vegetable-based, low-VOC inks,
and acid-free papers that are recycled, totally chlorine-free, or partly
composed of nonwood fibers. For further information, visit our website
at www.cornellpress.cornell.edu.

Cloth printing   10 9 8 7 6 5 4 3 2 1

Για τους γονείς μου με άπειρη αγάπη και ευγνωμοσύνη

Contents

Acknowledgments

Whoever lamented the solitude of academic work never had to do research in or about Russia. So many people made important contributions to this book, and my work is the product of their generous assistance. I cannot express the full extent of my gratitude to Sheila Fitzpatrick for her generous support and rigorous instruction over the years. At the University of Chicago where my research began, she tirelessly offered guidance and advice, and her creative influence runs throughout these pages. Ronald Grigor Suny helped me to identify and make sense of many key issues in the book, and I am especially grateful for his support and words of encouragement always. Colin Lucas provided constant support and important insights on earlier drafts of this work, and gave me the benefit of a comparative perspective. I also thank Richard Hellie and Misha Danos for their comments and suggestions. I feel very fortunate to have had a truly remarkable cohort at the University of Chicago. They helped me at various stages in the process, and their friendship and lively conversation so often transformed my work into pleasure. In particular, I thank Julie Hessler, Terry Martin, and Matt Payne.

The assistance of various scholars, archivists, and friends in Russia made this book possible. My warmest thanks to Nikolai Ivnitskii, Oleg Khlevniuk, and Sophia Somonova, whose friendship and assistance greatly facilitated my work in Moscow. In 1992, Tatiana Pavlova gave me permission to work in what was then a closed archive in Western Siberia. I extend my warmest appreciation to her, to the wonderful director of the Ialutorovsk archive, Nelli Vakulenko, and to the great staff there, especially Valentina Nikonova and Liudmila Bochkina. I have the fondest memories of my life in this small town and I thank those who received me so kindly. Finally, I owe an immeasurable debt to Sergei, Nastia, and Sasha Dubinski. They welcomed me into their home during various trips to Tiumen and Ialutorovsk, and assisted me through numerous difficulties relatied to work and everyday life. The material for this book could not have been discovered and presented here without the help of these dear friends.

My deepest appreciation to the special few who enormously enhanced and supported my work over the years: Deborah Camiel, Patricia Clifford, Renee De Nevers, Cori Field, Andrew Grant-Thomas, Maria Gough, Susan Hyland, James H. Johnson, Judith Kalb, Armando Maggi, Mark Marquardt, Alexander Ogden, Alexis Papadopoulos, Dan and Irina Peris, Marilyn Smith, Jeffrey Rossman, Valerie Sperling, Brian Taylor, and Myron Williams. I am very grateful to those who read drafts, assisted with illustrations, offered information on sources and archives, and gave me the benefit of their intellect at crucial moments in the process of my research: Dan Berkowitz, Svetlana Boym, Vladimir Brovkin, Eleni Gregoriadou, Steve Harris, Michael Herzfeld, Ippokratis Kantzios, Yanni Kotsonis, Mark Kramer, Larry Lessig, John Mickelson, Galina Moiseeva, Sally Falk Moore, Ben Polak, Sophia and Ivan Rabodzeenko, and Nana Tuntia. I also thank Christina Druck, Aliona Gregoriadou, Laura Heffner, and Debbie Maris.

My exceptional colleagues (past and present) at the University of South Florida deserve special mention. They read my work, offered guidance and advice, and created a stimulating and supportive work environment. In particular, I thank Giovanna Benadusi, Alejandro de la Fuente, Laura Edwards, Marcie Finkelstein, Kirsten Fischer, Robert Ingalls (who read the entire manuscript), Christine Lisetti, Victor Peppard, Darrell Slider, and Ward Stavig. I also thank my enthusiastic students at USF who have patiently received various parts of this book in classes, and who taught me to keep things simple. For financial support, I acknowledge Fulbright-Hays, the International Research and Exchanges Board (IREX), the Social Science Research Council (SSRC), the Center for Advanced Studies in Peace and International Cooperation at the University of Chicago, the University of South Florida, and the Mellon Foundation. Harvard University's Davis Center for Russian Studies also provided material support in the form of a postdoctoral fellowship, plus valuable input from a brilliant community of Russian scholars. I gratefully acknowledge Merrill C. Berman for his very kind contribution of the Radakov image. Roger Haydon, Teresa Jesionowski, and the anonymous reviewers at Cornell University Press gave generously of their time to significantly improve this work and to help make the book a reality. I am enormously appreciative.

Finally, I warmly acknowledge the important people who inspired me to pursue creative work and to study Russia: Paul Bushkovich, John Bushnell, Catherine Deans-Barrett, Douglas Kornelly, Anna Linden, Leon Lipson, Richard Panitch, Irwin Weil, and especially, David Joravsky. My kind and generous brother, Greg Alexopoulos, always provided moral support and financial aid without my even asking, for which I am profoundly thankful. My deep, heartfelt appreciation to my husband, Thomas W. Smith, whose constant love and support made the final year of this project wonderful and especially memorable. I am indebted to my amazing sister, Lia Alexopoulos, who helped me in innumerable ways, from the very beginnings of this project right down to its completion. This book is dedicated to my parents, George G. Alexopoulos and Pola Polydorou Alexopoulos, who taught me the pleasure and wonder of foreign places. For all they did for me, this is my modest gift.

GOLFO ALEXOPOULOS

Tampa, Florida

Introduction

They told me in Moscow that I would have to go to Siberia, and I imagined trekking through the snow in search of this mysterious archive that had never opened its doors to a foreigner. I was fortunate to meet someone who would drive me there, a historian himself who spent his entire life in Tiumen, the larger city two hours from this alleged archive. Sergei insisted that there could be no large warehouse of classified state records in the tiny agricultural town of Ialutorovsk, because no historian in the area, including himself, had ever heard of its existence. It was early in 1992, just months after the collapse of the Soviet Union, and a great deal remained unknown and open to discovery. But I began to share Sergei's doubts about my blind journey east when the address I had located in Moscow for this Siberian archive placed us on the remote edge of town. A tall concrete wall topped with barbed wire and an unmarked door made no impression from the street, but Sergei noticed it and pulled over to ask someone for directions. The policeman inside told us that we had reached our destination.

It was here that the Soviet regime stored personal records for the millions who were deprived of rights in the Stalin era and known as the *lishentsy*, a Russian word which literally means "the deprived" but is often translated as "the disenfranchised."[1] These voices from the 1920s–1930s were thought to have been silenced by the regime, yet this closed archive preserved over 100,000 case files that documented the lives of old and young, with artifacts such as photographs, newspaper clippings, questionnaires, character references, handwritten appeals to Soviet authorities and, in almost each case, the Kremlin's final decision to reinstate rights. A 43-year-old former tsarist official claimed to "deserve the

1

title and rights of a Soviet citizen," and a 72-year-old trader crafted a lengthy biographical narrative in which he asked officials for "the chance to live as a Soviet citizen without the onerous stigma of the *lishentsy*."[2] Members of the Party Central Committee, so notorious for rendering summary justice, devoted remarkable attention to the details of these personal narratives and, in many cases, chose to rehabilitate their victims. Who were these outcasts of the Soviet regime and how were they able to so vigorously and successfully engage the system that had expelled them?

The Identities of Soviet Outcasts

Every national community identifies its members and aliens, but Vladimir Lenin's revolutionary government approached this task like no other in history.[3] The full rights of membership in Soviet Russia's "great laboring family" was largely reserved for persons considered "proletariat" whereas the "bourgeois classes" represented Soviet outcasts or aliens. For Bolshevik leaders, class defined the new polity in an expansive and transnational way, as a political community of the world proletariat. Rejecting residency, ethnicity, and language as the criteria of citizenship in bourgeois nation states, Lenin's Bolshevik party instead defined the Soviet political community along class lines, consistent with the principle of solidarity among workers of all nations.[4] Shortly after the October revolution, class was so central in defining the new polity that foreigners who were members of the working class enjoyed "all the political rights of Soviet citizens" whereas Russian nationals of bourgeois origin were denied membership in the community of the proletariat.[5] For nearly two decades, people considered to have bourgeois identity represented Soviet Russia's noncitizen aliens and provided the contrasting image for defining the new proletarian citizenry.

A series of laws formalized Russia's ideological boundary, divided perceived bourgeois and proletarian elements, and granted the full rights of belonging to those with working-class credentials. The Bolshevik regime denied bourgeois elements rights that nations typically reserve for citizens, such as public assistance, military and civil service, and voting rights. According to Lenin, proletarian democracy "consists, first of all, in the fact that the working class are the voters and the exploiting masses, the bourgeoisie, are excluded."[6] According to the 1918 Constitution of the Russian Republic or RSFSR, the bourgeois classes who could not vote included perceived capitalist elements and distrusted holdovers from the old regime, namely: private traders, clerics, agents of the tsarist police and

White Army, persons who hired labor for the purpose of profit or who lived off unearned income, and all others believed to hinder socialist revolution in some way.

By the late 1920s, people without voting rights lost myriad other essential rights as well, such as access to housing, employment, education, medical care, and a ration card for essential food items, and many experienced more severe punishment like arrest and compulsory labor on the construction projects of Stalin's First Five-Year Plan. In Stalin's Russia, deprivation of voting rights meant much more than disenfranchisement as bourgeois aliens represented legal outcasts and enemies of the state. One man would write to Soviet authorities from his place of exile, "I've been deprived of all human rights and people can do anything they want with me and no one will defend or protect me. I can die of hunger, freeze from the cold."[7] From Lenin's 1918 Constitution that identified the various categories of bourgeois aliens to Stalin's 1936 Constitution, which formally abandoned them, disenfranchisement condemned millions to the status of outcast. Annual figures on the numbers of people without rights in the RSFSR remain inconsistent, but in the peak years of the policy the Soviet state bureaucracy registered roughly four million disenfranchised people.[8] This figure is probably deceiving and low as many dropped off the local state registries after their arrest or deportation by the secret police (*GPU-OGPU-NKVD*),[9] whereas others managed to evade the authorities and conceal their identity.

The present work examines the policy of disenfranchisement as a site where citizens, outcasts, and Soviet officials articulated the identities and attributes of those who belonged to their community and those who did not. Since the book represents a study of the uses and practices of inclusion and exclusion, it focuses on the decade 1926–1936. In these years, the campaign to excise alien social elements became coupled with a distinct "rite of passage" that restored rights to those who had undergone a personal transformation.[10] The elaborate system for returning rights to outcasts constituted a Soviet ritual of passage, as those who sought to re-enter Soviet society had to demonstrate their worthiness in prescribed ways.[11] The deprivation and the reinstatement of rights form two aspects of a single campaign to construct a national community of the proletariat. The mass, dual process of denying and restoring rights to outcasts offers a privileged site for examining the social and cultural content of a class-based political community that emerged during the formative years of Stalin's revolution.

Moreover, in the final decade of disenfranchisement policy, the penalties for being denied voting rights intensified sharply and created a class of outcasts among the enfranchised citizenry who faced popular suspicion and discrimination as well as arrest and deportation.[12] Also in these years, disenfranchisement became a campaign of mass mobilization and participation. Not only Kremlin leaders but also local officials, communities, and outcasts themselves engaged the process of classifying proletarian citizens and bourgeois aliens. People from various segments of society helped to define aliens and to determine both the range of acceptable citizen-selves and the terms of social membership in the Stalinist state. In his work on the making of France and Spain in the Pyrenees, Peter Sahlins argued that state formation is a two-way process and that local society constitutes "a motive force in the formation and consolidation of nationhood."[13] Similarly, in the vast territory of Russia under Stalin, local practices shaped the contours of the Soviet political boundary. Disenfranchisement and reinstatement of rights reveal the boundary of a new national community, the terms of exclusion and inclusion, and the characteristics of aliens and citizens as understood by citizens, state agents, and outcasts themselves. This work examines how class was lived in Soviet Russia, that is, how a broad population assigned bourgeois and proletarian identities.

Policies designed to excise dangerous alien elements from the civic body require extensive state and public participation for the surveillance, identification, and classification of individuals, and disenfranchisement was no exception.[14] The Stalinist campaign to purge society of nonlaboring, parasitic elements involved a massive mobilization of resources. On the one hand, the secret police pursued the so-called bourgeois specialists, private traders during the New Economic Policy or Nepmen, "former people" as well as the rich and exploiting capitalist class of peasants in the countryside, the reviled kulaks. One cannot precisely separate disenfranchisement from the campaigns of police repression that targeted class alien elements and other enemy groups in these years. But by focusing on a campaign of mass mobilization that involved ordinary civilians in a process of identifying aliens, one can begin to explore the various shades and layers of Stalinist repression, the popular cultural resonance of exclusionary policies, and the expansive yet unstable character of Soviet control.

Lenin's 1918 Constitution outlined the general categories of people marked for disenfranchisement, but formal law does not fully convey who was vulnerable to the loss of voting rights. Rather, the actual practices of classifying bourgeois enemies reveals the underlying assumptions that animate this law.[15] Sheila Fitzpatrick's studies of class identity in revolutionary Russia describe a policy of "ascribing class" in which the new Bolshevik regime "classed" its population, and people in turn adopted these forms of civic self-definition. Her work describes how the Communist

Party leadership determined bourgeois and proletarian identities according to such indicators as current social position, former (prewar or prerevolutionary) social position, and parents' social status or "genealogy." For example, Soviet leaders marked educated professionals, whom they grouped among the prerevolutionary privileged elite, as bourgeois specialists.[16] The personal questionnaire (*anketa*) in the dossiers of some outcasts highlights the importance that party officials placed on these and other indicators of identity, such as former estate (*soslovie*); profession and place of employment before 1914, 1914–1917, 1917–1919, 1919 to the present; income before 1917, before 1922, and since 1922; material position or property; service in the Imperial army, WWI, the Red Army, the White Army; trips abroad and the reason for foreign travel; past arrests, level of education; membership in a trade union or political party.[17] The party understood these as fundamental markers of a person's loyalty to the regime, which is why officials took exceptional interest in the biographical minutia of Russia's population.

In addition, cultural predispositions determined class ascriptions in fundamental ways. Orlando Figes and Boris Kolonitskii describe how the highly pejorative term "bourgeois" expressed various meanings for the participants of the 1917 Russian revolution, including foreigner, Jew, heartless and corrupt boss, speculative trader, parasite or one who profits from another's hunger, deceitful, greedy, rude, and arrogant, even well-dressed and articulate. In the late 1920s, despite their working-class credentials, Russians who labored on the Turksib railroad but expressed ethnic hatred toward Kazakhs bore the stigma of class alien elements for their chauvinistic behavior.[18] Lynne Viola also revealed that outsiders, marginal, educated people, and others were often grouped among the rural bourgeoisie, the rich peasant or "kulak" class.[19] Similarly, the familiar groups of undesirables fell victim to disenfranchisement. Those who lost their rights included social deviants and marginals such as prostitutes, gamblers, the infirm and elderly, tax evaders, embezzlers, ethnic minorities, and Jews, in particular. At a March 1929 meeting of the party fraction of the VTsIK Presidium, Aron Solts described how "the most diverse mix of people for the most varied reasons is being disenfranchised."[20]

Despite the haphazard nature of disenfranchisement on the ground, patterns of classification are evident, nonetheless. Ideology combined with local interests and cultural understandings to determine the identities of outcasts and citizens. In particular, the actions of local practitioners demonstrate that individuals reproduced an ideological schema that identified aliens as nonlaboring, privileged exploiters and citizens as the suffering, exploited laborers. A legal partition did not merely divide abstract proletarian elements from bourgeois aliens but, more concretely, distinguished productive laborers from parasitic elements and exploited victims from villainous exploiters. Party leaders, communities, and individuals attributed particular traits and behaviors to Marx's two opposing classes, and these personal characteristics determined the geography of Soviet Russia's distinct political boundary. The reviled "class alien elements" included not only the old regime elites but also the millions of others who committed the familiar inventory of disloyal and deviant acts that typically characterized class enemies.[21] Insiders and outsiders were defined not simply in class terms but in accordance with the attributes and behaviors that became synonymous with class.

Social Engineering and Stalin's New Citizens

The party's implementation of a formal rehabilitation mechanism in 1926 demonstrates its desire to not only institute a policy of exclusion and discrimination but also to engineer a new political community. Mikhail Kalinin, chairman of the Soviet Executive Committee (*TsIK*) argued that the Soviet Union was "creating a new man, whose characteristic traits must be quite different from those of the man who grew up in the capitalist world."[22] The Kremlin leadership insisted that revolutionary politics could refashion human nature and society, and this belief was shared by radical European movements elsewhere, for example, in France, Germany, Italy, and Yugoslavia.[23] Rehabilitation required that people abandon past activities, personal associations, and dependencies and instead demonstrate loyalty to Soviet power and public-sector employment. In order to be reinstated in rights, outcasts had to submit formal appeals to their local Soviet officials, and these typically included a petition narrative as well as letters of reference and attestations from neighbors, bosses, and coworkers. In each personal petition for the reinstatement of rights, Soviet officials looked for evidence of a converted outcast. If the practices of exclusion reveal the kinds of people who were vulnerable to the loss of rights, rites of passage illustrate the range of individually constructed and officially sanctioned citizen identities.

The party leadership pursued its goal of re-educating and transforming citizens in various spheres, as a number of historians have well noted. Studies concerning Soviet women, workers, and ethnic minorities, party affairs, and cultural policy describe how the new regime endeavored to make individuals a site for socialist construction.[24] The rehabilitation of outcasts provides a vivid picture of the Soviet social-engineering project, and in a unique context where people once considered enemies of the state represent the objects of coerced transformation. Although studies have concentrated on the exclusion of groups of people from the Soviet body politic, few explore questions related to the eventual social reintegration of some of these repressed groups. The story of those Soviet outcasts who survived years of repression and somehow managed to regain their rights illustrates the contradictions and opposing objectives of Soviet repressive policies. The goals of purging undesirable elements from the body politic and engineering a new Soviet person were not pursued in different domains, nor were these tasks the sole purview of either the secret police or, say, the trade unions and women's sections. Rather, the goal to coercively engineer a new society proved so fundamental and ubiquitous that even class-alien elements became the targets of socialist transformation.

How did outcasts respond to Soviet social engineering? As much as they were able, those without rights pursued civic incorporation in various ways. Writing about the victims of Auschwitz, Primo Levi stated that "If the drowned have no story, and single and broad is the path to perdition, the paths to salvation are many, difficult and improbable."[25] Similarly, for the disenfranchised, journeys to a life with simply more rights than none proved multiple and remarkable, although the Soviet regime insisted on a single path of its own design. Some people fled to new regions, forged new identity papers, or otherwise concealed their past.[26] Many others made successful appeals for the reinstatement of their rights, filing hundreds of thousands of petitions for rehabilitation and deploying a diversity of narrative strategies to vindicate themselves. Although the memoirs of Gulag prisoners describe how the secret police also accepted the petitions of prisoners and family members, anecdotal evidence suggests that sentences were rarely reviewed, much less reversed, on the basis of these appeals.[27] By contrast, many of the disenfranchised in the late 1920s and early 1930s managed to regain their rights or otherwise reintegrate themselves into Soviet society after enduring the hardships of discrimination, deportation, and forced labor following their loss of rights.

Case files of the disenfranchised include personal petitions for the reinstatement of rights, and this book's systematic sample of over five hundred of these petitions reveals a number of surprising elements. In the course of a decade characterized by the formation of a hegemonic Stalinist culture, party leaders consistently accepted a wide range of appeals for rights. The gatekeepers of the Soviet polity were supposed to reward successful personal transformations, to grant rights in exchange for demonstrations of loyalty and productive employment. From 1926 to 1936, the Central Electoral Commission, which included members of the Party Central Committee, accepted a number of often-opposing narratives at a fairly constant rate and did not necessarily favor petitioners who expressed loyalty to Soviet power and a record of socially useful labor. Contradictory principles and practices coexisted in matters of reintegration, and this complexity contrasts sharply with the seemingly homogenous cultural program of the prewar Stalin years.

Successful petitions for the reinstatement of rights reveal the often surprising preferences of party leaders, but they also reflect the lives and identities of Stalin's outcasts. For example, while studies have shown that party members who tried to redeem themselves before purge committees almost uniformly admitted their mistakes and offered stylized confessions in the hope of reinstatement, this pattern was not repeated by the disenfranchised. Appeals from Soviet outcasts only affirm the distinctiveness of party discourse as the disenfranchised, no less desperate than party members to avoid the harsh penalties of exclusion, hardly ever admitted wrongdoing.[28] Some emphasized their productive labor and loyalty, whereas others denied the charges or offered an emotional appeal, one resembling a traditional ritual lament. In the end, personal transformations of the kind the regime hoped to coerce were neither abundant nor uniform, as outcasts regularly offered a range of appeals. A number of works explore the effects of Bolshevik policy on the behavior and identities of individuals and address popular responses such as the internalization of Bolshevik values and practices, resistance and counter-narrative, atomization and fear, or conscious self-fashioning and role playing.[29] Although these studies are often viewed as incompatible, the evidence here suggests that they are not. The present work highlights the unstable and complex outcomes of Soviet social engineering and the various ways in which people confronted the demands of civic incorporation and personal transformation. I offer a mapping of the variety of outcasts' appeals in order to underscore the persistent coexistence of opposing, legitimate narratives in a Stalinist context.

Even at forced labor camps, the consequences of social engineering remained uneven and ambiguous. At OGPU-NKVD labor camps, the regime more brutally coerced outcasts to become productive laborers and undergo a personal transformation. Deportees who labored in the service of Soviet power and derived their material existence from the Soviet economy appeared as the most credible candidates for inclusion, and they well understood this. Ironically, the most severely punished of Stalin's outcasts, the prisoners in OGPU-NKVD forced-labor camps, requested rights with the greatest sense of entitlement. As one man wrote in his petition, "When I came to the labor camp I was immediately directed by the political section of the OGPU to the coal mines . . . where I have good references and over-fulfilled the technical norms . . . I deserve the full reinstatement of rights."[30] Here, the terms of political membership in which the state granted rights in exchange for an individual's productive labor are especially apparent. Stalin established the materiality of rights and their selective distribution in exchange for state service, but his policy created new expectations as well as new citizens.

In contrast to the forced laborers under OGPU-NKVD control, other petitioners made assertions not of an empowered, useful Soviet self but of a disempowered, weak self. Either by design or not, it appears that suffering, too, had become a Bolshevik value. Indeed, some outcasts spoke of their misfortune as though hardship entitled them to social membership. As one petitioner wrote: "I cannot exclude myself from the working class because my sufferings and deprivations are identical with theirs."[31] Accused of being socially harmful, some outcasts challenged this image by presenting themselves as completely innocuous, tragic figures, minor and insignificant, vulnerable, manipulated by persons as well as circumstances. Stories about the individual caught in a cycle of misfortune are similar in style, language, and emotional content. For this reason, I characterize these tragic narratives as a kind of ritual lament. Implicit in the lament is the notion that one cannot be blamed for trading, using hired labor, serving in the tsarist police, and so on, if one is essentially a tragic figure, condemned by unfortunate circumstances beyond his or her control. Both petitioners and Soviet officials apparently shared this common assumption, as laments were not only offered, but they were accepted. A life of suffering and exploitation could confer a Soviet identity.

Not all outcasts could or would transform their lives in the ways required by Soviet law, for this was not a uniform population. Many of the disenfranchised chose flight or concealment, whereas the elderly or disabled among them, together with others who could hardly earn rights through socially useful labor, sought other avenues of integration. Some were reinstated in rights after they secured the support of local officials, citizens, and employers, described the political and economic activities of family members, or recast their personal biographies by inserting themselves into a larger Bolshevik narrative.[32] In pursuit of rights, Soviet outcasts discovered how to effectively engage the system and how to construct both a meaningful identity for themselves and a persuasive identity for Soviet officials. As Stephen Kotkin has argued, Soviet policy proved both coercive and productive, that is, it established constraints that spawned formative and enduring behaviors.[33] On the one hand, outcasts seeking rehabilitation became schooled in a political exercise that involved refashioning oneself, soliciting positive character references, and constructing a compelling personal narrative. At the same time, successful adaptations only generated deeper suspicions among party leaders who wondered whether the practices and pronouncements of outcasts reflected sincere internal transformations or skillful acting. Even worse, they asked if these redeemed citizens were merely wolves in sheep's clothing. Since deceptive behavior represented a fundamental trait of the alien classes, Soviet authorities could never know for sure. In the end, the indeterminacy of social engineering led many party leaders to view the reintegration of outcasts as fundamentally threatening.

Class, Culture, and the Soviet Community

The Bolshevik regime sought to create an entirely new modern state, one based on class rather than residency or ethnicity, but the uniqueness and success of the Soviet political project should not be exaggerated. This first Marxist state identified certain characteristics of enfranchised citizens and disenfranchised aliens in a manner consistent with Europe's other revolutionary regimes. Anti-aristocratic and modernizing states often identified citizens as productive workers and aliens as idle parasites. Just as the Soviet regime attacked idle and parasitic elements as bourgeois remnants foreign to a nation of useful proletarians, the racial state of Nazi Germany also classified the "work-shy" and parasitic elements as "asocials" unfit for the national community.[34] For French revolutionaries as well, the nation constituted a collection of busy producers while the nobility was "foreign to the nation because of its idleness."[35] Moreover, class did not determine the distribution of material rights in the new society. In Soviet Russia, a privileged party elite, a "new class," ruled in the name of the workers, and the rights of access to shortage goods separated different segments of society, such as military personnel, scientists, party and trade union members, and ordinary workers.[36] The party leadership might have defined the Soviet "bounded citizenry," to use Rogers Brubaker's term, as an association of proletarian members, but the workers' state actually represented a composite of groups with varying rights and privileges.[37]

And yet, in a number of important respects, an ideology of class fundamentally informed the Soviet project to engineer a new political community. Stalin sought to establish a community of citizen-laborers in which productive employment and loyalty to the party program became people's central obligation and determined the distribution of material rights and privileges. Millions of people from the old bourgeoisie were executed or forced into exile, while others who scarcely resembled them had to abandon their "nonlaboring" lifestyles and secure "socially-useful labor." In addition, the Soviet regime appears unparalleled in the degree to which it underscored the population's material or economic "base," what Marx considered fundamental to social identity. More than other radical European leaders, the Marxist rulers of Soviet Russia acutely vilified exploiters and forcefully touted the significance of productive labor. In the decade 1926–1936, when disenfranchisement became a popular and dangerous weapon of exclusion, the majority of victims lost their rights for reasons having to do with past or present economic behavior. Both civilians and state officials participated in the meticulous inspection and registration of people's economic status and activities. They painstakingly scrutinized the population's material possessions and financial ties and characterized outcasts as nonlaboring parasites and exploiters. Just as physical and ethnic criteria primarily governed inclusion in the racial state of the Third Reich, economic conduct, financial dependencies, and sources of income fundamentally determined political identities in the classist state of Soviet Russia.

Finally, Soviet social engineering imposed a particular culture system in which opposing behaviors associated with the two classes provided the salient markers of insiders and outsiders. In Soviet Russia, the communist party leadership promoted a particular classificatory scheme of the kind that Clifford Geertz described, one comprised of "an underlying opposition of paired items" that were "mutually derivable from each other by logical operations" such as inversion.[38] If the bourgeoisie consisted of idle, privileged classes, nonlaborers, deceivers, and exploiters, the proletariat represented its opposite—the poor and sincere, oppressed, laboring, and exploited masses. Although values such as suffering and productive labor predated Marxism in Russia, it appears that Bolshevik ideology elevated them as dominant cultural values. Ann Laura Stoler has shown that where race provided the salient criteria for marking citizens, cultural differences established the contours of racial categories.[39] With regard to Bolshevik class categories, one can discern a similar pattern. When applied in Russia, the abstract ideological categories of proletarian and bourgeois identified certain concrete character types. Practices of exclusion and inclusion reveal how behavioral attributes and personal characteristics often distinguished bourgeois aliens from proletarian citizens and, in this way, determined the boundary of the Soviet political community. The present work concerns this formidable legal and cultural boundary and the people who crossed it in both directions.

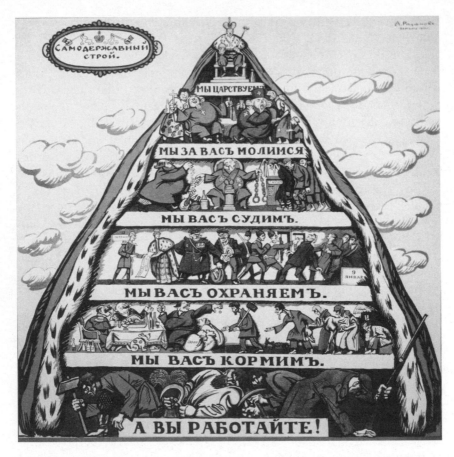

Aleksei Radakov, *Autocratic Structure*. 1917. From the Collection of Merrill C. Berman. Photo by Jim Frank.

1

Marking Outcasts and Making Citizens

"Autocratic Structure," Aleksei Radakov's political poster of 1917, features a six-tier pyramid with the tsar at the pinnacle and below him the words "We rule you." On the next rung, several corpulent priests enjoy food and drink, and the subscript reads "We pray for you." One level lower, fat magistrates sentence a scrawny public next to the words "We judge you." The middle rung of the edifice features ruthless prison guards and police above the description, "We protect you." Next, obese aristocrats throw crumbs at an emaciated peasantry and the heading reads "We feed you." At the large base of the pyramid, weary workers, peasants, and soldiers toil as the entire autocratic structure rests on their backs and shoulders, the injustice of it is expressed in the final statement "And you work." The poster captures a central message of Russia's Marxist revolutionaries, namely, that the ruling classes of the old regime lived off the labor of the working classes.[1] Uniformly described as "class enemies," these priests, judges, police, prison guards, landowners, and aristocrats who exploited the laboring peasants, soldiers, and workers represented the most notorious and reviled foes of Lenin's Bolshevik party. The enemies of the working class consisted of "bourgeois," "non-laboring," "privileged" or "exploiting" classes: those who lived off the labor of others and gave the proletariat only crumbs in return, as Radakov's pyramid so vividly illustrates. The Bolsheviks promoted the view of a Russian society consisting of Marx's two great classes: the exploiting parasites and the exploited laborers. This Manichaean picture also resonated with peasants and workers who so often reproduced it—well into the 1930s.[2]

13

Characters of Aliens and Alien Character

Years would separate these class aliens of Lenin's government from those vilified by the Stalinist regime, and although the two groups shared certain personal attributes and experiences, a great deal set them apart from each other. Nearly a decade after the Bolshevik seizure of power, the Soviet government revived, intensified, and expanded its earlier assault against the so-called class enemies. The "bourgeois aliens" as a group continued to be characterized as nonlaboring and exploiting elements throughout the 1920s, but their social composition would change fundamentally under Stalin. The Soviet government after Lenin would also establish a systematic redemptive ordeal for all segments of this enemy group. Bourgeois aliens possessed the hope of reentering Soviet society if they transformed their lives to conform with Soviet conditions. Outcasts who performed socially useful labor and demonstrated loyalty to Soviet power could be reinstated in rights. The story of Stalin's outcasts begins with an examination of a Soviet disenfranchisement policy which was distinctly twofold—it sought to both mark outcasts and make citizens.

The social groupings featured in Radakov's poster obviously benefited from autocracy, getting fat at the expense of emaciated laborers on whose backs their power and privilege literally rested. Since they had it so good under tsarism, these "former people" or vestiges of the Imperial past would be loath to embrace the new Soviet regime. The party largely believed that the true loyalties of the bourgeoisie would forever rest with the old system that protected their privileges. In 1919, a resolution of the eighth party conference argued that "the deprivation of political rights and any kind of restrictions on freedom is necessary exclusively as a temporary measure in the struggle against the efforts of exploiters to maintain or revive their privileges."[3] Russian and French revolutionary rhetoric virulently condemned the bourgeoisie and other enemies who might appear loyal to the revolution, but who merely "mask" their genuine interest in counterrevolution, the return of the old order, and the restoration of their power.[4] In the highly volatile revolutionary era, frequent repressive campaigns targeted these hidden and insidious forces. The fluidity and ambiguity of class categories in Russia, especially after the social leveling of the civil war, did not hinder the hunt for bourgeois class enemies.[5] The so-called "former classes" represented the main targets of the Soviet secret police or Cheka during the Red Terror of the civil-war period, when many lost their lives or were forced into hiding or emigration. Police repression against class enemies continued for decades with varying waves of intensity.[6]

In the postrevolutionary period, the persecution of class enemies proved very severe but at the same time quite arbitrary and inconsistent. Many members of the old bourgeoisie managed to avoid repression and even to secure a state job under the new regime. For example, in late 1919, one third of the employees at the People's Commissariat of Provisions (*Narkomprod*) were members of the bourgeoisie or intelligentsia, landowners and priests, while the mother of the prominent White Army general and baron, Petr Vrangel, worked in a Petrograd museum through the course of the civil war. In 1920, a survey prepared for Lenin specified that twenty percent of the employees in Soviet institutions were former landowners, priests, tsarist officers, high tsarist officials, or "bourgeois specialists" who had acquired their training before the revolution. A 1924 report by the Worker-Peasant Inspectorate, or Rabkrin, indicated that, with the exception of lower service and secretarial personnel, the People's Commissariat of Agriculture (*Narkomzem*) employed twice as many former gentry and nobles as workers and peasants combined.[7] Asked about their former tsarist identities when they applied for a job in the Soviet bureaucracy, class aliens often faced minor consequences if they made false claims in the early 1920s. For example, in 1924 a man was judged in a people's court for failing to disclose on a job application the fact that he served in the tsarist police. For concealing his past, he was only fined two rubles.[8] Finally, the life of a former White Army officer in the Siberia province (*krai*) illustrates the state's inconsistent treatment of the former people. His social origin officially petit bourgeoisie (*iz meshchan*), Okunev served in the Imperial Army since 1914, received a series of military awards, and supported the notorious White Admiral Kolchak during the civil war. After Kolchak's defeat, in order to avoid being deported, Obunev failed to register as someone who had served in the White Army, an offense for which he was sentenced in 1922 to five years deprivation of rights. The punishment was later commuted to two years, and although he remained on the OGPU special register of White Army officers, Okunev afterwards secured a state job and even became a trade-union member. In 1927, he lived as a Soviet citizen with full rights.[9]

At the same time, the bourgeois classes remained highly vulnerable to repression at the hands of the secret police and the courts. The class bias of the 1922 Criminal Code interpreted the transgressions of class enemies as political or counterrevolutionary acts, for which they faced harsh sentences and even the death penalty.[10] Bourgeois enemies encountered various forms of discrimination as well. For example, immediately after the Bolshevik seizure of power in 1917, the regime took steps to eliminate the political influence of the enemy classes through a policy of disenfranchisement. Formally barred from voting or serving in the local governing bodies or soviets, alien classes were also denied entry into the Red Army, assigned instead to serve in the rear militia (*tylovoe opolchenie*). This "unarmed worker battalion" of "nonlaboring elements" included disenfranchised men as well as convicts, administrative exiles, and other deportees between the ages of 18 and 45. Instead of military service, they were assigned to work as forced laborers in trenches, construction, timber, and other heavy industries.[11]

Soviet Russia's first constitution decreed that in the workers' state, labor constituted the central duty of all citizens, and the bourgeoisie or nonlaboring classes should be disenfranchised. The categories of people marked for disenfranchisement were listed in this 1918 RSFSR Constitution and later in the 1925 RSFSR Constitution, as well as the "Instructions on Elections to the Soviets," issued by the highest organs of the state bureaucracy, the RSFSR and USSR Central Executive Committees (*VTsIK, TsIK*), and the Central Electoral Commission, or CEC, subordinate to VTsIK.[12] Published in several editions and constantly amended, the instructions served as working manuals for local officials. The constitutions and electoral instructions specified the categories of aliens denied the rights to vote and to be elected to the local governing bodies or soviets, including: the exploiters or "class enemies" of Radakov's poster, namely, those who hire labor for the purpose of profit; parasitic elements or those who live off unearned income, such as interest money or income from property; capitalists such as private traders and middlemen; monks and other clerics of all faiths and denominations (*ispovedanii i tolki*); agents of the former police, gendarmes, prison organs, and security forces; White Army officers; and leaders of counterrevolutionary bands. At the same time, criminals and other social deviants would not find a place in the new order. The mentally ill or insane and persons sentenced by a court for crimes of profit or depravity (*korystnye i porochashchie prestupleniia*) could not exercise the right to vote either. This last provision illustrates an important aspect of exclusion, namely, that economic and moral deviance often determined class labels.

The constitution also allowed for a broader application of disenfranchisement beyond the categories of people explicitly denied voting rights and provided that "in the interest of the working class, the RSFSR deprives the rights of certain individuals and groups who exercise those rights contrary to [*v ushcherb*] the interests of socialist revolution."[13] In this way, any perceived enemy of the state could lose all rights. Lenin declared that his party would "disenfranchise all citizens who hinder socialist revolution."[14] In other words, one's enemy status was not exclusively determined by social origin or class but by conduct that others perceived to be anti-soviet.[15] Many lost their rights "as an anti-soviet element," "for not demonstrating loyalty sufficiently," "for having a way of life that is alien to Soviet power," and "as an ideologically alien element."[16] In its earliest laws, the Soviet regime explicitly associated aliens with people whose behavior could be considered harmful to Bolshevik power.

A broad set of behaviors, not simply political or economic but social and cultural as well, informed both the official and popular understanding of class enemies. Just as the Bolshevik party or ruling class defined itself according to certain behaviors, customs, and values, it also ascribed various attributes to the déclassé.[17] According to Bolshevik rhetoric, these anti-Soviet elements swindled and robbed the toilers who, unlike the idle and parasitic classes, led useful and productive lives. In 1917, Lenin called for "war to the death against the rich, the idlers and the parasites."[18] Behavior such as idleness and greed, and not simply economic or social status, defined the enemies of the revolution. In addition to behavioral attributes associated with their economic status, the sedentary old regime elites so vilified for thinking only of their own bellies invariably appeared obese. In the Bolshevik imagination, the oppressed toilers literally starved as the idle rich robbed them of the fruits of their labor. Priests, commercial traders, convicted thieves, and former landowners shared the appellation "class enemy" because of their conduct as nonlaboring exploiters. Party leaders also vilified bourgeois women as idle, nonlaboring "doll-parasites" who "lived at the expense of their husbands and lovers."[19]

Marx's bourgeois class might have represented an ideological abstraction, but idle people who exploited others were quite real for many in Russia. The party well understood this and repeatedly emphasized the behavioral attributes of the bourgeoisie, characteristics that effectively served in place of class and accounted for the broad resonance of class rhetoric. The power and meaning of Soviet Russia's abstract class categories derived from the cluster of behaviors ascribed to them. Aliens consistently represented thieves, embezzlers, speculators, manipulators, tax-evaders, and swindlers, as well as people considered to be arrogant, rude, socially deviant, or immoral.

Soviet Elections and Social Engineering

In a letter to Soviet authorities in the 1920s, a peasant asked why those who engaged in commercial trading or who served in the tsarist police or bureaucracy should be deprived of voting rights when, in fact, they all belong to a single state (*a vse eti liudi odnogo gosudarstva*).[20] Disenfranchisement appeared unjust to many, but the party leadership justified its policy in a number of ways. The alien classes lost the rights to vote and to be elected to the soviets because these disloyal groups could undermine Soviet power. Bolshevik enemies might infiltrate the local governing bodies and subvert party directives. After the Bolshevik seizure of power, soviets were established in rural areas, towns and cities, as well as workers' settlements (*poselki*).[21] The exact timing of elections to the soviets varied from one region to the next but all-Russian campaigns were conducted in the summer of 1926, winter/spring 1926–1927, winter/spring 1928–1929, winter/spring 1930–1931, and the winter 1934–1935. Deputies to the soviets could only be elected in tightly orchestrated contests from among the Bolsheviks' apparent constituency, the laboring classes. A campaign to revitalize the soviets (*ozhivlenie sovetov*) began in October 1924 and was primarily directed at nonparty peasants considered loyal to Soviet power, in order to encourage them to participate as both voters and delegates. Low-level soviet organs had to "draw in a broad mass of female workers and peasants."[22] The Bolsheviks promoted the election of women and national minorities to the soviets because they thought social groups with a history of oppression were their natural supporters. Membership in the local electoral commissions increased to include representatives from the trade unions, peasant committees (*krestkomy*), the communist youth organization (*komsomol*), and various national minorities. Local government needed to be purged of bourgeois elements and staffed with these proletarian representatives.

A central goal of the Bolshevik regime consisted in the social engineering of a new political community, one purged of alien elements and staffed with loyal laborers who would willingly implement party directives. Soviet elections served this goal by promoting political education and agitation, and the regular mobilization of nonparty workers and peasants. They provided the "most important school for the political education of the laboring masses" and the primary means of involving a broad cross-section of people in the task of building socialism.[23] Elections and voting also became what Moore and Myerhoff would call a "secular ritual," which functioned as a public display of ideological unanimity.[24] As in the case of revolutionary holidays and celebrations, electoral campaigns served the goal of mass mobilization and political education. They also provided an occasion for marking the boundary of the Soviet polity. At election time, Soviet officials recruited and registered a favored constituency and excluded from political participation those considered disloyal.

Officially called "electoral-accounting" campaigns, elections also helped party leaders to gather social data. For example, they used elections to ask what actions people considered to be exploitation (*zakabalenie*) of the surrounding population, the percentage of peasants from specific social groups who used hired labor and why, and what voters and disenfranchised people thought of the electoral instructions.[25] The leadership inquired into "the political mood, activities and demands of certain social groups" and sought information on counterrevolutionary actions (*vystupleniia*) and "the most egregious political mistakes and cases of gross [*grubyi*] disenfranchisement and distortions of class politics."[26] Electoral campaigns also provided an occasion for social and political census-taking, as the population with rights registered according to such indicators as social origin, ethnicity, party affiliation, and komsomol membership. Consistent with the regime's goal of population control and management, local officials had to submit detailed charts on the social origin, party affiliation, nationality, and gender of attendees at electoral meetings, the composition of rural soviets (*sel'sovety*) by economic status and occupation, gender, ethnicity, and party affiliation, as well as a breakdown by category of all the disenfranchised.[27] At election time, people literally stood up to be counted—according to a number of indices. Elections provide just another instance of how the Soviet regime diligently compiled all sorts of social data and scrutinized various characteristics of its population.

To be sure, the Bolshevik project of classifying and monitoring the public at election time was neither uniform nor systematic. No central electoral law for the RSFSR existed prior to 1925. In the early 1920s, campaign guidelines were established locally and with great variation, while a number of institutions maintained information on elections. In the Russian republic, elections were managed by the All-Russian Commissariat of Internal Affairs (*NKVD RSFSR*), until September 1925, when the party Central Committee transferred responsibility for electoral campaigns to the administrative organs—the TsIK Presidium of the USSR and the TsIK Presidia of the republics.[28] What appeared as a transfer of authority actually represented an extension of authority.[29] In 1925, according to a statement by the deputy director of the NKVD RSFSR, who was also a member of the Presidium of the Central Electoral Commission, both the NKVD RSFSR and the administrative organs maintained parallel and often duplicate functions during an electoral campaign. They were supposed to separately process statistical data on the campaign and issue reports to the CEC as well as to I. V. Stalin and V. M. Molotov, the party's agitation and propaganda department (*Agitprop*), members of the presidia of VTsIK and TsIK, the chairmen of the All-Russian and All-Union Council of People's Commissars (*Sovnarkom*), the Central Executive Committees of the autonomous republics, the provincial executive committees (*krai, oblast', guberniia*), as well as the editors of the newspapers *Izvestiia, Pravda,* and *Vlast' sovetov*.[30]

When the regime extended responsibility for elections to the soviets, the new cadre of peasants and workers, women and ethnic minorities, were supposed to assume the task of identifying aliens and citizens, perform agitation and propaganda work, and report on the population. The tasks of these governing bodies had been expanding steadily during the mid-1920s with the state's emphasis on industrial development. Although the party exaggerated the real power of the soviets, these local councils helped to implement policy in all matters from industry and agriculture to education and health and possessed coercive powers, such as the authority to impose severe fines or administrative exile. The social composition of the soviets seemed especially important given that these bodies participated in the high-priority work of an industrializing nation. In July 1926, the party central committee emphasized the need to continue engineering soviet membership with greater rigor, to bring more proletarian elements (non-party workers, poor and middle peasants) into the work of the soviets, use disenfranchisement more regularly, and eliminate class opponents.[31] Molotov identified the purpose of Soviet elections as "the complete taking over of the whole state apparatus by the working class," and he was determined to see this process completed as quickly as possible.[32]

Exclusion and the Campaign to Control Capital

The electoral campaigns of 1926–1927, 1928–1929, and 1930–1931 identified and excluded millions of aliens from the workers' state and thereby marked the boundary of the Soviet political community. These three elections in rapid succession deprived more people of rights than in any period before or since. The years 1928–1931 also witnessed the increasing severity of disenfranchisement as "deprivation of voting rights" became tantamount to complete marginalization and the disenfranchised corresponded to noncitizens or outcasts. All this occurred under the battle cry of class war against the bourgeois elements, the fat and idle old regime elites. However, in the peak years of class war 1928–1931, the party's rhetoric against the privileged classes concealed the social reality on the ground, namely, that disenfranchisement actually targeted an enormous diversity of ordinary people under the broad heading of "nonlaboring element." As was so often the case, people's conduct betrayed their class.

By the mid-1920s, when the Soviet economy had nearly recovered after the devastating effects of world war, revolution, and civil war, attention turned from restoring prerevolutionary productive capacity to expanding industrial production. Concerns about the need to "build socialism" and fears of capitalist encirclement also prompted this reorientation as communist party leaders sought to develop those industries that would strengthen and protect their fledgling regime. In December 1925, the fourteenth party congress adopted a policy which called for the rapid industrialization of the country. The new program also involved the expansion of the socialist sector or the concentration of all capital under state control. In this way, the party could quickly direct maximum resources into the priority sector of heavy industry. The party's industrialization drive seemed directly opposed to the activities of private traders who competed with the state for resources. The implementation of this industrialization policy began in 1926 with the government's sharp increase in capital investment in industry and a concurrent assault against private traders, those perceived to be diverting resources from the priority tasks of state.[33]

The industrialization drive highlighted the importance of staffing the soviets with a loyal proletariat and punishing alien classes who sought to sabotage party policy. Soviet industrialization coincided with an extensive campaign against various state enemies who might subvert the party's economic program. In 1926, the Soviet government sharply increased capital expenditure for industry and, at the same time, declared that the country was in a period of intensified class struggle (*obostrenie klassovoi bor'by*).[34] In September 1926, Stalin made clear in a letter to Molotov that "enemies of the working class" must be arrested and that "the struggle with them should be merciless."[35] His words signaled a crisis in the New Economic Policy or NEP and the beginning of the party's vigorous assault against private trade. Not a few party members strongly condemned this New Economic Policy of tolerance for private trade and small retailers, and for "capitalist and exploitative" activities such as the leasing of land and the hiring of labor. Members of Leon Trotsky's "Left Opposition," in particular, believed that the market economy of NEP was responsible for class differentiation and various forms of exploitation, sanctioned the accumulation of unearned income and idle lifestyles, and posed a fundamental threat to the proletarian regime. Although this faction was defeated at the fifteenth party conference in October 1926, its members' fears resonated with a party leadership that later called for "the definitive political isolation of bourgeois elements."[36]

Among the capitalist elements targeted for repression were the rural bourgeoisie, the prosperous peasants or kulaks. They effectively formed an official category of persons denied the right to vote because they engaged in economic practices that the constitution condemned as exploitative and nonlaboring, such as leasing land, hiring labor, and living off unearned income.[37] Applied most frequently in the campaign against the kulak, disenfranchisement was often the first in a series of repressive measures against this group of perceived rural capitalist exploiters. In 1926, months before the electoral campaign that witnessed the largest single jump in the percentage of the Soviet population disenfranchised, the head of the NKVD RSFSR and member of the Central Electoral Commission Presidium, A. G. Beloborodov, complained in a report to Molotov: "If one takes the general figure of the disenfranchised as a percentage of the voting-age population, then it must be acknowledged that one percent disenfranchised in the village is still insufficient [*vse zhe nedostatochen*] since the number of kulaks is no doubt higher than one percent."[38] Molotov took this to heart. In January 1927, he emphasized the need to raise the one-percent figure and offered planning targets for the numbers of people that should be disenfranchised in the campaign just beginning, setting the figure at 3–4 percent or, "even better," 5–7 percent.[39] In the 1920s, Soviet estimates of the number of wealthy peasant households generally stood at over three percent of peasant households. Therefore, if one percent of the rural population was disenfranchised in the 1924–1925 electoral campaign, many dangerous "capitalist elements" must be enjoying full rights.[40] It was time to rectify this situation.

Traders represented another group of perceived capitalist elements, and their numbers often overlapped with the kulaks. Restrictions on their commercial activities came first in the form of taxation. The license to trade involved a tax assessment (*okrad*) and proof that the tax obligation had actually been met. After the summer of 1926, the government sharply increased taxes on private industry and trade, subjected private traders to onerous railway tariffs, raised their rents for sites at bazaars, restricted their credit, and hiked their taxes. Economic measures against private traders were effective in driving many out of business and many others underground. In 1927, state organs and cooperatives controlled four fifths of all the country's trade (*tovarooborot*), a sharp change from the year before when private trade reached its peak in both the number of licensed traders and the volume of sales.[41] With the assault against private traders on the one hand and the promotion of government trade organs and cooperatives on the other, earnings outside the state economic structure became exceedingly restricted. Many ordinary peasants and small-time traders lost their rights for activities that were commonplace. One villager expressed the opinion that "soon they will disenfranchise all laborers [*trudoviki*] since all peasants fall under these [electoral] instructions."[42]

In the election of 1926–1927, with the government's assault against kulaks and private traders, the percentage of the disenfranchised population tripled.[43] No other campaign introduced so dramatic an increase in people without rights. Overall, the disenfranchised as a percentage of the voting age population in the RSFSR jumped sharply during the 1926–27 campaign and then remained relatively constant in the 1928–29 and the 1930–31 elections to the soviets. Although this figure then declined by about half with the election of 1934, the sharp drop in 1934 was not as considerable as the upward spike of 1926–27. The numbers of people without rights in the Russian republic or RSFSR jumped from roughly one percent to over three percent of the population, for a total of close to two million people.[44] In his report to the fifteenth party congress in December 1927, Stalin continued his class-war rhetoric, insisting that the party needed to "limit the growth of capitalist elements" and "by various means," although the victims of this policy could hardly be characterized as capitalist exploiters. In the summer of 1927, a Rabkrin report declared that the leasing of land "in all regions of Russia" was "a general practice." Even Stalin acknowledged in July 1928 that the campaign against private trade meant that "we are driving out of trade thousands and thousands of small and medium traders."[45] Peasants who earned kopeks as scavengers (*krest'ian-sborshchiki*) were losing their rights after "collecting scattered raw materials (rags, bones, hoses, glass, paper, etc.)" for resale.[46] Despite the regime's public rhetoric that its policy targeted the privileged classes, disenfranchisement could apply to large segments of the Soviet population who simply engaged in some form of commercial activity.

In the late 1920s, people lost rights as "bourgeois, nonlaboring elements" largely because of their economic activities and dependencies. For the Bolsheviks, economic behavior formed the base of social identities. The Bolshevik leadership considered source of income and acts of exploitation to be chief determinants of political identity and allegiance. This was true even in the case of religious clerics, as rabbis, mullahs, pastors, priests, and shamans were condemned for living off unearned income and exploiting the masses.[47] The Council of Commissars included among the indices of rich peasant or kulak farms the presence of family members who trade or lend money or who live off unearned income and specified that "this category includes clerics."[48] The party Central Committee's Anti-religion Commission noted that decisions on the voting rights of members and leaders of religious sects should consider whether these persons received their primary source of material support (*soderzhanie*) from religious organizations.[49] Income served as an important factor even in the disenfranchisement of clerics, as their preaching was considered to be exploitative and a means for generating nonlaboring income. Still, party officials believed that clerics posed a fundamental threat to the regime, which is why increasing numbers of people lost their rights under this category. The legal definition of clerics expanded in the late 1920s, as VTsIK placed missionaries and preachers (*propovedniki*) under this classification in January 1927, and a Central Electoral Commission decree of October 1928 even included kosher butchers (*evreiskie rezniki*) as clerics because they "perform religious [*kul'tovye*] duties."[50] In 1928, evangelical Christians also lost their rights as clerics because the state perceived them as preachers.[51]

Disenfranchisement did not target the old privileged elites so much as the conduct associated with them, such as perceived economic exploitation and idleness. Like the representations of the old regime elites of Radakov's poster, alien status corresponded with nonlaboring, exploitative, and parasitic behavior. If the regime had declared a class war against the former people exclusively, the battle would have been more contained because of the limited number of priests, White Army officers, and former landowners in Russia. Yet the "intensified class struggle" of 1926–1931 was a total war, with mass participation and millions of victims. In this country where behavior so often determined class, the party waged a broad and vicious battle against all people who might have exhibited one of the many reviled attributes of the bourgeois classes. Persons perceived as nonlaboring or parasitic could be stripped of rights and classified as noncitizen aliens.

Bolshevik propaganda grouped rich peasants, private traders, and bureaucrats together as nonlaboring elements and thieves. The official rhetoric often associated the disenfranchised with crooks or embezzlers, people who stole from individuals and the public.[52] Stalin attacked alien elements who had "burrowed into our organizations like thieves."[53] Similar to the capitalist exploiters, the bureaucrats were condemned as "robbers of public funds," and on the anniversary of the revolution on November 7, 1928, the official slogans were "down with the kulak, the Nepman, and the bureaucrat."[54] In his memoir, a criminal investigator in the Leningrad regional court, Lev Sheinin, implied that attacks against the urban traders or Nepmen were related to the assault against official corruption or the stealing of state funds. Revenue inspectors were arrested along with the Nepmen, accused of taking bribes for lowering the Nepmen's taxes.[55] Illegitimate sources of income determined one's status as an alien. Exploiting classes represented parasites and thieves, and this is even illustrated by the kinds of people with whom they were so often grouped. In one publication, the enemies in the soviet were described as "two kulaks, three thieves, one bootlegger, two embezzlers."[56]

Attacks continued against anti-Soviet elements who robbed public resources and diverted capital from state control and the all-important task of industrial production. The worst wave of repression coincided with Stalin's "revolution from above" in 1928–32 and the adoption of the First Five-Year Plan of industrialization and the collectivization of agriculture.[57] Attacks against the kulak and other class enemies sharply intensified during this period that Sheila Fitzpatrick described as "Cultural Revolution" or militant class war.[58] Members of the party leadership warned of how class enemies deceived Soviet power by holding positions in the state bureaucracy. In October 1928, Avel Enukidze warned that the Soviet institutions contained "material from the old bureaucracy . . . former ministers, gendarmes, generals, etc." Just two months later, Sergo Ordzhonikidze expressed a similar conviction that many of the former White Army officers, priests, merchants, and tsarist officials who had been purged from Soviet institutions following the Shakhty trial had already found new employment within other institutions; others noted that "former officers of Kolchak, Denikin, Petylura etc.," who had been purged, had found new positions, and "some of them were members of a trade union and drew unemployment benefits."[59] Many of the former people who had been deprived of rights in earlier years were now flatly labeled kulaks as well, as electoral lists of the disenfranchised became de facto lists of local kulaks.[60] The term kulak was often attached to former White Army officers and priests, for example.[61] Preparations for the 1928–1929 elections to the soviets took place at a time when the secret police or OGPU was rounding up all kinds of perceived anti-soviet elements, including the "former people," kulaks, bourgeois specialists, and private traders. In the first months of 1928, many local markets were closed, and peasant "speculators" were prosecuted under a 1927 provision of the 1926 Criminal Code, article 107. Implemented at the time when the assault against private traders was just beginning, article 107 was not regularly enforced until the end of 1927.[62] The OGPU sentenced private traders, and arrested, imprisoned, or deported former landowners, priests, and so-called "bourgeois specialists." In 1927, forty percent of the over 10,000 former landowners still living on their estates were deported.[63] When, in December 1929, Stalin urged the "liquidation" of the rich peasants or kulaks as a class, those who had been disenfranchised faced dekulakization and deportation as well.[64]

The Great Transformation in the Ranks of Class Aliens

More people were disenfranchised in the campaign of 1928–1929 than in any other election to the soviets. The local electoral commissions of 1927 were purged in preparation for the next elections in 1929, and "class alien and socially dangerous elements and persons deprived of electoral rights" were also purged from the party and army.[65] Many local officials believed that the message from the party was to disenfranchise as many as possible, that is, to err on the side of too many disenfranchised rather than too few. The Chairman of the RSFSR Central Electoral Commission, A. S. Kiselev, served in the Party Central Committee from 1925 to 1934 and held the position of VTsIK secretary since 1924. According to this top official in charge of disenfranchisement, the difference between the 1928–1929 and 1925–1926 campaigns was that "the administrative department [of the soviets] didn't issue instructions—disenfranchise as much as you can, otherwise you'll be taken to court."[66] Local officials reasoned that in the environment of the First Five-Year Plan, it was politically safe and wise to push for higher target figures.[67] For example, one Moscow official reported in 1929 how in the city "it was announced that all housing administrations that do not provide a correct list of the disenfranchised would be prosecuted [*otdany pod sud*]," and after these instructions were issued, local officials decided "just in case" to disenfranchise more than was necessary.[68]

As more people became the victims of disenfranchisement, the composition of this outcast group changed fundamentally. Although the disenfranchised included priests, landowners, and other class enemies, in the late 1920s, these "former people" faced severe repression at the hands of the secret police, while officials of the soviets apparently managed lists of the disenfranchised that more often included dependents and capitalist elements. In 1926, the new electoral legislation revised the constitution's categories of disenfranchised people and made possible a dramatic shift in the composition of the disenfranchised. The first All-Union Electoral Instructions, published by TsIK on September 28, 1926, and by the RSFSR republic executive committee or VTsIK on November 4, 1926, broadened the constitutional categories of the disenfranchised. Focusing its attack against capitalist elements, the party significantly expanded the categories that condemned commercial activities. Explicitly citing past economic behavior for the first time, the Instructions deprived rights to "those who trade or have traded," "those who live or have lived off unearned income," or "those who use or have used hired help." None of the other categories was so extensively broadened in Soviet law.

Moreover, the 1926 Instructions added dependent family members of the disenfranchised to the groups of people who should be deprived of rights. Prior to these Instructions, dependents did not constitute a legal category of the disenfranchised but were referred to only indirectly in Soviet law. With the 1926 Instructions, family members of all who lost their voting rights (except those disenfranchised by a court or for mental illness) shared the fate of relatives "in those cases where they are materially dependent on the disenfranchised persons and do not have socially useful labor as a source of their own existence." As in Imperial Russia when the legal status of women and children derived from husbands and fathers, Soviet disenfranchisement directly affected children and wives of male heads of households.[69] At the same time, Soviet Russia's concern with economic dependency multiplied the stigmatizing effects of disenfranchisement, leading to instances where men lost rights for being dependent on their trading wives or for being the brother of a trader, and young men were disenfranchised because their mothers traded or their uncle owned a mill.[70] Moreover, contrary to the letter of the law, mothers lost rights because of the counterrevolutionary activities of their sons, and fathers because their sons were arrested and sentenced. Thus every family member disenfranchised potentially condemned parents, spouses, children, even siblings.

Beginning in 1926, disenfranchisement became a basic weapon in the party's arsenal against nonlaboring elements, and this led to a dramatic change in the composition of the disenfranchised as a group. Prior to the publication of the 1926 Instructions, dependent family members made up only 9 percent of the disenfranchised in the urban and rural districts of the RSFSR.[71] By 1929, dependents, usually women and young adults, made up 35 percent of all of the disenfranchised in urban areas and 49 percent of the rural disenfranchised.[72] The fact that family members lost their rights as dependents largely accounted for the sharp increase in the numbers of disenfranchised people after 1926.[73] In the early 1920s, people deprived of rights were predominantly White Army officers, entrepreneurs (*predprinimateli*), former tsarist policemen and security officials, clerics, counterrevolutionaries, and bandits whose names appeared on the formal register of the Soviet secret police. For example, in 1924, 70 to 80 percent of the disenfranchised in the provinces (*guberniia*) of Amursk, Arkhangelsk, Penza, Tomsk, and Tula, as well as the Far East province (*krai*), were classified among these groups.[74] Although many "former people" were repressed by the secret police before the soviets could register them as disenfranchised, there were fewer landowners, White Army officers, and priests in Russia than there were persons who ever (in the past or presently) used hired labor, lived off unearned income, engaged in trade, or were financially dependent on someone disenfranchised. The latter groups comprised 81 percent of the disenfranchised in the North Caucasus province (*krai*) in 1927;[75] 75 percent in the Moscow province (*oblast'*) in 1931,[76] and 80 percent in the RSFSR in 1929.[77] After 1926, the vast majority of those without rights could attribute their fate to financial dependency on someone disenfranchised or to their own past or present economic activities.

The Creation of Outcasts

Stalin fundamentally redefined what it meant to be denied voting rights, which by 1930 implied severe political and economic marginalization. In the First Five-Year Plan period, when the revolutionary state expanded to control nearly all economic resources, the disenfranchised were denied economic rights and condemned to life at the margins of society and at the edge of subsistence. Denied state employment and denounced as parasitic nonlaboring elements who did not engage in socially useful labor, the disenfranchised faced exclusion from a socialist sector that thoroughly dominated economic life. Many of these outcasts had even less access to material resources than the victims of deportation and resettlement, who often earned a paltry sum and ration for their work under forced labor conditions. As aliens without rights and dangerous social elements, the Soviet disenfranchised also confronted the likelihood of arrest, deportation and forced labor. Their status resembled that of Jews and Gypsies in the Third Reich who were similarly vilified as parasites, thieves, and idlers, purged from civil-service posts and the armed forces, subject to severe discrimination and economic ruination, denied social welfare benefits open only to citizens, and made victims of intensifying police repression.[78]

From 1927–1930, a series of increasingly severe laws stripped the disenfranchised of their most elemental rights. In 1930, one Soviet legal expert wrote that "to deprive one of voting rights in our case means excluding that person from social-political life."[79] Kiselev characterized disenfranchisement as "a very serious punishment,"[80] and others described how people without rights had much more to lose in 1929 than in 1926: "Then, they didn't say that they'll expel your kids from school, remove you from your job, the trade union, evict you from your apartment, etc. This year, now that the campaign has expanded broadly [*shiroko razvernulas'*], they talk about this."[81] The observation was shared by Kalinin, the head of TsIK, when he described what it meant to be disenfranchised in 1929: "Do you understand what disenfranchisement means? It's like putting someone against the wall. . . . This isn't simply deprivation of voting rights; it means depriving [someone] of all rights. . . . For us now, being deprived of voting rights is like being deprived of life. . . ."[82] Stalin's outcasts could not participate in any aspect of Soviet life from adoption or guardianship to education, housing, and employment. The disenfranchised were barred from conducting legitimate economic transactions, and they could not assume any legal profession (defender, judge, people's assessor, investigator, and so on). By 1930, alien elements were effectively condemned to the criminal sentence "deprivation of rights" that denied all civil rights.[83] They lost the right to work in state institutions or factories or to serve in the Red Army. They could not join a trade union or adopt a child, and they were denied all forms of public assistance, such as a state pension, aid, social insurance, and medical care, as well as state housing.[84]

Commissariats and cooperative organizations issued additional directives that imposed restrictions on the rights of the disenfranchised, and this diversity of state organs participated in making outcasts. For example, the Commissariat of Agriculture required that the disenfranchised pay higher fees for state agricultural services and assistance, and the All-Russian union of cooperatives issued directives denying the disenfranchised shares and a ration book.[85] In 1930, the Commissariat of Justice described a "massive filing of court suits on the eviction of the disenfranchised from municipal housing."[86] The disenfranchised could not participate at the general meeting (*skhod*) of rural residents, and they could not acquire, maintain, or use firearms or ammunition for firearms, whether for hunting or sport.[87] In 1927, Molotov attacked the predominance of the wealthy peasants in the agricultural cooperatives; soon, the disenfranchised were barred from membership in collective farms, as well as industrial and agricultural cooperatives.[88] Their children could not enter the komsomol or postsecondary schools.[89] From 1928, with the gradual introduction of the ration system, these outcasts were denied food rations that by 1930 applied to such staples as sugar, tea, bread, butter, oil, meat, eggs, and potatoes, and rationing continued until 1935.[90] Living outside the state rationing system was not easy. One man claimed, "If they take my mother's ration ticket, then I will be forced to starve."[91] Such severe economic and social discrimination proved most oppressive for people without rights. "Surely," one disenfranchised man argued in a petition to Soviet authorities, "this is a monstrous punishment."[92]

During Stalin's revolution, chronic and acute shortages of goods strengthened the mandate for disenfranchisement. By depriving a broad array of rights to millions of people, the state eliminated the need to supply a large segment of the population at a time of acute shortage. The savings were not lost on Soviet officials. Stalin refused to have his industrial ambitions checked by the reality of limited resources. In a letter to Molotov dated July 1925, the leader spoke of the importance of building the country's military industry "because without that they will beat us with their bare hands," and he identified the "serious danger" of "squandering some of the kopecks we have accumulated" since "we suffer from a shortage of capital."[93] During the bread crisis in 1928 that led to the beginning of rationing, A. Mikoian argued that a country with limited resources should not supply everyone with bread but only the workers, in whose name the Bolsheviks ruled: "Why must we supply the full 100 per cent of the population? Why must we supply the Nepmen?"[94] Local government organs also recognized the financial benefit of denying free services to the disenfranchised or charging the disenfranchised fees for certain services. In the Leningrad province (*oblast'*), one public-health office issued a circular to health institutions and professionals in 1930 instructing them to "quickly end free medical care" to the disenfranchised "except in psychiatric cases and those which are highly infectious [*ostro-zaraznye*]."[95] Instead, the disenfranchised were to be charged fees for services at pre-established rates for everything from operations to abortions to dental work. In another case, a government decree in January 1927 withheld the right of free public education from the children of some of the disenfranchised, but the RSFSR Commissariat of Enlightenment (*Narkompros*) complained that there simply was not enough money to extend the privilege of free education so broadly. Consequently, the decree was revised to apply to children of all categories of the disenfranchised.[96] It appears that the chronic shortages of the First Five-Year Plan period encouraged party leaders to deny disenfranchised groups access to the state's limited resources such as housing and food rations. At the same time, socialist construction itself, the building of a centrally-planned economy and the promise to supply the laboring class, implied the exclusion of alien classes. Soviet citizens represented those for whom the state provided material support, whose economic base was the socialist economy. Class enemies who acquired their income through deception, theft, and exploitation would have no right to the state's resources, the fruits of socialist labor.

By the late 1920s, the numbers of people disenfranchised rose sharply, and the figures are probably understated because jurisdiction over millions of disenfranchised people shifted from the soviets to the secret police following arrests and deportations. In 1928, private traders were often sentenced to article 107 of the Criminal Code that punished speculation, and the campaign to eliminate the kulaks led to the deportation of millions. For example, a Leningrad man deprived of rights as a former trader in 1926 was criminally sentenced by the OGPU in 1929 to 3 years exile under article 118 of the Criminal Code.[97] Another was deprived of rights in 1927, dekulakized and deported in 1930.[98] A man from the Ivanovo Industrial province (*oblast'*), deprived of rights as a craftsman (*kustar*) for using hired labor, died in a hospital of the OGPU labor camp in Siberia (*Siblag*) in Tomsk in 1932.[99] The disenfranchised stood on a slippery slope in which the loss of civil rights often resulted in arrest, deportation, and forced labor.

Many people without rights were forced to work on major construction projects of the First Five-Year Plan, such as the Turksib railway linking western Siberia and Central Asia, and the hydro-electric station on the Dnieper River.[100] On these work sites, they carried special passports that denied them mobility, and they lived separately from other workers.[101] All categories of the disenfranchised were represented among the prisoners of the country's various forced-labor camps. The son of a priest disenfranchised in 1928 for working as a deacon was deported to work in the Donbass coal mine for two years, 1929–1931.[102] Orthodox priests and bishops worked in the large construction projects such as Magnitogorsk, wearing "their hair long; in some cases it fell to their waists" but nonetheless "hard at work with pick and shovel."[103] During the First Five-Year Plan period, the loss of rights was but one, often the first, in a series of repressive measures directed against the perceived enemies of Soviet power.

At the same time, disenfranchisement policy possesses certain elements that distinguish it from other instances of Stalinist repression. In particular, disenfranchisement included an elaborate rehabilitation mechanism as early as 1926. Together, the deprivation and the reinstatement of rights comprised a single policy directed at changing people's identities and their relationship to the state. In the latter half of the 1920s, disenfranchisement sought to force economic and social transformation: to concentrate capital in the hands of the state and compel people to enter the industrial labor force. Like the party purge committees, the soviets regularly evaluated petitions for reinstatement, but here the appeals process served the goal of social engineering. The Stalinist regime deprived people of rights during the First Five-Year Plan period in its effort to redirect resources and change individual identities, or the economic behavior and dependencies that determined them.

The Ritual of Rehabilitation

A mechanism for the reinstatement of rights sought to transform Soviet aliens into laboring elements and useful, loyal citizens of Soviet power. The rehabilitation mechanism was used with greater frequency in response to the worst excesses of disenfranchisement in the late 1920s, but its ori-

gins and significance long predated them. On October 13, 1925, VTsIK issued its first republic-wide instructions on elections to the urban and rural
soviets, and this document dictated how local electoral commissions
should be formed throughout the republic as well as how officials should
decide cases of disenfranchisement and process petitions for the reinstatement of rights. Once a campaign ended, administrative organs had to establish commissions to review complaints and petitions from the disenfranchised regarding the reinstatement of rights. The procedure for
receiving appeals and deciding on rehabilitation was further elaborated in
the Instructions of the following year, November 4, 1926. The 1926 Instructions that called for the broad disenfranchisement of commercial
traders and family dependents also formalized a procedure for the reinstatement of rights.[104]

Disenfranchisement policy included an elaborate rehabilitation mechanism that encouraged aliens to reacquire rights. Officially, outcasts could
be reinstated in rights if they engaged in socially useful labor and demonstrated loyalty to Soviet power.[105] In order to become a citizen, people had
to change their economic base, as it were, and acquire a record of state-
sector employment. As with so many other Soviet initiatives, the campaign
to deprive and reinstate rights compelled people to perform various redemptive acts of service for Soviet power. In particular, rehabilitation elevated state-sector employment as the vehicle for securing all rights, both
political and economic. The disenfranchised, especially private traders and
dependents such as women and children, had to both abandon their exploitative, parasitic, and nonlaboring ways and secure public sector employment or socially useful labor. The system for reinstating rights was
based on the belief that productive labor could potentially transform nonlaboring elements into useful citizens, although party members embraced
this idea with varying degrees of conviction. More fundamental state-
building concerns also provided the rationale for the rehabilitation system.
The party's drive to build socialism and industrialize Russia's economy required that the state harness all productive labor.

Soviet rehabilitation policy intended neither to offset the excesses of disenfranchisement nor to provide amnesty for alien elements. Party leaders
refused to grant rights automatically to even the wrongly disenfranchised,
and people had to formally appeal for their rights, regardless.[106] For almost everyone, the path to inclusion was neither effortless nor direct.
Rather, outcasts were required to submit a petition with supporting documents and make a persuasive case for the reinstatement of rights. Rehabilitation was not supposed to be summarily granted but earned through
labor and loyalty. As Elizabeth Wood characterized a phenomenon com-

mon to other European revolutionary regimes, "One could never passively exist in this new society but must rather actively demonstrate one's worthiness to belong in the body politic."[107]

The 1926 TsIK Instructions roughly divided the categories of the disenfranchised into two groups for the purpose of rehabilitation: (1) those who held positions in the coercive apparatus of the old Imperial state, that is, former police, workers in the prison establishment, gendarmerie, and so on; (2) persons belonging to the "class of exploiters," such as landowners, the bourgeoisie, and religious clerics. In these Instructions, the first category could be reinstated in rights only by a special decree from the Presidium of the All-Russian Central Executive Committee. Former police needed to demonstrate two things, that they presently engage in productive, socially useful labor and are loyal to Soviet power. The exploiting classes also had to demonstrate loyalty to Soviet power but were required to engage in productive, socially useful labor for no less than five years. Kremlin officials fixed a work requirement for capitalist elements, perhaps because the soviets only decided rehabilitation in these cases without the need to consult other organs, such as the secret police. Party leaders might have felt it necessary, therefore, to establish minimum requirements for local officials to follow.[108] Finally, the children of people deprived of rights, who were minors before 1925 and lost their voting rights simply for being financially dependent on a disenfranchised parent, could be reinstated if they engaged in socially useful labor.

Although citizens had to demonstrate loyalty to Soviet power, labor in the service of the state's economic goals proved essential for the majority of the disenfranchised. Since economic relations and dependencies largely determined political allegiances, it was assumed that people who derived their main source of economic support from the state would likely be loyal to Soviet power. Thus not surprisingly, in February 1927, shortly after publication of the 1926 Instructions, several changes to the criteria for rehabilitation re-emphasized work for nearly all categories of the disenfranchised. First, those deprived for economic transgressions could be reinstated in rights if they were members of a trade union.[109] And former tsarist police and prison workers could be rehabilitated just like the former bourgeoisie, that is, by their local executive committee if they worked in industry or engaged in socially useful labor for at least five years and demonstrated their loyalty to Soviet power.[110] That same year, another category of disenfranchised people was granted the possibility of rights in exchange for work and loyalty. The TsIK Presidium on November 2, 1927, declared an amnesty for White Army officers which removed many of them from the special register of the OGPU.[111] It appears that since the secret police scrutinized the loyalty of this group, no five-year minimum work record was required of for their rehabilitation. Still, former White Army officers had to demonstrate current employment in soviet or social (*obshchestvennye*) institutions and trade-union membership. Members of this group could also be reinstated if they fought on the side of the Red Army and "participated actively in the armed defense of Soviet power."[112]

Petitions for the Reinstatement of Rights

As the number of outcasts increased and the penalties for disenfranchisement became increasingly onerous, people flooded various officials—housing administrations, trade unions, police departments, and local government—with complaints and petitions for rehabilitation.[113] One Soviet official noted that "no one wants to be disenfranchised, so they all file petitions for their reinstatement [of rights]."[114] Local authorities probably devoted more time to such letters than they did to disenfranchisement. An official described the reinstatement of rights as a process in which "people wander from one government agency to another [*po vsem instantsiiam*], our commissions overburdened and crushed by the quantity of petitions."[115] Some people without rights wrote repeatedly until they received a positive decision from an electoral commission at any level of the state hierarchy.[116] Others were rehabilitated only to be denied rights again, as in the case of a Latvian man who was disenfranchised in 1922, reinstated in rights in 1930, disenfranchised again in 1931, reinstated in 1933, disenfranchised in 1935, and finally reinstated again in 1936.[117]

As with disenfranchisement, decisions regarding the reinstatement of rights were made locally by the soviet electoral commission. Rejected petitions moved up the administrative hierarchy to the next electoral commission for review, with the Central Electoral Commission serving as the highest appeal organ.[118] At the end of 1926, the CEC established its own subcommission for reviewing complaints on disenfranchisement and petitions for the reinstatement of voting rights. I. I. Kutuzov became chairman and A. A. Solts was named vice-chairman of the subcommission until its dissolution in 1936. Other members of the subcommission included I. Raab, the secretary of the Central Electoral Commission, and representatives from the Commissariat of Justice, the NKVD, OGPU, and the VTsIK Department on Nationalities.[119] In March 1929, the CEC secretariat discussed the establishment of visitation hours for private citizens at the office of the subcommission, but it decided instead that Kalinin's reception room (*priemnaia*) would expand its functions to receive persons deprived of voting rights.[120] Sometimes the Procuracy investigated complaints of wrongful disenfranchisement and dekulakization, and the courts also participated in rehabilitation when cases involved people sentenced by a court to deprivation of rights.[121] In the 1920s, many former tsarist policemen, guardsmen, and military personnel also wrote to the VTsIK Amnesty Commission for the reinstatement of their civil rights as well as for the return of confiscated property and the reversal of their deportation order, but the Amnesty Commission rejected the vast majority of these petitions.

In the late 1920s, the volume of petitions for rehabilitation jumped sharply and then continued to increase steadily throughout the 1930s. Between the 1925–1926 and the 1926–1927 campaigns, the Central Electoral Commission received only 469 complaints concerning wrongful disenfranchisement for an entire twelve-month period while there were 600,000 persons without voting rights in the RSFSR.[122] Yet in the first nine months of 1927 the number of petitions increased over twenty times to nearly 11,000.[123] In the 1928–1929 campaign, the Moscow City Soviet reported that district (*raion*) electoral commissions had received over 44,000 petitions from the disenfranchised, while the Moscow provincial commission handled as many as 150–200 per day.[124] In 1929, VTsIK received 35,542 complaints total, and this jumped to 17,000 in only the first two months of 1930.[125] The volume of petitions probably underestimates the number of individuals who depended on these appeals for rights. As one local official emphasized at a Central Electoral Commission meeting in 1929, each petition determined the fate of several individuals. "The number of complaints cannot be compared with the number of people disenfranchised. You know, we disenfranchise a peasant along with his family. There were instances in which 7 complaints were filed, yet they write that 60 people are complaining. It turned out that [the 7 complaints were from] half [of the disenfranchised] since there were dependents."[126]

People from each of the outcast categories submitted petitions and complaints for the reinstatement of rights to the CEC, and the volume of letters generally reflected the composition of the disenfranchised population. For example, in the 1925–1926 campaign, officials in the Urals reported that their most active petitioning group consisted of former policemen and gendarmes, followed by the wives of clerics "who 'swear' that they don't live off their husband's earnings."[127] Yet the number of petitions from people classified as former police declined sharply from 1928 to 1935, as did those from clerics. In the 1926–1927 campaign, the Central Electoral Commission subcommission reported 66 percent of petitions received from men, 34 percent from women, and over half of all petitions (53 percent) from peasants.[128] This trend continued, for in 1929 the CEC received its largest segment of letters from the Central Black Earth province and of those petitions reviewed, peasant petitions constituted the greatest share (40 percent).[129] The profile of petitioners seems to reflect the fact that most of the RSFSR's disenfranchised were from rural areas, outnumbering urban noncitizens by nearly three to one in the campaign of 1930–1931.[130]

People without rights often avoided local officials and sent numerous petitions directly to Moscow on the assumption that central authorities would be more sympathetic.[131] Of all the Soviet leaders, M.I. Kalinin, as chairman of VTsIK, provided the most popular address for the disenfranchised. He received everything from personal visitors to telegrams from the disenfranchised who worked under forced-labor conditions on Siberian construction projects. Many letters addressed to Stalin were passed on to VTsIK by the Party Central Committee. The media provided another recourse. The disenfranchised frequently asked the press for information and even intervention on their behalf. One newspaper, *Krest'ianskaia gazeta,* received many peasant letters on the question of voting rights in the 1920s, asking what persons could legally be disenfranchised and what assistance or options were available for those who were disenfranchised.[132] Appeals to the radio and print media also included requests for advocacy.[133]

A degree of randomness and unpredictability characterized the practice of reinstating rights; nonetheless, distinct patterns are evident in rehabilitation. Some petitioners clearly had more hope for regaining their rights than others. For example, groups closely monitored by the secret police, such as priests, White Army officers, former landowners, and tsarist officials were the least likely to be reinstated in rights. In these cases, loyalty was apparently more important than socially useful labor, and a determination by the secret police regarding the political worthiness of the petitioner proved essential. At a 1929 meeting of VTsIK, Kutuzov described how the Central Electoral Commission handled the cases of former White Army officers: "All those White Army officers who served in the White Army but were crossed off the OGPU register [*sniaty s ucheta OGPU*] we rehabilitated; all those whom we did not rehabilitate are on the GPU register."[134] In addition, the Central Electoral Commission doubted the redemptive potential of religious people like Adventists, Mennonites, and Evangelicals, and they along with Orthodox priests and nuns typically appeared at the end of Commission protocols among the petitioners flatly refused. In addition, many of those with prerevolutionary titles had their appeals denied. The wife of the former Leningrad assistant Governor General A.A. Goncharova was rejected in 1930, as was a former countess and the wife of a former land captain.[135] When he petitioned for the reinstatement of rights in 1927, the assistant to the librarian of the Lenin Public Library since 1918 was rejected by the Commission as "a marshal of the nobility" (*predvoditel' dvorianstva*).[136]

While the Central Electoral Commission reviewed an increasing number of petitions from 1927 to the peak year of 1932, its approval rate averaged around 50 percent, with the lowest point in 1928 when it approved only a quarter of petitions.[137] The CEC generally approved a higher percentage of cases than lower-level administrative organs because local officials often feared being perceived as "soft" on anti-soviet elements. Leaving it to central officials to undo their excesses, local authorities told one Central Electoral Commission representative that in depriving rights, "it's better to overdo it than not; you over there can just correct things" (*luchshe pereborshchit, chem naoborot, a vy tam uzh ispravite*).[138]

Rates of rehabilitation, like disenfranchisement, varied regionally and in some cases proved substantial. In the city of Iaroslavl in 1929, less than 30 percent of the petitions sent to local electoral commissions for the reinstatement of rights were approved.[139] According to 1929 figures from the Moscow province, 82,046 people were deprived of rights. Of these, 44,297 or 54 percent filed a petition with their district (*raion*) soviet executive committee for reinstatement. In most cases, the petitioner's request was granted. In 56.7 percent of the petitions reviewed, the petitioner was reinstated in rights; 43.3 percent were rejected, and 5.2 percent were not reviewed. As a result, 28 percent of Moscow's disenfranchised population reacquired rights.[140] In the Uzbek SSR during the 1928–1929 campaign, the Commission reinstated rights in only 11 percent of the cases it reviewed.[141] Although the percentages increased in 1929, republic officials still reinstated rights for fewer than half the petitions. The Central Electoral Commission of the Tatar republic reinstated rights in nearly 40 percent of cases from rural areas and 25 percent of cases from urban areas.[142] In 1935, the Central Electoral Commissions of the Belorussian and Turkestan republics reinstated rights in only 13 percent and 23 percent of the cases they reviewed respectively, while the Central Executive Committees of other union republics reinstated rights in between 32 percent and 37 percent of the cases they considered.[143] Republic Central Executive Committees and their electoral commissions were harder on petitioners than was the VTsIK Central Electoral Commission in Moscow.

Patterns of Inclusion and the Citizen Profile

The factors that influenced how Soviet officials decided cases for the reinstatement of rights reveal what they considered to be the basic criteria for inclusion. In the dossiers of the unsuccessful petitioners, one encounters a persistent pattern of negative characteristics just as successful petitioners shared a common stock of positive personal attributes. Successful cases of reformed aliens often reflected the pattern of a short-term transgression followed by a decisive change in behavior that took the form of state service and employment. The typical pattern is expressed by members of the Central Electoral Commission in a case from 1927: "He traded in 1921 for 8 months in his workers' settlement after which and to the present day he served in state and cooperative institutions; a trade union member."[144] Rights were generally reinstated in those cases where petitioners had served in the Red Army, participated in social work, held a party or trade union membership, had separated from a disenfranchised parent, or otherwise demonstrated an independent source of income. It appears that a record of Red Army service provided the surest way of acquiring rights, yet most acquired rights after demonstrating a life transition. Outcasts were supposed to have stopped the activity that had caused their disenfranchisement, and any indication to the contrary provided grounds for rejection.

In certain cases, life transitions had to be emphatic and displayed by political proclamations, volunteer work, and other evidence of re-education. People who carried the especially damaging stigma of former priests had to not only publicly renounce the cloth (*publichno sniat' san sviashenika*) but also engage in anti-religious work and be a member of the league of the militant godless (*bezbozhniki*). For example, although he was disenfranchised "as a former priest without a five-year work record," a man from the Leningrad province was reinstated in rights in 1927 because he "officially renounced the cloth [*otreksia ot sana*] in 1924." The daughter of a priest was reinstated in rights because she "works as a trade-union and party delegate of the party women's section [*zhenotdel*], and works for the elimination of illiteracy." A former psalmodist described how after abandoning his work in the church he began to "politically re-educate" himself and attend political lessons.[145] Those disenfranchised for their religious ties were often compelled to make personal transformations public and unambiguous.

Economic conduct and dependency constituted fundamental criteria when officials decided whether to reinstate rights. This is vividly illustrated in the case of Zoia Orlova whose petition was rejected. An investigator noted that she "should be disenfranchised because according to the neighbors she herself doesn't do anything; her husband does something, they live well, they have a servant."[146] Orlova seemed to possess characteristics of the privileged classes, as she lived off unearned income and employed hired labor. For a woman seeking rehabilitation, her own employment proved just as important as the status of the husband. For example, a woman disenfranchised for living on unearned income from an apartment that she and her first husband rented was reinstated in rights because she "lived off the income of her second husband" who worked on a Volga steamship and was a trade union member.[147] A Tambov woman disenfranchised for trading had her rights reinstated because she was supported by a husband who worked in Soviet institutions.[148] One woman traded because her "drunken husband was unemployed," and the Central Electoral Commission reinstated her rights since she "divorced him and married a Soviet worker."[149] Female petitioners invariably noted the occupation of their husbands whether or not the spouse caused their disenfranchisement, and Soviet officials confirmed the critical importance of a man's status when they routinely noted the economic activities of husbands in the case files of women. Still, the goal of Soviet policy was to force women from a state of financial dependency on men to one of material independence, and even popular films from 1926–27 reinforced this important party mandate.[150]

Political re-education and loyalty also provided important markers of the Soviet citizen but could be expressed in different ways. The rehabilitated included those who saved the lives of party members, Red Army soldiers or others during the civil war, had a relative who participated in the attack on Alexander II, or suffered Siberian exile for their political activities under the last tsar.[151] In petitions for the reinstatement of rights, women claimed that their husbands were partisans who helped the Reds, while men described being taken prisoner by the White Army or making good friends with Red Army soldiers who saved their lives. Parents regained their rights because sons served in the party, OGPU, or the Red Army, or because a child perished on the front fighting for the Reds. The process of petitioning for rights compelled people to rewrite their personal narratives and to accentuate elements of their past that linked them to the Bolshevik grand narrative.[152] People refashioned themselves as Soviet citizens and offered a new identity in order to persuade authorities that they did not deserve the "class enemy" label, yet their success in regaining rights speaks to the preferences of Soviet officials. Approved petitions reveal the attributes that state authorities considered essential for social inclusion.

In order to understand the criteria that guided official decisions to grant rights, one would need to look beyond the laws on rehabilitation to the actual practices of Bolshevik authorities, such as their patterns of decision-making. These patterns expose the primary attributes or behaviors that officials ascribed to citizens and to the alien classes. For example, rejected appeals included those cases where a petitioner possessed foreign ties or ties to alien elements, a criminal record (particularly involving theft, bribery, or embezzlement), an unofficial source of income, or demonstrated deceptive behavior. Those who ever went abroad could not expect to be reinstated in rights unless some factor, such as local support for a petition, could offset this especially damaging attribute.[153] One case was rejected because the petitioner received unearned income in the form of "200–300 rubles a month from daughters in America."[154] Consistent with the official characterization of aliens as people who stole public resources, rejected cases included those of men sentenced for embezzlement and a woman whose husband was convicted for giving bribes.[155] Also rejected was the appeal of a man who worked as an underground lawyer, earning undocumented income in the process of writing complaints to Soviet authorities on behalf of peasants.[156] Others had their petitions rejected after being purged from Soviet institutions for "ties to an alien element" or "treating people rudely,"[157] or denouncing local peasants sympathetic to Soviet power during the civil war.[158]

Of all the attributes typically associated with the alien classes, it appears that Soviet officials felt especially threatened by the bourgeois class's tendency to trick others, mask true intentions, present false appearances, and commit counterrevolutionary acts surreptitiously [*tikhoi sapoi*]."[159] Evidence that petitioners might have hidden their social identity represented the ultimate damaging mark in someone's dossier. Wherever mention was made in the official summary of the case that the petitioner "masked" a true identity, officials categorically rejected the request for rehabilitation. Unsuccessful petitioners included men who concealed their disenfranchisement or time served in the former police, who had "a fictitious act of separation" (*fiktivnyi razdel'nyi akt*) from a father who was a priest and who hid his service in the White Army by assuming a false name.[160] One woman who remarried failed to be rehabilitated because she was "in fact" not divorced from her first disenfranchised husband.[161] A man whose record of service seemed appropriate for rehabilitation had his petition rejected because "local authorities view his reinstatement of rights negatively since . . . he was sentenced for concealing the fact that he was disenfranchised."[162]

Soviet officials articulated the defining characteristics of aliens and citizens in the process of deciding cases on disenfranchisement and the reinstatement of rights. What emerged from the practices of reinstatement as the fundamental features of the new citizen? Those who coveted membership in the new socialist society had to demonstrate that they abandoned their former economic activities, severed old dependencies, acquired a record of state-sector employment, and displayed loyalty to Soviet power; they could not have a criminal record especially for such economic crimes as embezzlement or theft nor ties to foreigners and other alien elements. Finally, like the French revolutionaries who insisted on transparency and authenticity and the Italian fascist Mussolini who described his supporters as "those who harbor a pure soul in their heart," the Bolsheviks put an extraordinarily high premium on sincerity.[163] Soviet citizens had to demonstrate transparency, and people who concealed any aspect of their damaging past remained an alien.

Conclusion

Bolshevik leaders excluded representatives of the old regime elites, the exploiting and nonlaboring elements featured in Radakov's 1918 poster, from participation in their new society. Former landowners, White Army officers, priests, tsarist officials, and capitalist exploiters could have no place in a new proletarian state where honest labor distinguished the Soviet citizenry. In party imagery and rhetoric, these parasitic classes who hoarded the country's resources in the days of tsarist rule represented the most prominent and visible targets of disenfranchisement. Yet by the late 1920s they hardly constituted the majority of outcasts. In 1926, the party began to implement a policy of rapid industrialization that resulted in the expansion of the socialist sector and the accumulation of capital under state control. Party leaders viewed private traders as capitalists whose economic activities frustrated the industrialization drive by manipulating supply and diverting resources from the state's priority sectors. Not surprisingly, 1926 also witnessed the implementation of a new electoral law that explicitly identified a much broader range of commercial behavior as punishable by disenfranchisement. The consequences of this expanded attack against economic activity that the party considered exploitative and nonlaboring became evident immediately in the 1926–27 electoral campaign, when Radakov's reviled classes fell to comprise just a small proportion of the total number of people deprived of rights. Now the majority of outcasts consisted of dependent family members of the disenfranchised, or persons who had hired labor, lived off unearned income, or engaged in private trade. Still, Russia's street traders and former landowners shared certain fundamental attributes. While the profile of the disenfranchised had changed, the negative attributes associated with them had not.

Moreover, Stalin's First Five-Year Plan of economic restructuring and the resulting expansion of state power, changed the meaning of disenfranchisement. No longer a matter of voting rights in the soviets, the stigma of disenfranchisement denied people access to work, housing, education, medical care, a pension, and a ration card. The Stalinist regime made the consequences of being denied voting rights so severe as to imply complete political, economic, and social marginalization. By the late 1920s, the disenfranchised became Stalin's outcasts. At the same time, prior to Stalin's consolidation of power, the party leadership had coupled this instrument of exclusion with a mechanism of inclusion that made the reinstatement of rights possible for those who redeemed themselves before the state. The 1926 electoral law that severely punished a broader range of economic activity also granted fundamental rights in those cases where people had abandoned their nonlaboring lifestyles (namely, private trade or financial dependency) in favor of socially useful labor (namely, state-sector employment). Rehabilitation would be granted to those who engaged in socially useful labor and demonstrated loyalty to Soviet power. The system of exclusion and inclusion compelled people to dramatically change their economic conduct, seek public sector employment, and profess their allegiance to Soviet power in exchange for fundamental rights. In this period of acute shortage, the party leadership sought to minimize the fiscal obligations of an expanding welfare state. Stalin would supply deficit goods such as grain and housing only to those people whose productive labor served the interests of his rapidly industrializing country.

Victims of disenfranchisement and beneficiaries of rehabilitation exhibited the characteristics of the Bolsheviks' aliens and citizens, and reveal how Soviet officials marked the boundary of the first socialist society. Although this boundary was highly imprecise, the 1918 Constitution established broad legal categories for the disenfranchised and provided that people whose behavior could be deemed anti-Soviet would lose their rights as well. However, even in the light of this important discretionary component, the Soviet political community did not emerge as a randomly constituted entity. The party leadership did, in fact, try to engineer a political community consistent with Bolshevik ideology and the pressing needs of a rapidly industrializing state. Aliens represented capitalist elements—exploiting, deceptive, nonlaboring types—while the Soviet citizen was distinguished by productive labor and honest service to the state. Bolshevik culture reveals certain underlying patterns, for not just any attribute evoked the image of the bourgeois alien or proletarian citizen. In their laws and public statements regarding disenfranchisement and in their decisions on the reinstatement of rights, party officials excluded from the body politic those identified as thieves and parasites, foreign elements and pretenders, and extended full rights to persons believed to be sacrificing, useful toilers whose soul was transparent before the state.

Isidor Frikh-Khar, *The Shashlik Vendor*. 1928. © State Russian Museum, St. Petersburg, 2001.

2

Faces of the Disenfranchised

For those whose job it was to enforce the laws on disenfranchisement, the categories of bourgeois aliens proved ambiguous. Kremlin authorities who monitored local practices concerning the deprivation of rights tried in vain to clarify confusing cases and offer more precise policy guidelines. In addition, numerous individuals and agencies helped to compile the lists of the rightless and, as a result, local practices of disenfranchisement reveal a range of alien identities that have no apparent reference to official policy. More surprising, however, than such irregularities in the application of outcast categories are the consistencies. Across Russia, distinct and often striking patterns of classification are also evident when one examines how aliens were identified on the street and in their communities.

Actual practices of disenfranchisement suggest that central and local authorities were generally guided by similar motives when they marked outcasts. Both groups focused their attention on the need to maintain power, control the distribution of shortage goods, and discipline deviants. Moreover, consistent with a party policy that tied social identity to economic conduct, the frequent targets of disenfranchisement were those whom others identified as embezzlers and thieves, exploiters and parasites. The party characterized aliens as exploiting, nonlaboring elements that robbed and deceived, and local officials and communities consistently disenfranchised according to these behavioral markers as well. Although the identity of local aliens often coincided with the party's targeted enemy, the relationship between central instruction and local implementation was far from consistent. On the local level, some of the traits associated with bourgeois elements resonated more strongly than others. For example, local practices of depriving rights demonstrate that attributes of bourgeois elements

45

such as arrogance, rudeness, and foreignness expressed especially potent meanings and accounted for numerous cases of disenfranchisement.

Moreover, communities all across Russia generated similar yet striking interpretations of a party policy that selectively distributed shortage goods to those who engaged in productive labor and demonstrated conformity with the community's predominant values. Certain patterns of disenfranchisement reveal a set of distinctly local preferences regarding who should be deprived of all rights. On the ground, weak and marginal members of a community filled the ranks of outcasts. People limited by physical disability or old age lost their rights because they could not participate fully in the life of a group or make a productive contribution. Others who engaged in behavior considered unacceptable or deviant in some way were also vulnerable to complete marginalization. The lists of the disenfranchised included the poor, invalids, and the elderly, as well as gamblers, prostitutes, and polygamists. Rates of disenfranchisement were much higher in areas with large non-Russian populations. Practices of exclusion demonstrate the degree to which communities extended membership to the able-bodied and productive, and to persons who complied with the dominant group's values and standards of behavior.

An Ambiguous Policy

In 1925, someone from the Urals described in a letter to the editor of the peasant newspaper, *Krest'ianskaia gazeta,* how ordinary peasants were deprived of rights.

> The rural soviet called in 25 people and announced, "You are all deprived of voting rights. The fine is 4 to 20 rubles." We all began asking why and one of them said—"You, you used to trade and you, you were a church elder and you, you were sentenced by a court. . . ." Look at the peasant's situation. He can't be a craftsman, he can't be in business or they deprive him of his rights and give him a fine. He is strangled by these unjust accusations. Whoever at any time traded or served under the Tsar or at any time was sentenced by a court is damned.[1]

The categories of disenfranchised people proved too broad and ambiguous, and it did not take long for local officials to discover that the law applied to most of the Soviet population. The fundamental ambiguity of the policy presented a constant problem for members of the party leadership who served on the Central Electoral Commission. Established in September 1925, the VTsIK Central Electoral Commission was responsible for managing the implementation of disenfranchisement policy on the ground. With an office in the Kremlin, the Commission commanded a broad audience at its meetings, including representatives from the newspapers *Bednota, Pravda, Izvestiia,* and *Krest'ianskaia gazeta,* the RSFSR Press Bureau, the NKVD RSFSR, the secret police (*GPU-OGPU-NKVD*), the Party Central Committee, the Supreme Court, the Central Control Commission, as well as from the VTsIK Department for Nationalities, the VTsIK Statistical-Political Department, and the Commissariat of Justice (*Narkomiust*).[2] These and other institutions were deeply involved in the work of the CEC whose control over elections, disenfranchisement, and the reinstatement of rights affected almost every organ of government. Since the loss of rights touched on issues from housing and insurance to taxes, institutions such as the RSFSR Procuracy, Commissariats of Justice and Finance, and the Social Security Administration (*Glavsotsstrakh*) deluged the Central Electoral Commission with inquiries regarding the types of persons who should be disenfranchised.

Correspondence between state institutions demonstrate the degree of confusion within the upper ranks of government over the proper application of the categories, but it was largely local officials who bombarded the Central Electoral Commission with requests for clarification. What about persons who simply sang in a church choir but were not psalmodists or assistants to the priest? Since the owners (*soderzhateli*) of both private sewing and foreign-language schools were not deprived of voting rights unless they earned a profit, was one safe if the school was not profitable? Did the former people include tsarist postal workers? How should officials classify the postreform Justice of the Peace (*mirovyi posrednik*) or people who performed the bible readings during church services? The Mari autonomous oblast asked what the Instructions meant by "materially dependent" with reference to family members of the disenfranchised. One puzzled citizen inquired: "Was an elderly disenfranchised man dependent on his grown son or the other way around?"[3] Each regional soviet submitted questions that reflected its particular experience as well. The Central Black Earth region inquired about the family members of rich peasants or kulaks who had been deported; the North Caucasus asked about traders, the Siberian regions needed clarification on counterrevolutionaries.

Local officials were often confused in rehabilitation cases as well, unclear about what exactly constituted loyalty, for example. The Worker-Peasant Inspectorate (*Rabkrin*) of the Vladimir province (*guberniia*) asked for clarification on the meaning of the term "loyalty," suggesting that the Commission specifically indicate what counted for loyalty—service in the

Red Army, social work, or what? In 1928, the Smolensk provincial executive committee asked the Central Electoral Commission pointedly, "What could serve as evidence of loyalty?" CEC policymakers spoke as though the outcast categories were self-evident and offered only an oblique and curt reply: "the understanding of 'loyalty' is sufficiently defined and requires no further explanation from the center."[4] Frustrated by the apparent impossibility of precisely applying the legal categories, local authorities criticized the CEC for issuing confusing instructions, if guidelines were issued at all. One Moscow official argued that "in all the newspapers . . . there are very few instructional articles that explain the law, the constitution, in an accessible way [*populiarno*]."[5] Another official from the Moscow province (*oblast'*) complained that the 1930 Instructions had "many contradictions" and "provide dubious explanations."[6] The Nizhnyi Novgorod provincial soviet executive committee complained about the "lack of precision and clarity" in the use of the term "trader," and party leaders acknowledged that instructions on disenfranchisement were ambiguous. Even a member of the CEC, A. A. Solts, admitted that "everyone is to blame, including the Commission" for cases of wrongful disenfranchisement.[7]

Although reluctant to issue precise directives, CEC authorities were forced by their subordinates to decide myriad ambiguous cases. So they ruled, for example, that a monk who had not yet taken his monastic vows should be disenfranchised, and officials of the Provisional Government of 1917 could not lose their rights because "former" referred to "tsarist."[8] Nonetheless, Moscow authorities repeatedly distanced themselves from their own ambiguous law, urging local officials to judge "case-by-case, individually" and not "mechanically, formally." For example, when the Procuracy asked whether persons who bought and sold meat scraps as cat food should be disenfranchised, A. S. Kiselev could only offer the standard reply, namely, that "each case should be decided individually."[9] Sometimes, central authorities offered fixed criteria in order to help local officials determine exploiters from simple peasants. For example, those who own fishing boats of 35 or more tons or who rent out their fishing boats of 5 or more tons were considered exploiters, whereas all others were not.[10] However, such precise directives were rare. The language of disenfranchisement law as demonstrated by the 1926 Instructions relied heavily upon terms of degree. The policy itself depended on subjective determinations, as officials had to judge whether someone was a petty (*melkii*) or big-time (*krupnyi*) trader, an occasional or temporary exploiter of labor, or served in the White Army as an officer or rank-and-file (*riadovoe*) soldier. If peasants employed others or lent money and equipment "systematically" or "continuously," they were being exploitative. Those who employed others to the extent that their economic activity could be characterized as "beyond the limits of a laboring household" (*trudovoe khoziaistvo*) also represented exploiters. These critical judgments became the responsibility of local officials who decided what economic activity could be considered "laboring" or which undesirable activity occurred "continuously." The persistent problem of identification, of how to spot a person deserving of disenfranchisement, was simply inherent in the language of the law. The party leadership sketched a broad policy outline and addressed only some of the inherent ambiguities in the legal classifications while leaving others deliberately vague. Kremlin authorities did little to ensure uniformity and regularity in the application of their policy. This, plus the fact that many people and institutions were involved in constructing the lists of the disenfranchised, made multiple interpretations of who should be deprived of rights seem truly inevitable.

Lists of the Rightless

Local circumstances and preferences frequently determined who would be deprived of rights. Not only was the electoral law ambiguous, but many people took part in its implementation. Strictly speaking, the executive committees of the local electoral commissions (*izbirkomy*) under the soviet executive committees (*ispolkomy*), the low-level organ responsible for managing the electoral campaigns, compiled the lists of the disenfranchised and published these registers of the rightless in the press. The city or rural electoral commissions made sure that lists of the disenfranchised were "compiled, reviewed, confirmed and published."[11] Lists of the disenfranchised were maintained alongside a variety of other lists that the administrative organs managed, such as the lists of voters, the deceased, the mentally ill, and those arrested. People feared and reviled the electoral commissions. In one district, a group of local peasants collectively petitioned demanding that all of the members of their electoral commission be deprived of rights.[12] The register of noncitizens was ominous and despised, and from Voronezh to Karelia to the Urals, reports circulated of lists being vandalized.[13] For example, in the city of Kurgan in the Urals province, reports described the mutilation of publicly displayed lists during the 1926 campaign.[14]

As legal and statistical documents that confirmed rights lost, lists were important to the disenfranchised, local officials, and central authorities alike. In theory, the registers included the date and cause of a person's disenfranchisement and might also provide the names of any dependent family members, a short history of each person's wrongful activity, current occupation and occupation before the revolution, tax rate and payment history, number of family members capable of work (*trudosposobnyi*), and a property assessment with mention of the barn, home, and livestock. Yet few lists of Soviet outcasts represented carefully constructed legal documents, and some were never formally compiled at all.[15] As late as 1928, the Caucasus region of Ingushetia had no figures on the disenfranchised or the composition of the electoral commissions, and Samara lacked a formal register of the disenfranchised.[16] Central authorities also complained that lists were compiled without verification but from personal petitions or denunciations, hearsay (*so slov*), or "personal information from the members of the electoral commission."[17] Local officials offered the following explanations for why certain people lost their rights: "We all know them, that's why we disenfranchised them"; and "Everyone knows that he traded."[18]

A variety of organs participated in constructing the reviled register. At the factory level, local trade-union committees compiled lists of disenfranchised people, although these had to be ratified by the district electoral commission.[19] Tax authorities also provided local officials with information on a person's occupation and income and thereby played an important role in placing people in the list of disenfranchised. The finance office kept records of trading licenses and the tax payments of individuals and of people who traded or paid certain taxes. For example, the disenfranchised included peasants who paid a higher tax rate, such as a fixed quota (*tverdoe zadanie*) or an individual tax assessment (*individualnoe oblozhenie*), presumably for earning more as rich peasants, although such taxes often represented punitive and arbitrary assessments. In 1929, the Belorussian TsIK claimed that the individual tax "leads directly to the loss of voting rights" and many cases confirm this.[20] While consulting with various state institutions to help them compile lists of the disenfranchised, local officials also mined other sources. For example, the Moscow provincial executive committee justified the disenfranchisement of a former trader in 1929 on the grounds that "in the [municipal directory] *All Moscow* for 1911 and 1913 he is listed as a merchant . . . [his wife] was listed in *All Moscow* as a merchant's wife [*kupchikha*]."[21]

In the cities, the housing management (*domoupravlenie*) identified aliens residing in urban apartment buildings, new residents and old. Suspicious persons were turned over to the police who worked with soviet officials to compile a list of the disenfranchised. In 1928, the Moscow soviet declared that lists of the disenfranchised should be based primarily on information provided by the housing administration.[22] A report to Kiselev in 1929 on the Moscow province noted that the task of "compiling the list of the disenfranchised was in fact in the hands of the housing administrations" and that the process occurred with little oversight from other organs.[23] Shortly thereafter, the Central Electoral Commission issued a secret report to Stalin on the subject of the disenfranchised, asserting that the housing administrations in the cities were in reality responsible for drafting the list of outcasts. Complaining about "a transfer of the functions of state organs to the housing management," the report explained: "In the cities, and even in Moscow, the lists of the disenfranchised are in fact compiled by the housing managements. . . . These lists are confirmed formally by the district electoral commissions."[24]

The involvement of a variety of people in the process of disenfranchisement, the existence of chaotic and incomplete lists of the disenfranchised, and the addition of names because of rumor or hearsay all contributed to making the process of depriving rights highly irregular. At the same time, this situation reveals the extent to which local officials and communities were able to put their stamp on the implementation of the policy. In a 1930 VTsIK report on the Lower Volga province (*krai*), officials condemned the practice of what they described as "the formation of independent 'central electoral commissions' that have usurped the rights of the electoral commissions of the soviets."[25] Educational institutions, trade union and factory electoral commissions, as well as workers' brigades participated in identifying class enemies.[26] Not strictly the job of soviet officials, disenfranchisement mobilized various segments of society in a mass campaign to identify bourgeois outcasts. Not surprisingly, ambiguities in Soviet law and the involvement of a broad cross-section of the population in the campaign of exclusion often produced divergent outcomes. Nonetheless, remarkable consistencies in the practice of marking outcasts are also evident across this vast territory.

Common Enemies

A policy of depriving rights was well received by some local officials who, like their bosses in Moscow, used disenfranchisement to silence opponents and maintain power. Many people were cast out following disputes with local officials. In 1925, a NKVD RSFSR report claimed that people were losing their rights for "being critical towards authority,"[27] and for years disenfranchisement was justified for actions such as "insulting the chairman of the rural soviet and for insubordination,"[28] and "disrupting a meeting."[29] Peasants were deprived of rights for "criticizing the activity of the township soviet executive committee [*volispolkom*],"[30] others "for actively levying criticism," and "cursing the policies [*meropriiatiia*] of Soviet power and the party."[31] Disenfranchisement routinely victimized those who resisted Soviet policy. For example, the grain crisis of 1928 caused some local officials to disenfranchise peasants who opposed the state's confiscation of their grain. In the North Caucasus, a man was deprived of rights because "he concealed his crops."[32] Fifty-seven peasants in the Volkhov raion were deprived of voting rights in 1929–1930 for refusing to join the collective farm.[33]

Just as the official policy of disenfranchisement targeted the opponents of Soviet power, on the ground the policy was often applied against personal enemies. Many spoke of being deprived of rights because others were settling "personal scores" (*po lichnym schetam*)[34] or "hated me."[35] The nearly 20 percent disenfranchised in one village in the Caucasus resulted from the fact that rival clans (*rodovye gruppirovki*) tried to deprive the other of rights.[36] Disenfranchisement served as a convenient instrument of revenge against personal enemies.[37] One man from the Western oblast claimed that he was denounced as a former tsarist policeman by someone who was the subject of his own letter of complaint. The accused tsarist policeman explained that because of his work on the factory's wall newspaper "there's a lot of resentment against me" (*na menia mnogo zlykh*).[38] A woman also described how her family's personal enemies used disenfranchisement as a weapon of revenge: "I'm not supposed to have citizenship rights [*prava grazhdanstva*] simply because someone wanted to get rid of my brother, the pilot, another had to settle on our farm, a third had to marry my sister, but she wouldn't agree, so it was necessary to make us disenfranchised, kulaks and counter-revolutionaries."[39]

Also like their party leaders, people used disenfranchisement as a weapon in the perennial struggle over scarce resources. They punished their neighbors for hoarding goods in short supply, that is, "for not helping their neighbors and fellow villagers by giving them grain."[40] During the famine in 1933, a man was disenfranchised for not lending grain. "Nearly 100 activists from my village asked me for a loan [of grain] without payment [*bez otdachi*] and I refused. Then they told me personally in the face that 'we can fix you' [*podobrat' kliuchi pod toboi*], which is what they did."[41] People also lost rights when neighbors coveted their urban apartment, an especially scarce commodity in the overcrowded cities of the late 1920s and 1930s. A home reflected one's wealth, and people lost rights because their neighbors believed they had "a nice home" or "a nice, new home."[42] A Moscow man claimed that the housing management deprived him of rights in 1929, and because of a "housing squabble they even wanted to evict me from my apartment."[43] A Moscow woman, outcast as a homeowner, was the target of the secretary of the housing management. Her son described how the woman's adversaries really wanted her living space:

> Today some fool [*durak*] came from the housing administration and said that my mother is disenfranchised and that the disenfranchised are enemies of Soviet power. . . . How can a sick, elderly, 70-year-old woman be an enemy? Twice they issued a suit in court to have her evicted. . . . The housing secretary really wants her apartment [*ploshchad'*] so he can set up and marry off his daughter and son.[44]

One Moscow man was condemned as an alien element and accused of hoarding shortage housing space, but V. N. Lenskii's other annoying behaviors prompted the denunciations that ultimately led to his disenfranchisement. An inspector for the Worker-Peasant Inspectorate for nine years, Lenskii made a habit of arrogantly flashing his Rabkrin documents and challenging the authority of those who managed his Moscow apartment building.[45] The chairman of the housing administration, a certain Kolesinskii, wrote Rabkrin SSSR concerning their inspector who discredits the organization "at every step," and claimed Lenskii was exposed as an alien element during the administration's effort to "unmask" and evict a group of resident Nepmen or private traders. Lenskii, he said, "openly sympathized with Nepmen" and belonged to a group of "bourgeois anti-soviet elements" in the building whom he tried to protect from eviction. Moreover, on Lenskii's comfortable salary of 200 rubles he is "the only one in the building who maliciously fails to pay his rent [*zlostnyi neplatel'shchik*]." He never pays voluntarily, forcing the housing administration to continuously turn to the courts—in nine cases of five months each—to enforce payment. Lenskii's failure to pay was especially intolerable given that he had more than his share of living space. He lived with his wife and child in a four-bedroom apartment "while many in our building are huddled together, several people to a room that's crowded and damp." Like others charged with being alien elements, Lenskii was condemned for the principal behaviors commonly attributed to bourgeois elements, namely: arrogance, rudeness, extravagance, hoarding scarce resources, and failing to pay monies owed.

For his part, the inspector seemed confident in his ability to disarm his accusers. Lenskii bragged that if anyone brought charges against him, he would use his connections (*blat*) and have Rabkrin pressure the court to drop the charges (his accusers condemned him as litigious). Kolesinskii complained that Lenskii also rented out part of his large apartment space for income, thus marking him as someone who "lived off unearned income." According to the writer, Lenskii was simply "an anti-societal element in the extreme."[46] The accuser also sent a denunciation concerning Lenskii to Rabkrin SSSR in which he made the claim that Lenskii was the son of a priest who studied in a religious academy, married the daughter of a Moscow merchant, and had "bourgeois relatives" including a disenfranchised person who lived with him. In addition to his many apparently annoying and unacceptable qualities, denouncers also noted that the man whose name sounded like the leader of the Russian revolution was actually a certain Svinobaev.[47] No action seemed to flag an alien element so much as concealing one's true identity. If masking a non-Russian ethnic identity were not enough, another denunciation from a different author charged Lenskii with being a speculator, an arrogant and ill-tempered man, and an "immoral element" (*razlozhivshiisia element*). Lenskii denied that he had bad manners and rude speech and claimed instead that while others "spoke sharply and rudely, I answered them calmly." He accused those carrying out evictions in the apartment of being impolite, while he defended his own proper behavior.

In fact, the inspector's behavior was quite central to his case. One man even wrote in defense of Lenskii's manners and proper speech, testifying that he never invoked the rude language he was accused of using.[48] Such charges of egotism and rudeness carried political significance because disrespectful, insulting behavior epitomized the bourgeoisie. The famous Russian revolutionary Leon Trotsky actually wrote a mini-treatise on manners where he condemned the "feudal" rudeness of the old nobility toward inferiors, so Lenskii's behavior seemed to provide additional evidence of his alien and anti-Soviet character.[49] Keenly aware of the damaging nature of the charges, Lenskii vehemently denied accusations that he behaved rudely and falsified the number of residents living in his apartment. He claimed that he had a five-member family and that all the fuss about his apartment was generated by a member of the housing administration who wanted the place for himself.[50] For his part, Lenskii demonstrated his own skill at denunciation and vilified his accusers as "former traders, sons of priests, and people who are trying to acquire my apartment."[51] His case demonstrates that social origin and ties to alien elements were no less important than conduct in determining the identity of bourgeois aliens. Lenskii's perceived offensive, arrogant, bullying, greedy, and deceptive behavior ultimately did him in.

As Lenskii's and other cases demonstrate, nonlaboring, deceptive, and rude actions marked people as bourgeois. Unacceptable behavior became an indicator of spoiled identity, and the disenfranchised were described as "a card-player and middleman in the selling of livestock."[52] A local official classified the "former people" (*byvshie*) in his community as "traders, criminals, thieves, drunks, etc.,"[53] and citizens who wrote to Stalin referred to "White parasites" in their communities.[54] Persons were deprived of rights as "a criminal element," "an embezzler," "a hooligan," "a horse thief."[55] In Moscow, one woman lost her rights as "the mother of a deported hooligan,"[56] and another because her husband was administratively exiled for embezzlement.[57] Others were sentenced by a court to deprivation of rights for tax evasion and bribery.[58] In the Penza gubernia in 1924, one county (*uezd*) deprived the rights of all bootleggers and persons discovered stealing timber.[59] In party discourse as well as on the ground, the noncitizen represented someone who demonstrated rude, disorderly, or deviant behavior and who stole from the public either through speculation and trade or by avoiding taxes, embezzling funds, or hoarding resources.

Official Bolshevik sources branded the class aliens as deceptive, exploitative, nonlaboring elements and thieves, and the public often reproduced this image. For example, in 1929 the tailor from Moscow, Leonin Golobachev, was accused by his neighbor in a communal apartment of exploiting "poor, proletarian masters" and "paying them pennies [*groshi*]" while giving "false information to the housing committee about his earnings in order to reduce his rent and hide his income tax from the finance office."[60] The fact that angry neighbors vilified people like Golobachev as tax evaders and exploiters confirms the resonance of this image. As Sarah Davies notes, the popular notion of exploitation was that those in power did not work themselves but rather lived off the labor of others, and this "was often expressed through the use of the concept of theft," the belief that both peasants and workers were being robbed of the fruits of their labor by the thieves and swindlers (*zhuliki*) who were in positions of power.[61]

The case of Maria and Fedor Talbert from a village just outside Leningrad further illustrates how aliens represented nonlaboring, exploiting elements and thieves for much of the public as well. Formally, the cause of their disenfranchisement was the exploitation of hired labor, but they were also accused of concealing income and cheating the state by failing to pay taxes. Fedor insisted that the allegations were the result of "incorrect and false denunciations" and "unfounded petitions from people who lie and are angry with me." His wife, Maria, claimed that the charges came from "my enemies." According to Mrs. Talbert, the entire local soviet blamed her for their sentence of embezzlement and drunkenness, so in retaliation they "promised to deport me and my family."

The Talberts themselves were the victims of a denunciation that was addressed to the Novgorod prosecutor from Avgust Bordanovich Griunberg. Lengthy, caustic, and detailed, it expressed the kind of economic resentments that caused many to lose their rights as bourgeois aliens. Griunberg characterized Talbert as a "prosperous, cushy former trader, speculator, and extortionist" and his wife as the daughter of a "terrible former Petersburg policeman" with all sorts of close connections to other disenfranchised people. Fedor worked in the raion soviet as an agronomist, Maria in the rural soviet as the auditing commission chairman, and in their "Latvian colony" the couple established "one of the premier" kulak households. Their sons were "hooligans," feared by the villagers. According to Griunberg, son Viktor beat one man unconscious, but his parents consoled the victim with wine and money to avoid a court sentence for their son. No doubt, the writer knew them quite well, for he included details about their lives before they moved to the "Latvian colony" (for example, the murder of Mrs. Talbert's father and Mr. Talbert's older brother), and about their economic dealings—how they made their money, when they were taxed, and when they avoided taxation.

The Talberts' economic activity and income provided most of the material for Griunberg's denunciation. More than any other aspect of their character or lives, the denouncer took the greatest interest in their prosperity, describing them as traders with a Midas touch. Mrs. Talbert, in her job as a canteen worker (*bufetchitsa*), sold good wine at a premium and could afford to keep servants and maids for herself. Talbert made use of timber from a certain forest area but did so while avoiding the authorities. The writer was clearly suspicious of how forestry officials seemed to bypass Talbert, as though he had bought everyone off. While Talbert cut firewood, the denouncer claimed, the town was short of timber to build a fire station. Once again, the predominant image of the alien was that of the greedy individual who consumes needed public resources.

According to their accuser, the Talberts were "getting rich everywhere without shame and without conscience,"[62] and these charges surfaced at a time when party members were also being purged for "the cult of good living."[63] Talbert was denounced for having a huge orchard and garden, every kind of agricultural machine and tool, and a luxurious home. His trading was extensive and diverse—he sold pelts as well as apples from his own orchard annually for 300–500 rubles—and much of the income he earned he managed to hide from tax officials. Moreover, he hired day laborers more than 50 days a year to assist with his grain and potato crops.

The damaging letter also mentioned how father and son were hunters and were sentenced and fined for poaching. The writer claimed that it was "impossible" to "describe all the pranks of the Talbert family" and declared emphatically that "it is necessary to deprive the Talbert family of voting rights."[64]

Although the Talberts were denounced primarily for their economic practices, ethnic and religious prejudice featured prominently in this case as well. Griunberg maligned the "Latvian colony" and identified the Talberts as religious people, devoted to the local Lutheran pastor (who, he eagerly noted, had just been arrested). In this respect, the case of the Talberts' disenfranchisement is not unusual. Deceptive economic behavior was often attributed to non-Russian ethnic groups. The party leadership did not explicitly associate trading and ethnicity, but the patterns of disenfranchisement make this correlation unmistakable. It appears that disenfranchisement served as a coercive weapon against ethnic minorities as well, in the years just preceding the mass deportations of various nationalities.[65] Anti-capitalist rhetoric often associated the "merchant-thieves" with foreigners and Jews, and even Nikolai Bukharin called for "a struggle against Nepmen of all nationalities, Jews included."[66] Rates of disenfranchisement were highest in communities with large non-Russian populations. In Stalin's Russia, aliens were very often non-Russians.

Targeting Ethnic Minorities

In December 1928, the central committee noted that "the nearer to the periphery, the worse the social composition of the electoral commissions."[67] Ethnic minorities, such as Germans, Poles, Estonians, Chinese, Kazakhs, Ukrainians, Uzbeks, Tatars, Turkmen, and Georgians resided in the periphery of the Soviet Union, and they possessed disproportionately large numbers of disenfranchised people. The Soviet bureaucracy did not maintain statistics on the ethnic composition of the disenfranchised, but areas reporting unusually high percentages of people without rights tended to have large non-Russian populations. For example, the Kiev gubernia reported 6.5 percent disenfranchised in 1923, and the Odessa gubernia nearly 5 percent in 1924.[68] The disenfranchised as a percentage of the voting population in the North Caucasus province was as high as 3.8 percent in the 1925–1926 campaign and jumped to 8.3 percent in the 1926–1927 campaign.[69] In the Volga German ASSR, one district (*kanton*) reported an increase in the number of disenfranchised from 4 percent in 1926 to 10 percent in 1927.[70] In the Taganrog okrug in 1927, reports circulated of "abuses by the district electoral commission in the disenfranchisement of German settlers [*nemtsy-kolonisty*]."[71] Another frequent target of disenfranchisement, noted in 1926, were Kazakhs returning to the RSFSR from emigration.[72]

Methods of accounting for and tracking the population without rights hardly represented an exact science, and figures on the numbers of outcasts often vary between sources. Nonetheless, one can see a striking pattern of ethnic enclaves reporting higher than average numbers for their disenfranchised population. In the electoral campaigns of 1926–27 and 1928–29, the RSFSR reported roughly 3–4 percent of rural and 7–8 percent of urban residents disenfranchised as a percentage of the voting-age population. Compared with these overall numbers, 13 percent of the voting-age population was reported disenfranchised in the Kalmykia ASSR in 1928–29, and the Crimea ASSR listed 8.7 percent without rights in 1928–29. The Moscow oblast deprived voting rights to 3–6 percent of the voting age population in 1928–29, at a time when the North Osetia oblast reported 7.6 percent, the Buriat-Mongol ASSR 7.6 percent, and the Crimea ASSR 8.7 percent disenfranchised. In urban areas, the Tatar ASSR registered 12 percent disenfranchised in the 1926–27 election to the soviets, and the Uzbek SSR outcast as many as 13.7 percent in the 1928–29 campaign. Moreover, the exclusion of ethnic groups did not suddenly emerge as a pattern in the late 1920s. Even as early as the 1924–25 election to the soviets when the RSFSR had disenfranchised 1–3 percent of the population, cities like Odessa and Zhitomir disenfranchised 9.9 percent and 11.3 percent respectively.[73]

The writer Isaac Babel, a soldier in the Red Army during the civil war, described how Jewish residents of the Ukraine and eastern Poland asked him if the Bolsheviks would allow freedom of trade.[74] Whatever expectations they had of a reprieve under Bolshevik rule, their hopes were quickly shattered in the years that followed. Jewish communities tended to be the hardest hit by disenfranchisement after the government assault on private trade. In 1929, two towns in the Smolensk gubernia, both noted for their very high rates of disenfranchisement, were composed of a "large percentage of Jews who trade openly but without a license and sometimes with only a rank one license."[75] Rudnia, just northwest of Smolensk near the border with Belorussia, and Pochinok, just southeast of Smolensk, were characterized by central authorities as "big trading towns" in which only half the local residents had private plots (*zemel'nye nadely*). Of the local residents, 30 percent in Rudnia and 64 percent in Pochinok were deprived of rights. Roughly half of the disenfranchised in each town were classified as former traders, whereas most of the others lost their rights as dependents. A VTsIK inspector characterized the majority of these traders as "traders of rank one licenses who trade from hawker's stands and from tables: decorated spice cake, apples, candy, donuts, cakes, and so on. All the goods of each of these traders can be bought for one-and-a-half to two rubles."[76] In the trading town of Pochinok, sixty-four percent of the local residents were deprived of rights.[77] One man described the predicament that led to the disenfranchisement of so many Jewish subjects in his petition for the reinstatement of rights: "It is well known that Jews, as one of the most oppressed nationalities under tsarism were not allowed to work the land at all, so most of them were forced into crafts [*kustarnyoe remeslo*]; until 1927 this hulling mill was my family's only means of existence."[78]

Tatars, Germans, and Chinese were also classified as traders and speculators and disenfranchised in large numbers. A 1925 report from the Amur gubernia noted that in districts (*raiony*) along the Chinese border as much as 50 percent of the local population was disenfranchised because they were believed to have been involved with contraband.[79] The pattern continued for nearly a decade. In 1934, an inspector from the VTsIK Presidium made a trip to the city of Orenburg to check on the electoral process, and he reported the inappropriate disenfranchisement of Chinese nationals who engaged in trade.[80] In 1927, some villages in the Tatar republic had as many as 20 to 50 percent of their residents disenfranchised for trading.[81] This three-to fourfold increase over the preceding year was largely attributed to what one official described as "speculators [*baryshniki*] particularly in the Tatar settlements."[82] A 1929 report by the electoral commission of the Tatar autonomous republic noted a "high percentage of disenfranchised persons in the cities of the Tatar republic."[83] In a village of the Saratov gubernia, a group of Tatars was disenfranchised simply because "Tatars are considered traders, secondhand dealers [*barakholshchiki*]."[84]

Economic practices alone did not flag the Soviet alien. Non-Russians also lost their rights for reasons having to do with ethnicity and religion, as disenfranchised aliens appeared culturally distinct from the enfranchised Russian citizenry. If not prejudice, then ignorance often accounted for the disproportionately high numbers of disenfranchised people among ethnic minorities. In the regions of the Far North, large numbers of people from the indigenous populations of the Chukchi and Nivkhi were disenfranchised as shamans.[85] In the Buriat-Mongol republic, over 6 percent of the population was reported disenfranchised in 1931, at least twice as high as the average percentage of disenfranchised from the ethnic Russian regions. The reason given for the high number of disenfranchised was the nearly 9,000 Buddhist lamas who were classified as clerics and accounted for over half of the people deprived of rights.[86] There was one lama for every 32 people in the republic, a ratio several times higher than for Orthodox priests in Russia.[87] In Georgia, Muslims were disenfranchised "as sectarians" (*kak sektanta—miuridy*).[88] In the Kokand okrug, an official entered a mosque and disenfranchised all the indigenous people (*tuzemtsy*) inside; then he expelled all peasants (*dekhkan*) wearing a turban (*chalma*) from a meeting of the poor peasantry.[89] In 1933, a Moscow man lost his rights "as a Jewish butcher." The protocol of this case did not mention that the man was selling kosher meats, just that he was slaughtering animals "by the Jewish method" (*po evreiskomu sposobu*), suggesting that it was the kosher practice and not the fact of selling meats that caused the butcher's loss of rights.[90] Non-Russians were much more likely to lose their rights than Russians, and for reasons related to their economic practices as well as cultural traditions.

It is unlikely that local officials and communities disenfranchised ethnic minorities with blatant disregard for party instruction. Ethnic minorities were often suspected of political disloyalty, and in the Caucasus region of North Osetia, a number of people were disenfranchised on the suspicion that they had ties to nationalists (*narodniki*).[91] Implementers of Soviet policy understood the need to follow the spirit and letter of central directives or, in the least, present the appearance of compliance. In any case, a consensus emerged that embezzlers, parasites, thieves, and tax evaders, as well as ethnic minorities represented appropriate targets. Practices of exclusion demonstrate that central authorities and local communities shared a set of values concerning the character traits of Soviet aliens. At the same time, while local patterns of disenfranchisement often reveal a striking degree of coherence with the Bolshevik bourgeois enemies broadly defined, they at times expose distinctly local preferences. Communities also advanced different terms of normative identity from those generated in Moscow.

Marginalizing Social Deviants

The Bolshevik leadership condemned behaviors such as drunkenness as conduct unbefitting a citizen, and the public also outcast those who exhibited disagreeable or asocial ways. People whose behavior was considered deviant, inappropriate, or offensive, or whose actions violated social norms and customs often landed among the rightless. For example, in Armenia a man was deprived of rights as "a strange character" (*kak tipa*), and in Moscow, a man was disenfranchised as "dubious" (*somnitel'nyi*).[92]

In 1926–1927, there were also instances of people with venereal disease (*venneriki*) being excluded from the list of voters.[93] Others were disenfranchised as "stupid" (*glupye*), "rowdy" (*buzotery*),[94] "on the suspicion of cattle-stealing," "not on good terms with his wife" (*s zhenoi ne v ladakh*), "as an incorrigible drunk," "as an imbecile" (*pridurkovatyi*), "as an unreliable element."[95] In the Borisoglebsk uezd in 1925, the local NKVD RSFSR reported cases of people disenfranchised "for prostitution, religious fanaticism, and causing squabbles [*za skloku*]."[96] A peasant was deprived of voting rights in Sverdlovsk because "he prophesies from the bible the end of the world" (*prorochit s biblii konets mira*).[97] In Belorussia, another peasant was condemned for damaging a hayfield; they said he was a "babbler" (*gorlopan*).[98] Heavy drinkers were also disenfranchised in Iakutsk ASSR, and one citizen from the North Caucasus even asked his local officials: "Why isn't there a slogan, "Comrades who drink can't be elected to the soviet?"[99]

Local exclusionary practices demonstrate that many considered card players and gamblers wholly unworthy of rights. In Azerbaidzhan, people were disenfranchised as "a ladies man" (*babnik*) and as a "card player and gambler" (*kartezhnik*).[100] Card players were also disenfranchised in the Don okrug, the Riazan, and the Iakutsk regions.[101] In one village, the rural electoral commission disenfranchised an entire group of card players and gamblers because they played at the bazaar and lured peasants into losing money.[102] Here, card players surely exhibited bourgeois traits of theft, deception, and economic exploitation. Still, all these disenfranchised card players prompted the Central Electoral Commission to issue a pointed telegram to the Iakutsk TsIK in 1929 which stated: "According to a strict reading of the VTsIK 1926 Electoral Instructions, card playing is not grounds for disenfranchisement."[103]

Rude, hostile, and abusive people also became victims of disenfranchisement. Some lost their rights for swearing (*rugatel'stvo*), or for being a bandit, a scum (*svoloch'*), a hooligan, or a brewer of moonshine (*samogonshchik*).[104] Outcasts were marked for being "a harmful element," "for treating his wife and children rudely,"[105] and "for beating the children,"[106] as domestic violence often provided cause for disenfranchisement. A variety of unacceptable lifestyles and occupations were also condemned, from polygamy to gambling to prostitution. Local officials deprived people of rights for being a sorcerer (*koldun*) or a dark character (*temnaia lichnost'*). In Moscow, others who lost their rights were fortune-tellers (*gadalki*).[107] One man was disenfranchised for "having two wives," and in 1931, the conference of soviets in the Chechen autonomous oblast petitioned the Central Electoral Commission with a suggested addition to the Instructions—that men with more than one wife be disenfranchised.[108] The Central Electoral Commission rejected the inclusion of this item in its laws.

Women often lost their rights for behavior deemed unacceptable, such as prostitution or an unwillingness to marry early. In the years following the revolution and into the 1920s, party leaders regularly associated prostitution with unearned income and characterized prostitutes as nonlaboring elements who did not hold productive jobs in the state sector.[109] Thus, although central authorities in Moscow often condemned the local habit of disenfranchising prostitutes, the practice did adhere with official criticisms of prostitution as a form of exploitation, unearned income, and unproductive labor. Officials disenfranchised a Moscow woman as "someone without specific occupation." When authorities from the Commission asked what this meant he was told: "We disenfranchised her because she sometimes engages in prostitution."[110] In the Crimea, Bashkir ASSR, and Moscow, women lost their rights as prostitutes.[111] Women's sexual behavior was also punished in a case originally reported in the newspaper *Bednota* and discussed in official correspondence. In the 1928–1929 campaign in a village of the Penza okrug, unmarried women were denied rights as nuns. When asked why the 20-year-olds were included on the list of the disenfranchised, the local electoral commission explained, "They are nuns [*monashki*]. . . . It's very simple. If they haven't married by the time they're twenty, in our view, they're considered nuns and so don't have voting rights in the rural soviet."[112] In the Vladimir gubernia, women were also disenfranchised for "not having married."[113] It appears that this particular instrument of coercion was used to manage women's sexual behavior and relations with men.

Although local preferences usually converged with a policy that marked aliens according to certain types of economic conduct, communities also had their own ideas about who should be outcast. Local patterns of disenfranchisement reveal that people were repeatedly excluded for reasons having to do with unacceptable behavior, perceived social deviance, or cultural difference, and for a way of life that did not comply with social norms. Those perceived as social deviants became the country's political outcasts. Persons who already stood at the margins of their communities represented the most likely candidates for exclusion.

The Poor and Weak Become Outcasts

In 1930, one man wrote an anonymous letter to Stalin describing how licensed private traders of rank two,[114] poor street vendors, were being disenfranchised although they hardly resembled the capitalists that the state sought to eliminate:

> [T]his disenfranchised person is subject to every misfortune, people call him what they wish, he is left without work . . . even his family can't find a job anywhere. That means that the disenfranchised and their families have to die of starvation. . . . not only that, but you say you're deprived of rights and they'll kick you out of your apartment and leave you in the cold. And for what?? For trading rank two, without any hired help, with only your own personal hard labor in a 2.5 x 2 booth haggling like a parrot in a cage and carrying your things around on your back like a pauper. . . . This miserable trader can't be harmful to the government when all the goods in his booth are worth 80–150 rubles."

The writer described the disenfranchised petty street vendors as unfortunate and miserable people who worked on their own and without hired labor. So poor and unskilled, they had no other choice but to trade. In contrast, he argued, those better educated, with the means and foresight to accommodate themselves to Soviet power, avoided becoming its victims. The writer repeated the charge often made by party leaders, namely, that clever and manipulative former people had acquired legitimate work and even drew social assistance from the state.

> And all the former people [*byvshie liudi*] before the revolution and now are rolling in the dough [*kupalis' syr v masle i seichas kupaiutsia*]. Since they are better educated and understood the future perfectly they tried not to trade and instead found a position for themselves in institutions, while paupers like myself kept on trading and were left not only without other work but even without bread. Meanwhile, the former people live and work just like they did before 1917, and some of them are even too old to work and are collecting aid from the Soviet government.[115]

If nothing else, the writer's general claim about the disenfranchisement of the poor is well supported by the evidence.[116] The sick and elderly, petty and part-time traders, women, invalids, and people who traded apples, seeds, hay, pudding (*kisel'*) were regularly deprived of rights. Under central pressure to compile lists of bourgeois aliens, local officials often disenfranchised marginal people, and this pattern is consistent with Lynne Viola's findings concerning groups that were especially vulnerable to dekulakization.[117] In Moscow, hawkers or street vendors were stripped of rights for buying dead dogs, selling flowers, pigeon feed, and loofahs, and in Tambov a man was disenfranchised for selling the dresses of his deceased wife.[118] Some invalids were given a free license to trade in place of a pension, yet they were often deprived of rights for holding a trader's license.[119] One man complained: "They gave me a free license so that I could feed myself; they gave me no pension and now they deprive me of voting rights."[120] Ice-cream vendors on the streets of Moscow, Leningrad, and Kharkov were disenfranchised as traders because local officials reasoned that "if we disenfranchise one, we have to disenfranchise them all."[121]

Poor and petty traders also became vulnerable to the deprivation of rights when forced to act as covers for other large-scale traders. More established entrepreneurs tried to protect themselves from the government's attacks against private trade by pressuring their vendors to have the trading licenses issued in their own names. A member of the party wrote a memo to the Central Electoral Commission of the Tatar TsIK, reporting this problem in 1927: "A rich peasant of the village gives [a farm laborer] money and says, 'The money comes from me, and you take the rank two license out in your name and trade meat; all profits received we split down the middle.' The farm laborer is forced to accept these terms . . . and in this way . . . he is disenfranchised while the rich peasant who anticipated all this and was afraid of being disenfranchised did not take the license out in his name."[122] A woman from Ostrov told of a similar arrangement in which she was manipulated by Fedorov, the proprietor of the tea shop that employed her. "They didn't let Fedorov trade anymore and then he said to me, 'You want to work and you don't want to starve?' He suggested I take out a license to trade in my name. . . . I wanted to feed myself and help my children so I decided to take the license, although I worked as an employee."[123] Leaders of the party's women's sections in the 1920s argued that this problem was especially acute among women who, hard hit by the unemployment of the NEP years, were forced to trade in the local flea markets where they constituted a small bird of prey for hucksters and speculators.[124]

The government's assault against private entrepreneurs often had the effect of actually targeting the poor and vulnerable, as more established and experienced traders found ways to get around the law themselves. Laws against trading in the late 1920s caused many small-scale consumer industries to close, yet the artisans employed in these factories remained dependent on their previous employers. Under pressure from their former bosses, they took out trading licenses in their name yet relied on their former employer for capital and the marketing of their goods.[125] Many traders described how they took out a license in their own name "but, in fact, I traded not with my own capital [*sredstvo*] but with someone else's entirely."[126] After borrowing money to trade, one man described himself as the furthest thing from a capitalist: "Trade without one's own means, that is itself a kind of slavery also."[127] The image that such narratives convey is of Soviet outcasts as oppressed laborers, victims of the wealthier traders who continue their commercial activities with impunity.[128] All the while, it is these exploiters who, in fact, should be disenfranchised.

The poor were also subject to disenfranchisement for living off "unearned income." Under this classification, cooperative peasants who received state assistance were often deprived of rights, a fact that generated concern from those within the Soviet bureaucracy who understood that these agricultural workers were not well-to-do. In 1927, the Soviet Center of Agricultural Cooperatives wrote to the Central Electoral Commission about the alarming rate of disenfranchisement among shareholders (*paishchiki*) and members of the governing board of agricultural cooperatives. Cooperative shareholders who employed hired labor and craftsmen who accepted government credits for agriculture were especially vulnerable.[129] Similarly, the USSR Central Agricultural Bank wrote the CEC a secret memo in 1927 complaining about the disenfranchisement of peasants who were associated with agricultural credit unions. Peasants who acquired machines on loan for winnowing, sowing, and reaping were disenfranchised because they rented out their machines and used the income to help pay off their loan. This led one group of citizens to ask their officials in 1929: "How can poor and middle peasants develop their land [*khoziastvo*] so as not to fall on the list of the disenfranchised?"[130]

Soviet law also disenfranchised those who received rent or other "unearned income," and when applied, this category deprived rights to many underprivileged people who simply received some form of non-wage payment. For example, peasants who worked as shepherds were disenfranchised as private contractors (*podriadchik-pastukh*).[131] Women who received alimony were also deprived of voting rights and classified as "living off unearned income."[132] In Moscow, Riazan, and Vladimir provinces some people who received alms were consequently identified as living off unearned income.[133] Others lost their rights because they "lived off old food reserves" (*zhivet starymi zapasami*).[134] Women who read prayers over the dead (*chitalka po pokoinikam*) were denied rights on the suspicion that they received unearned income in the form of funeral food (*kutia*) and the dresses of the deceased.[135] In fact, it appears that the prohibition against "unearned income" targeted women disproportionately as they were more likely to derive economic support from barter and gifts, rent payments, alimony, or their husband's income. Interestingly, this pattern of excluding dependent women is also evident in the prerevolutionary Russian and Ukrainian village where women who begged or relied on the aid of others were more likely to be stigmatized as witches.[136] Because of their material dependence and informal economic practices, women were especially vulnerable to exclusion.

In communities throughout Russia, the disenfranchised hardly reflected the features of a privileged or exploiting class. Central officials no less than local authorities grouped peddlers and small merchants among the bourgeoisie.[137] A secret memo to Stalin in 1930 noted the disenfranchisement in urban areas of anyone who had any sort of position in the tsarist regime.[138] Relatives or simple acquaintances of the disenfranchised were sometimes condemned as dependent family members, regardless of whether they were financially dependent or nonlaboring.[139] The Instructions called for the disenfranchisement of people who regularly employed laborers because this practice was considered exploitative, but many who hired labor in Soviet Russia hardly qualified as exploiters. Peasants who needed a few extra hands during the harvest were often classified as exploiters of hired labor. In one village, nearly half the peasants were forced to hire seasonal workers during the harvest and, as a result, they were all threatened with disenfranchisement.[140] In a town outside Sochi one man complained in 1927 to the editor of the journal *Sovetskoe stroitel'stvo* that people lost their rights simply because that year "there was a good harvest of fruits and vegetables." As a result, many who hired temporary workers to help them gather the harvest then became disenfranchised. Commenting on this injustice, he remarked boldly: "To disenfranchise according to the Instructions, one would have to first of all disenfranchise the entire electoral commission, for I too used hired help and the other members also. You yourselves know that if [we were] to follow the Instructions, [we] would have to disenfranchise 75 percent of the population."[141]

The prohibition against the hiring of labor resulted in unusually large numbers of people without rights. The estimates of peasant households that employed hired labor ranged from around 15 percent in the Leningrad and Western regions to as high as 30 percent in Siberia, Transcaucasia, and the Ural region. Moreover, only half of rich peasant or kulak households hired labor, and the employment of others was practiced by all classes of peasants, mostly middle and poor peasants. Similarly, small craft industries employed nearly three-and-a-half times as many workers as the big capitalist entrepreneurs, and these small entrepreneurs, far from being a rich class, probably earned less on average than low-level Soviet officials.[142] In the Far North nearly three quarters of the Kolyma nomads could be classified as kulaks and feudal lords.[143]

Under the category of clerics, many ordinary lay people were condemned as bourgeois aliens. Several electoral commissions disenfranchised people simply for believing in God, and in one village of the Rubtsovsk okrug a woman was deprived of rights for baking communion bread (*prosfora*) for the church.[144] Church watchmen also lost their rights, as did those who sang in church choirs.[145] In Siberia, a singer was disenfranchised "as the leader of a choir—an amateur." Others lost rights for simply having ties to religious persons, even if the "ties" appeared exploitative; for example, in the Kaluga gubernia, a man was disenfranchised as "the land laborer for a priest" (*batrak u popa*).[146] In a letter to Molotov, one man claimed that he was disenfranchised as a former priest because of his nickname. "I was disenfranchised for allegedly being an Old Believer priest. In fact, I was never a priest; there isn't even a house of prayer in our village. But my nickname on the street [*ulichnoe prozbishche*] is priest [*pop*]; they disenfranchised me on the basis on my nickname."[147]

In cases concerning the mentally ill (*umalishennyi*), one encounters the most striking evidence of how the weakest elements of society were the most vulnerable to disenfranchisement. Although this provision affected men considered "possessed" (*oderzhimyi*), women were particularly vulnerable to losing their rights under the "mentally ill" classification.[148] One woman was disenfranchised as "insane" without a medical document attesting to her insanity but simply "on the opinion of the neighbors," while another woman was deprived of voting rights as a "mentally ill pensioner."[149] The category "insane" also applied to many others including some with physical disabilities. In the village of Velichaiko, eighty people were disenfranchised as "insane" for having neurological disorders.[150] Others lost their rights because at one time they had suffered from depression (*stradali dushevnym, nervnym rasstroistvom*).[151] In one case, someone was disenfranchised as "the family member of an insane man."[152]

Those with a handicap or disability, the sick, or elderly who could not make a productive contribution to the community often became the victims of disenfranchisement. The Tatar republic in 1927 reported cases of the disenfranchisement of the blind, persons without legs (*beznogie*), and those who were deaf and dumb (*glukhonemye*).[153] In the winter 1925–1926 in the Urals oblast, lists of the disenfranchised included persons who were crippled, blind, mute, and deaf, and so on, "simply because they suffered from such great physical deficiencies."[154] One rural soviet referred to residents who were mute as "disenfranchised by nature" (*lishennye ot prirody*).[155] People were deprived of rights as "an epileptic," "having a nervous illness" (*nervno-bolnye*), "sick" and "feeble-minded" (*slaboumnye*).[156]

To a striking degree, patterns of disenfranchisement mirror other exclusionary practices in Russia. In the prerevolutionary peasant commune, the collectivized Soviet village, and even post-Soviet local communities, weak and unproductive members or persons entitled to social welfare assistance were frequently excluded because they posed a financial burden on other members. In Tsarist Russia, "some communes preferred to exclude families and individuals who could not provide for themselves in order to reduce welfare obligations and tax liabilities and to reclaim land allotments and other resources for stronger, more independent members." The main reasons why a commune in Tambov chose to cast out certain members as military recruits included the men's theft, laziness, irresponsibility, poverty, and disability. Patterns of exclusion as evidenced by the community's choice of army recruits also demonstrate that "the commune saw in recruitment a way to rid itself of poorer and less productive households, especially those that were likely to default on taxes and dues." In the years just before the Bolshevik revolution, the Imperial state deemed that only productive elements of the population could join cooperatives. Excluded from membership were traders and other "exploiters" and "speculators" who were not engaged in productive labor, but rather misdirected resources and weakened the state's tax base. One sees a similar practice in the collectivized Soviet village where "the non-able-bodied and the weak came to be seen as living violations of the new moral economy."[157] Other examples of exclusion from the Imperial and Soviet eras reveal a strikingly similar pattern in which productive labor and economic self-sufficiency determined social membership.

Central reports concerning local practices of disenfranchisement contain repeated references to how the elderly and those with physical disabilities were being deprived of rights, probably because of their entitlement to disability and retirement pensions.[158] For example, one pensioner from the Moscow oblast complained that when he asked the raion social-security department (*strakhkassa*) for his pension he was rejected; shortly thereafter the raion soviet informed him that he was deprived of voting rights.[159] Entire groups of people were disenfranchised "for inability to work" because they were 55–60 years old, and these are significant ages because men of 60 and women of 55 could be eligible for pensions. In Viatka province men over 60 and women over 50 were disenfranchised as too old to work; those who did not cultivate land or pay taxes were also deprived of rights as nonlaboring elements.[160] In 1925, the chairman of the Voronezh gubernia electoral commission described the disenfranchisement of all older men and women: "There was a case in which the township soviet executive committee of Nizhnedevtsk uezd put together the list of voters and all men over 55 and all women over 50 did not appear on the list. Thus they were deprived the right to vote on the grounds that they are not capable of working [*netrudosposobnye*] according to the Labor Code and do not have the right to vote. . . ."[161] In numerous cases throughout Russia, communities disenfranchised all residents over 50 or over 60.[162] One woman described how she and her husband were deprived of rights because she was the only member of a five-person family who was capable of working in the collective farm. "Since my husband was sick, paralyzed, and plus had two young children, and his father was an old man with tuberculosis, I was the only one [in the family] who could work in the kolkhoz. In November 1935 my husband and I were once again disenfranchised, that is, when my husband was not in good health and couldn't even move at all and his elderly father was in the same condition."[163] In Armenia, people were disenfranchised for being over the age of 50.[164] In 1929 in the Armavir okrug, people around 58–60 years of age, especially widowed women, were deprived of rights.[165] In the Vladimir gubernia in 1929, one county (*uezd*) disenfranchised all women over 50 years of age.[166] This pattern of disenfranchising the elderly appears to have punished women in particular.

The party leadership was aware of the fact that ordinary citizens, often weak and marginal people, lost their rights in great numbers. In 1929, the chairman of the Central Electoral Commission, Kiselev, asked members of the VTsIK Presidium, "What is the social position [*polozhenie*] of those who are disenfranchised?" and proceeded to offer the following portrait of Moscow's disenfranchised: "She has two kids, receives alimony, and now works as a cleaning lady; she's the mother of a person on disability and receives a 30 ruble pension; . . . he's disenfranchised for trading seeds and apples . . . he's disabled and receives a pension . . . they disenfranchised a people's court judge, a member of the party since 1918; they disenfranchised a 22-year-old student for serving in the police at a time when he was 11 years old. . . . they disenfranchised singers in the church, they disenfranchise for hooliganism, for literary earnings. . . ."[167] Party leaders themselves recognized that local patterns of exclusion created a diverse group of outcasts and that many of them were ordinary people who simply worked for meager earnings or who received a pension.

What could account for the exclusion of weak and poor members of a population? For decades in Russia, the non-able-bodied, elderly and weak members of the community, such as widows, did not fare well in the struggle for scarce community resources. Such groups could not effectively assert their claim to shortage goods. It appears that local leaders in Russia distributed resources primarily to other heads of households who supported young families. Perhaps the community relied on private charity to care for the infirm and elderly. Moreover, those who identified outcasts made certain calculations about whom they could afford to exclude. Local officials throughout Russia apparently shared the view that depriving rights to those already marginal was a safe path of compliance with Soviet instruction. In an atmosphere of class war where officials felt pressured to disenfranchise a certain percentage of the local population, those without powerful advocates or loud voices were especially vulnerable. An inspector during the campaign of 1928–1929 expressed it this way: "The soviets followed the path of least resistance and took the middlemen [*maklaki*] and card-players whom it was easy to disenfranchise because they're the poor who won't turn to anyone [*nekuda ne poidet*] and won't complain. [The rural soviet] didn't disenfranchise those who by virtue of their power exercise authority."[168]

It appears that decisions about whom to disenfranchise were also shaped by local officials who sought to protect themselves and some members of their communities. First, these authorities worried about their own safety, given the risk of retribution. For example, in the city of Samara, electoral commissions were "afraid to disenfranchise their own [*lishit' svoego*]" for fear that they would be killed or become the victims of arson in retaliation. One local official was severely beaten by those whom he was intending to disenfranchise.[169] In addition, officials tried to protect those they liked or believed to be undeserving of punishment. In the Vyshgorod township, local authorities chose not to disenfranchise in a case where "the father is disenfranchised but the son is a good guy [*paren'*], plays the accordion; no need to disenfranchise him." Local officials refused to disenfranchise persons who "lend their cart to poor peasants" or were "desirable members of the community." A report on the campaign in the Caucasus noted cases in which "kulak elements and traders as well as dependent members of their family are not disenfranchised and are sometimes even defended by poor peasants." In the Urals oblast in the winter 1925–1926, a priest was not disenfranchised because local officials claimed that he was "a completely Soviet man."[170] Hiring poor peasants was viewed by some as an act of public service rather than exploitation. Local authorities also demonstrated a reluctance to deprive people of rights when they appeared harmless and protected individuals by classifying them in a favorable way. For example, in Kolomna and the Kolomenskii uezd, the police and administrative organs registered all former nuns as housewives. Local officials from the Sarapulskii province suggested granting voting rights to several mullahs because they were less "harmful" than the muezzin who looked like kulaks but were not disenfranchised.

Believing that the muezzin should be disenfranchised rather than the mullahs, local officials gave several mullahs in this raion agricultural tax breaks as poor peasants.[171]

As in the case of dekulakization, some officials hoped to protect their communities from the intrusions of central policy, so they resorted to tactics of evasion or resistance. In acts of defiance, many simply reported to their superiors the lack of any enemy classes whatsoever, saying "we have no one here to disenfranchise" or "there is a complete absence of people for disenfranchisement."[172] In 1925, the Voronezh province White Army officers were not disenfranchised because the soviet argued that "we have way too many of them."[173] One local soviet kept a man off of the list of disenfranchised because "he's old, he can't harm anyone."[174] Local officials also artificially expanded their lists with the names of children. Even small children appeared on the registers of disenfranchised as local officials tried to satisfy their superiors while at the same time leave their own communities relatively unaffected. In the North Caucasus and elsewhere, children between eleven and sixteen years of age were discovered on the list of the disenfranchised,[175] and one rural soviet in Komi included on its list children under the age of one.[176] Officials also padded their lists with the names of those who had died, left the region, or already regained their rights.[177] In the Smolensk gubernia, Irkutsk, Orenburg, and elsewhere, the register of outcasts included those who no longer lived in the village.[178] In a town outside Sochi, the list of the disenfranchised had only two people on it in 1926, and they were both deceased.[179] In one such case, Moscow authorities offered the following sarcastic directive: "The VTsIK Presidium would like to clarify that when questions about the disenfranchisement of certain persons are under consideration, discussion can only be about living persons and by no means about the dead."[180]

Local officials found themselves in the difficult position of having to provide names of outcasts to fulfill the target figures of their superiors and also protect themselves and their communities at the same time. For this reason, they frequently padded their lists with the names of those who would be the least affected by disenfranchisement, including children, the dead, and people who had already left the village. One man described how he sold his property, horse, and cow and left for Siberia in 1927 with his family to work, as he said, for wages and "as a proletarian." In 1933, he asked his rural soviet for a document (*spravka*) verifying his social origin and was told that in 1929, during his absence, he and his family were disenfranchised.[181] In his application for rehabilitation, one former trader answered the question "When were you deprived of rights?" with a simple "I don't know"; another responded, "I have no way of knowing when they disenfranchised me."[182] The causes of disenfranchisement were frequently unknown as well. "I myself don't even know the reason for my disenfranchisement," one woman remarked. Another whose husband was deprived of rights claimed, "We didn't even know when and why they deprived us of rights." A woman described how several days after the election "I learned through several people that I was deprived of rights. For what and how—I don't know—but from private conversations [I learned it was] apparently for trade."[183]

Officials practiced sneaking names onto the lists of the disenfranchised. A Urals man, deprived of rights after leaving his village, later described his experience: "In December 1928 or January 1929 they deprived me of voting rights in absentia [*zaochno*], after I had lived away from home for nearly a year and they didn't send me any kind of notification about this. Now when I came home for my usual vacation I asked people why I was deprived of voting rights and they said they didn't know: 'They didn't announce [anything]; we just heard that you were deprived of rights at the meeting of activists.' "[184] Sometimes, the surprise proved most alarming. Under the threat of eviction, people who discovered that they were outcast raced to gather the necessary documents proving that they deserved the reinstatement of rights. The victim of a false denunciation, one Muscovite faced eviction when he desperately tried to vindicate himself. He implored his former city soviet: "I have enclosed documents that attest to [my socially-useful work record] and ask that you grant me back my voting rights or at least send me immediately the reason why I was disenfranchised and when. If you fail to send me this information I will lose my job and housing in Moscow."[185]

Conclusion

The actual faces of Soviet Russia's disenfranchised become apparent when one examines not Bolshevik posters, but the local practices of depriving rights. The legal categories of the disenfranchised as delineated in the constitution and the electoral instructions often proved confusing and ambiguous, enabling local authorities to exercise license in the application of Soviet law. Still, the outcomes of policy implementation do not appear entirely incoherent. Rather, distant localities made similar decisions regarding whom to disenfranchise. Patterns of disenfranchisement across Russia suggest that local communities shared certain preferences regarding the kinds of people who should be subject to exclusion. On the one hand, local victims like Lenskii and the Talberts shared many of the same attributes that the party ascribed to the bourgeois classes. They and others were cast among the ranks of aliens because their neighbors believed that they behaved like exploiters, thieves, parasites, and nonlaboring elements. Local patterns of disenfranchisement also indicate that non-Russians were more likely than ethnic Russians to be grouped among the alien elements. Economic factors as well as cultural prejudice informed local exclusionary practices.

The particular concerns of local officials and communities also played a significant role in shaping the course of disenfranchisement. On the ground, people used the deprivation of rights as a weapon against personal enemies or the community's disruptive and marginal elements. Officials also sought to protect themselves against retaliation, defend local residents, punish social deviance, and satisfy central authorities by padding the lists of outcasts. More surprisingly, however, the most defenseless members of a community were especially vulnerable to exclusion. The poor, weak, and elderly apparently provided safe targets for people who had to satisfy the demands of their superiors to identify and punish enemies, but who also wanted to minimize the disruptive effect on their friends and communities and even backlash against themselves. At least some local officials and citizens believed that such individuals would be less likely to protest their disenfranchisement or retaliate against their accusers. What outcry could one reasonably expect from people who left the village, the incarcerated or institutionalized, the young, sick, female, disabled, the elderly, and the petty merchants? In fact, Soviet officials, perhaps to their surprise, did indeed hear these people talk back.

Konstantin Chebotarev, *In the Canteen*. 1932. © State Russian Museum, St. Petersburg, 2001. From *Soviet Art: 1920s–1930s, Russian Museum, Leningrad*. New York: Harry N. Abrams, Inc., 1988. By permission of the Museum.

3

Dangers, Disappearances, and False Appearances

In 1929, at the height of disenfranchisement and sufficiently early in its implementation, a number of Kremlin officials raised concerns about the course of their policy. Former traders and sons of priests who once were considered dangerous seemed less so after years of work in Soviet industry, at least according to some Bolshevik authorities. Certain party leaders complained about good Soviet citizens disenfranchised "formally" for being the daughter of a priest, as in the following Central Electoral Commission report that quoted from the Ivanovo newspaper *Rabochii klich:*"Here's a more typical example of such formalistic decisions: citizen Kineshmy-Lebedeva was disenfranchised as the daughter of a priest [*sluzhitel' kulta*]. Meanwhile, [she] has worked in Soviet institutions [*na sovetskom sluzhbe*] for 10 years . . . and has good references from the local trade union committee [*mestkom*]."[1] Some in the party would have surely labeled this daughter of a priest a "masked alien" working in Soviet institutions, but others considered the ten-year work record tantamount to naturalization. One official from the Moscow province (*oblast'*) questioned: "Is it really expedient to deprive the rights of a worker with a 20-year work record simply because he gets a 1,000 or 1,500 ruble income for renting part of his home?"[2] Similarly, the chairman of the Central Executive Committee or TsIK, M.I. Kalinin, disagreed with the disenfranchisement of a worker and former nobleman in 1929: "a former nobleman [*dvorianin*] works in Soviet institutions for 6–7 years for 50–70 rubles and you disenfranchise him. That can hardly be right."[3] The chairman also wondered whether Soviet power should really fear clerics. "A priest [*pop*] isn't a dangerous element," Kalinin claimed in 1929, "he isn't going to resort to adventurism [*ne poidet na advantiuru*]."[4]

Others questioned the notion of the trader as socially harmful, as in the case of one Moscow man who argued that he did not exploit but rather helped unemployed comrades when he hired them, and a petitioner from Dagestan who claimed "I traded but I wasn't harmful to society. . . . I helped everyone in any way I could."[5] Not everyone viewed trading as a negative activity worthy of such severe official sanction. For example, a Tatar man living in the Crimea described those who helped him to trade as saviors rather than enemies. Unemployed with many dependents, he proved unable to feed his family until he opened a coffee shop "thanks to the help of good people."[6] From party officials to the disenfranchised, many failed to accept the idea that all traders, priests, and dependents represented dangerous elements.

Then there was the absurdity of what one outcast described as an innocent child living "in hunger because his grandpa was a petty trader."[7] The irrationality of a policy that vilified relatives of "former people" for generations was not lost on party leaders. One official argued that this purge campaign would have to be abandoned soon before it appeared utterly senseless.

> At one time we had former people; now it turns out we have the children of former people. It looks like soon there will even be the grandchildren of the former people's children. How far will this go? . . . If a man is 74 years old and he is the son of a former trader, then surely he is not himself a former trader. . . . children of former people, grandchildren of former people, great grandchildren of former people—we can't carry on like this.[8]

Moreover, patterns of disenfranchisement were such that the most unfortunate individuals appeared on the list of the disenfranchised for having traded apples in a time of unemployment or for hiring a nanny for an invalid family member. The standard, indeed formulaic, complaint from central authorities about local disenfranchisement practices involved an image of dangerous political reversals or inversions. Poor, naive invalids were losing their rights while exploiting, crafty speculators continued to live normally or even quite well. A 1930 cartoon from the satirical paper *Krokodil* illustrated the problem when it featured members of the former bourgeoisie enjoying life in a luxurious apartment. After apparently taking numerous bribes, the housing manager earned the praise of these class enemies for how he "obtained ration tokens for us, helped with exemption from the reduction of living space and takes minimum rent as from the unemployed. It's a pity there are not enough such people in the party!"[9] It was widely believed that the former privileged classes remained so, while ignorant poor folk became disenfranchised.

The notorious "abuses" by local officials to which central authorities so often referred described a policy turned upside-down and backwards. In 1929, Kiselev claimed that those who by law should not be disenfranchised were, while the real "exploitative elements" continued to enjoy voting rights.[10] Kalinin made a similar assertion that year, claiming that peasants of moderate wealth or middle peasants faced disenfranchisement, whereas rich peasant kulaks did not.[11] Central authorities repeated this observation to illustrate a policy gone completely awry, as in the following 1931 remark from I. I. Kutuzov, head of the Central Electoral Commission's subcommittee on reviewing complaints of wrongful disenfranchisement: "In this electoral campaign . . . you see that often they disenfranchised those who previously worked in factories but lost their ability to work and must engage in small trade [*torgovlishka*] or, for example, a widow burdened by a large family who can't work in industry so does wretched trading [instead]. . . . Yet big-time sharks, of whom there are still many unfortunately, they weren't exposed . . . because they're more sly than the small-fry [*meliuzga*] whom we disenfranchised."[12]

As the weak, poor, and unfortunate filled the ranks of outcasts, party officials grew increasingly alarmed about the presence of unmasked enemies. Believing that those who truly deserved to be disenfranchised were avoiding detection and escaping punishment, Kremlin leaders pushed a campaign of exposure (*vyiavlenie*) so that the lists of the disenfranchised, as Kalinin emphasized, included "all persons who by law should be disenfranchised."[13] In the 1928–1929 campaign, cities like Shakhty and Groznyi established special commissions for exposing the disenfranchised (*komissii sodeistviia po vyiavleniiu lits, lishennyikh izbiratel'nykh prav*).[14] Moscow factories had commissions "for exposing the disenfranchised" at the workplace.[15] Tales of exposure described how these special commissions, together with organizations like the housing managements and the komsomol, "turned up" enemies in their midst: "In Moscow, the housing units expose the disenfranchised . . . [in one case] a resident in the house was Agnia Nikolskaia (who now teaches English in the Timiriazev Academy), the daughter of the former Minister of Internal Affairs, Protopopov, . . . and the komsomol member, A. V. Chikarev, an agent for the dissemination of literature, who turned out to be the son of V. Ia. Sorokin, the former prominent worker of the police department."[16]

The sharp increase in the numbers of outcasts in Moscow during the 1928–1929 campaign was attributed in part to this intensive effort to "expose" the disenfranchised.[17] For Soviet officials, the real enemy constituted a phantom, always unmarked and elusive. And so they worked not only to "compile" the lists of the disenfranchised but also to "verify" them, to ensure that no one went undetected. This concern to track and expose the disenfranchised was expressed in a report by the Moscow City Soviet to the Central Electoral Commission in 1929: "In Moscow last year there were 43,000 [people disenfranchised] but now 63,000 have been exposed. In the provinces and rural districts this year there were 43,223 exposed while in the last electoral campaign there were 37,449. What's the percentage in the gubernia? 4.3 percent. But in Moscow we still don't have accurate figures but it's around 3 percent. We think that in Moscow we still haven't fully exposed [the disenfranchised]. [The newspaper] *Rabochaia Moskva* maintains that there are 133,000 disenfranchised people unexposed. . . . In every district [*raion*] 40–60 people are working to verify the lists."[18]

Officials sent from Moscow to report on local electoral campaigns returned with descriptions of how the truly privileged had escaped all official sanction and even occupied positions of authority, whereas the poor became victims of disenfranchisement. A member of the 1929 Central Electoral Commission Plenum reported the following: "I was in Sevastopol. There, a citizen filed a complaint concerning wrongful disenfranchisement. An official document was enclosed indicating that they deprived her of rights as a homeowner. When I went out to review the case it turned out that she lives in a small shack [*khibarka*] and has seven kids. In that house, horrible poverty reigns. Her trading consists entirely of going with her eldest son to the dump [*na svarku*)] and collecting rags in order to then re-sell . . . they often disenfranchise those who should not be deprived of rights while, on the contrary, an alien element creeps even into the party." In a similar story of a policy turned upside down, one official described the life of a woman with six children who washed clothes for a living and was deprived of rights for selling ice cream two years earlier. At that time, she served as the maid for a certain Piskarev who was not disenfranchised, although he earned a large income from his house.[19] In March 1929, Kalinin described the way in which Moscow officials made decisions on whether to disenfranchise, calling their practices "formalistic, mechanical," "callous," "an un-communist, purely bureaucratic deviation . . . worse than a right deviation."[20]

Adding further to the problems associated with the policy, a number of Soviet institutions objected to the disenfranchisement of valuable employees. In 1929, the Commissariat of Enlightenment complained about the large numbers of teachers deprived of rights. The assistant commissar, V. N. Iakovleva, stated in a secret memo to the Central Electoral Commission that work in education would suffer as skilled employees were disenfranchised, for "not always is there a sufficient reserve of qualified cadres to quickly replace the disenfranchised."[21] In another case, G. V. Chukhrit of the People's Commissariat of Trade (*Narkomtorg*) complained that average peasants who earned very little providing eggs for the state were nonetheless deprived of rights for "engaging in the buying and reselling of agricultural products." He tried to persuade the Central Electoral Commission to allow these peasants to gather eggs for the state because their disenfranchisement could "very seriously harm our efforts to carry out the egg campaign."[22] The campaign to deprive rights seemed ineffective and counterproductive to many; to others the policy looked even worse.

Conditions for Counterrevolution

Disenfranchisement, Lenin believed, would make it possible for the Bolsheviks to maintain power in the delicate period of transition after the revolution. In 1919, he confidently asserted that in a couple of years the leadership would be able to boast that "we have been able to hold on [to power] . . . namely because we included in the Constitution that certain persons and groups be deprived of rights."[23] If Lenin trusted that disenfranchisement would be responsible for preserving the Bolsheviks' grip on power, by 1929 some party leaders seemed convinced that, on the contrary, the practice of depriving rights might actually threaten the stability of the regime. At a March 1929 meeting of the party fraction of the VTsIK Presidium, Solts described a policy run amok. "When I came here . . . already within two days I felt that something is not normal here and I turned to Mikhail Ivanovich [Kalinin] and said to him that a peculiar phenomenon [*osoboe iavlenie*] is occurring, something unbelievable—party members, workers, wives of oppositionists, whoever—the most diverse mix of people for the most varied reasons is being disenfranchised."[24] Kalinin claimed that disenfranchised "communists have come to me who were literally crying."[25] Central authorities feared that they ran the risk of alienating their own constituency and destabilizing the regime, that when a printer is disenfranchised because his wife once traded apples, "we mostly defeat [*b'em*] ourselves and not others."[26] Moscow was teeming with angry residents, as Kiselev described at a meeting of the party faction of the VTsIK Presidium in 1929. The ease with which people were being disenfranchised had caused an "uproar," a bad atmosphere, a dangerous mood in the capital. "[I]n Moscow, there's an unbelievable uproar [*podnialsia neveroiatnyi shum*]. . . . One can simply tell that an atmosphere has been created that isn't good. They disenfranchise right and left because of personal vengeance. One man moved another's pot on the stove so out of vengeance [*mest'*] the other says, 'I'm going to go and tell and they'll deprive you [of rights]'. . . . Moscow is big and a mood has been created that is unfavorable [*neblagopriiatnoe*]."[27]

Party officials could hear the mood on the street in numerous letters of complaint, as people without rights submitted angry, sarcastic, and indignant remarks to Soviet authorities. Lenin once wrote that peasants "could not rise in rebellion, they are only able to petition and to pray." But he did not consider that some petitions were at times modest rebellions.[28] Not a few petitioners included in their letters a sharp indictment of the individuals and policy that condemned them. Reminding Soviet authorities of poverty in the workers' paradise, one woman declared with irony, "even if I wanted to exploit hired labor, how could I with only 3.5 desiatins [of land]?"[29] The son of a deported kulak, identifying his petition as "from a worker," unabashedly criticized the leadership: "What kind of policy from our leaders is this? [*chto za politika nashikh rukovoditelei*]."[30] One petitioner used bitter sarcasm when offering the requisite assurances to Soviet authorities that he had no connection to his alien parents. He described how his father was imprisoned in 1928 and deported in 1929, and remarked, "in this way, I have no ties with him."[31]

Some outcasts expressed their disillusionment with Soviet power and charged the party leadership with hypocrisy. A man deprived of rights and excluded from the collective farm along with his son argued that his expulsion "completely contradicts the policy of Soviet power that all peasants should be brought into the kolkhoz."[32] A man described how his children tried to enroll in school but faced rejection because of their disenfranchised father, and this "at the same time that [political] slogans speak of the need to study."[33] As Foucault noted, "resistance is never in a position of exteriority in relation to power"; the party's own values and slogans shaped these written expressions of opposition.[34] In a letter dated 1931, an administrative exile, deported first to Solovki and then to Arkhangelsk, spoke of the failures of Bolshevism: "If I once believed . . . that I live in a country run by the proletariat, in a country where the leadership is waging a fierce battle with the exploiters of the laboring population, a struggle against inhuman treatment of the lower classes, etc., etc., and that only in this country I could count on defense and support in every respect—then now I am convinced that people look at me like I'm scum [*svoloch'*]." He asserted most emphatically, "I am bitterly disillusioned."[35]

Ethnic minorities often expressed their disappointment with how the principles and practices of Bolshevism diverged. In particular, Jewish outcasts frequently spoke of the regime's hypocrisy and their own shattered optimism, how Jews lost their rights under Soviet power just as they had under tsarist rule. Bolshevism had truly failed the Jews because nothing had improved. "In tsarist times . . . when I petitioned for the right to live in any place [*pravo povsemestnogo zhitel'stva*], I was rejected as a Jew. And now, I am refused rights for other but no less formal reasons. . . . Persecuted in the past, I even remain in the present without full rights."[36] In the following petition of a Jewish refugee from Poland, one encounters a similar sense of indignation and injustice. Despite his persecution under the Tsars, flight from Poland, and military service during the civil war, he continued to be deprived of rights. He wrote with irony:

> When there was the revolution in Russia and the power of the workers was established, I fled to Russia. Having experienced all the delights [*prelesti*] of living under the yoke of tsarism, being eternally persecuted only because I was Jewish, I thought that in a free country I wouldn't experience any kind of persecution, no limits on my rights as an individual and citizen. . . . And so, given all my working life, my active participation in the battle on the front, continuous persecution by the tsarist government, the fact that I, knowing that the workers established power, fled from the persecution of exploiters, [given this] they deprive me of voting rights [and] simply because, under necessity, I engaged in petty trade for a short time.[37]

Disenchanted subjects seemed to appear everywhere, in the rural areas and the capital, among Russian and non-Russian minorities. A man from Dagestan also described Bolshevik hypocrisy and a life unchanged. "It has been asked: under the Tsar we were subservient [*nam gnuli spiny*]. Could it really be that they'll despise us under Soviet power too? I think not because Soviet power generally accommodates the laboring peasant of Dagestan, yet at the same time it deprives me [of rights] in 1928. . . . I worked 1919–1926 for the good of my people and hardly deserve such contempt."[38] Some warned that the continuation of such injustices would harm Soviet power. "All this injustice doesn't benefit but only harms the state because intense hostility comes from this," warned one writer, "The entire peasant population views Soviet power with hostility."[39] In 1929, Kalinin went so far as to say that the current process of disenfranchisement had the potential of generating counterrevolutionary activity in the capital: "Moscow is not a provincial city; here you never can eliminate counterrevolution just as the former capital was not able to eliminate revolutionary activity. Therefore, I think that first of all a directive should be issued so that the disenfranchisement of laboring elements is approached with great caution [*s suguboi ostorozhnost'iu*]."[40] The directive that Kalinin called for was issued months later.

Ambivalence and a Mild Retreat

In all probability, voices of popular opposition and the leadership's own worries regarding counterrevolution influenced the decision to ease certain discriminatory measures as early as 1929. A circular from the People's Commissar of Justice, N. V. Krylenko, specified that the disenfranchised could not be evicted from their apartment if they currently earned a "laboring wage" (*trudovoi zarabotok*).[41] The Russian Central Association of Trade Unions issued instructions that persons deprived of voting rights should keep their trade union membership and could not be fired from work for one year after their disenfranchisement if they had filed a petition for the reinstatement of voting rights.[42] Moreover, disenfranchisement could not serve as the sole reason for imposing certain sanctions. For example, a circular of the NKVD and the Commissariat of Justice specified that disenfranchisement alone could not justify the eviction of people from their apartment.[43] The following year the Soviet government initiated even broader measures that signaled a mild retreat in the pace of disenfranchisements as well as the party leadership's ambivalence about the success of its policy.

In 1930, the government did appear to lighten certain sanctions against the disenfranchised, remove bureaucratic barriers to employment, and reaffirm the legal exceptions to the categories of disenfranchised people. In his infamous article of March 1930 entitled "Dizzy with Success," Stalin condemned the excesses committed by local officials during the campaign of forced collectivization and dekulakization.[44] Only weeks later, TsIK issued its own statement concerning abuses in a decree "on eliminating violations of USSR electoral legislation."[45] This and subsequent laws banned such discriminatory practices as the indiscriminate confiscation of ration books; the denial of medical care, legal assistance, and housing; the expulsion of alien children from school; and the disenfranchisement of family members who are not dependents.[46] The law also emphasized that organs such as the housing management, local trade union committees, and collective farms did not have the authority to disenfranchise people.[47] In 1930, the NKVD issued a circular that the eviction of people without rights from state and municipal housing can only take place "on general grounds established by the appropriate laws," while "in the existing legislation there is no prohibition against the disenfranchised living in municipal housing."[48] Nonetheless, these restrictions appeared hollow as policymakers condemned only those discriminatory measures "that have not been provided for in USSR or RSFSR legislation." For example, the Central Electoral Commission maintained that instructions to deny the disenfranchised shares in cooperatives and ration books "correspond to the state and party line" and need not be changed.[49] The discriminatory policy against the disenfranchised remained fundamentally intact.

In addition, the party leadership urged a systematic review of petitions for the reinstatement of rights, and the formation of special commissions to verify lists of the disenfranchised for the purpose of rehabilitating those wrongly classified. In particular, the person who filed a complaint of improper disenfranchisement now had certain advantages over the petitioner who simply appealed for reinstatement, since the former was not subject to discrimination while the appeal was under review.[50] For this reason, many chose to file complaints and stave off the broader penalties of disenfranchisement. At the end of 1930, an official from the Western oblast recognized this legal incentive to claim wrongful disenfranchisement and argued that outcasts "always send multiple complaints so that they have cause to say that 'a complaint was filed and so no restrictions concerning disenfranchisement can be applied to me.' Daily there's a line of disenfranchised people and they're waiting for an answer. They know that they [should be] disenfranchised, but they complain anyway."[51]

In reassessing these cases, officials referred to the various legal exceptions to the categories of disenfranchised persons. In the Instructions on Elections to the Soviets, those formally protected from disenfranchisement included petty traders, lay worshipers, and small craftsmen, peasants who sold their goods at the market or who hired help because of illness or mobilization, and factory workers with ties to the village who employed hired labor for the months they worked in the cities.[52] These people were often disenfranchised regardless, but now the government took steps to reaffirm this section of the electoral instructions. Since 1924, invalids from civilian labor and military service were largely protected from disenfranchisement if they engaged in trade, and the state now reaffirmed that invalids who engaged in trade on a free license of "rank one" for personal production (*na lichnye promysly*) could not be disenfranchised.[53] The Central Electoral Commission generally rehabilitated those who traded during the 1922 famine and the acute unemployment of 1927–1928, or if trading involved minor activities such as baking bread out of one's home. In 1929, the Central Electoral Commission reaffirmed that homeowners who belonged to the "laboring categories of the population (blue-and white-collar workers, their family members, as well as the unemployed, invalids from work and their families, and others) do not qualify as disenfranchised."[54] With militant class war waning, the government reaffirmed existing laws regarding those who should be shielded from the loss of rights. Acknowledging that the most vulnerable segments of society had lost their rights in the period of intensified class struggle, the party issued these decrees to emphasize that the poor and invalid were legally protected from the loss of rights. In 1930, the flurry of decrees did not mark a change in policy so much as an affirmation of the formal exceptions to the categories of the disenfranchised.

Party leaders also considered local economic conditions and people's value to the state when they assessed whether someone should be disenfranchised. In 1930, the Central Electoral Commission issued a circular that listed the kinds of production in which craftsmen could use hired labor due to "technical conditions."[55] Subcontractors in the sale of alcohol were considered private traders and subject to disenfranchisement, whereas subcontractors in the distribution of newspapers (*pechati*) were not.[56] Regional economic variation and "particular local conditions" were also studied in order that the economy of any single region would not suffer disproportionately from disenfranchisement. For example, in 1928, the CEC Presidium asked the NKVD RSFSR to supply information on the degree to which workers and peasants generated rent income from their homes, while other officials monitored the large numbers of disenfranchisement in a village of the Kaluga province (*guberniia*), where "there are a whole line of peasants there who buy and sell hay."[57] For example, tobacco, grape, and other crop-growers were allowed to use temporary hired help, and peasants in the Urals region could hire two seasonal workers.[58] Finally, VIPs were not supposed to lose their rights, as is evidenced by a 1929 protest by Procuracy officials to Kiselev after the Kremlin hospital's consultant was disenfranchised.[59]

Foreign nationals constituted another group protected from disenfranchisement, particularly since their loss of rights created problems with foreign embassies.[60] One case that attracted special attention in Moscow involved American World War I veterans. The Commissariat of Finance received numerous complaints from U.S. veterans and pensioners who, because they received money from abroad, experienced "various forms of oppression," including disenfranchisement. The heirs of U.S. veterans faced expulsion from trade unions and the komsomol; veterans themselves were fired from their jobs, excluded from the collective farm, evicted from their homes, and dekulakized. Calling such treatment of U.S. veterans and their heirs "completely wrong," the Commissariat sought to rectify the situation.[61] In March 1930, the Commissariat of Finance sent a memo to the NKVD of seven areas, including the Ukraine, Russia, Belorussia, Uzbekistan, and the North Caucasus, with copies to their respective Commissariats of Finance, about this problem. The memo condemned the treatment of heirs of U.S. World War I veterans who lived "in various cities and rural areas of the USSR" and received a pension from the U.S. government. The pension was issued in dollars to the Soviet Central Bank, which then distributed the money to the appropriate individuals in rubles. The Commissariat stressed that there was "nothing wrong" with this, for the arrangement served the state's "well-known hard currency interest" because "hard currency from abroad remains in the USSR Bank." Therefore, the transfer of money to heirs of U.S. veterans should continue, and U.S. veterans and pensioners should not be subject to "any forms of oppression and persecution."[62]

The retreat of 1930 consisted in the government affirming the formal limits of disenfranchisement and the legal exemptions to the categories of people who should be deprived of rights. Central officials began to urge caution in disenfranchisement and provide more clarification about who should and should not be deprived of rights. VTsIK emphasized that participants in counterrevolutionary bands and former officers and bureaucrats of the White Army who served in the Red Army and took active part in the defense of the Soviet republic should not be disenfranchised.[63] The Supreme Court determined that the fact that someone received money from abroad in the form of pension, alimony, or insurance could not itself serve as grounds for classifying the person as a nonlaboring element and imposing limitations on his rights.[64] People who requested a passport for the right to live in certain cities or settlements (*naselennye punkty*) and whose passport application was rejected could not be disenfranchised for this reason alone.[65] These laws do not reflect a reversal in party policy but only an affirmation of the formal limits on disenfranchisement that were virtually ignored at the highest levels of the state bureaucracy during the period of militant class war. How seriously people took these statements remains an open question, as those reinstated in rights faced continued discrimination because of popular suspicion and fear. Speaking at a meeting of the Central Electoral Commission in 1931, Kutuzov described this problem in the Moscow oblast: "When [formerly disenfranchised people] show the rural soviets a decree from the Moscow electoral commission or the Central Electoral Commission for the reinstatement of rights, the rural soviets tell them that it makes no difference to them [*eto im ni po chem*]; they'll continue to [keep them] disenfranchised."[66]

Finally, in 1931, VTsIK issued a decree forbidding state institutions from requiring that citizens present a document to prove that they had voting rights. For example, the Commissariat of Labor typically required citizens to present documentation confirming their voting rights when they approached labor and insurance offices with requests for employment or a pension. After publication of the VTsIK decree, this requirement was rescinded.[67] Although local officials routinely required citizens to demonstrate their right to vote before they could be eligible for housing or education, policymakers condemned the practice, arguing that it created "unnecessary work" for officials who had to issue such documents.[68] Organizations were instead urged to use inquiries and questionnaires if they wanted information on someone's past, which meant that individuals could deny their disenfranchisement and assume the risk of being found out. This is what many chose to do.

Tracking an Elusive Enemy

When the satirical writers Ilf and Petrov described the case of a class enemy, a pharmacy owner and son of alien elements who had himself confined to a mental institution in order to avoid the authorities, these popular humorists caricatured the sad reality of people doing whatever they could to protect themselves against repression.[69] Party leaders long understood that concealment and flight were common responses to disenfranchisement. In April 1928, a provincial executive committee asked the Central Electoral Commission to mandate that the disenfranchised be registered when they move to another district (*raion*), but many CEC officials considered this effort hopeless. A member of the Moscow City Soviet, speaking before the Central Electoral Commission in October of that year, noted: "We take account of everything from manure to garbage, but we don't keep track of [*ne uchityvaem*] the class enemy and it is impossible to."[70] When the Central Electoral Commission referred the suggestion to the NKVD, the latter admitted the impossibility of tracking an elusive group like the disenfranchised: "A significant portion of the population, particularly the rural population, lives on RSFSR territory without a passport [*propusk*]. It is obvious that under such conditions it would be impossible [*neosushchestvii*] for the soviets . . . to keep a record of all persons deprived of voting rights."[71] In 1931, the Central Electoral Commission ultimately rejected a plan requiring outcasts to register with the local authorities whenever they move to a new place of residence.[72] Various draft proposals on the establishment of a nationwide, permanent account of disenfranchised persons who changed their place of residence were ultimately scrapped as inexpedient (*netselesoobraznyi*).[73] Thus, although policymakers complained about the failure to identify aliens and to keep adequate account of the disenfranchised, they had few practical ideas for a possible remedy. Attempts to maintain reliable statistics on the number and movements of the disenfranchised were consistently dismissed as futile.

Although data on the numbers of disenfranchised people were notoriously problematic, party leaders devoted a lot of attention to these numbers. Any fluctuations in the number of people disenfranchised generated great debate and anxiety. Indeed, the inconsistent manner in which party leaders interpreted these figures reflected their deep ambivalence about the practices of exclusion and inclusion. In 1929, VTsIK requested data from local officials on "the increase and decrease in the number of disenfranchised, in the city and in the village, as compared with the previous campaign."[74] Fluctuations in these figures were watched carefully, and the Central Electoral Commission would even send investigators to determine why some regional figures changed abruptly, either up or down.[75] Kalinin called this highly quantitative approach to disenfranchisement policy "uncommunist" and thoughtless: "the figures look right, so we're satisfied [*tsifry podkhodiashchie i my spokoiny*]."[76] However, often the figures did not look right, and in such cases interpretations of the statistics varied widely. For example, decreases in the numbers of people without rights could be condemned as evidence of official neglect and weak class vigilance or touted as an indication of more "exact accounting" and a successful effort to address the excesses of the previous campaign.[77] In March 1929, Moscow officials seemed confused about how to interpret the sharp increase in the numbers of the disenfranchised. They wondered whether there was gross underreporting in the previous campaign's accounting, or some striking sociological change (*sotsial'nyi sdvig*) in the city, or whether the increase was indeed due, as anecdotes claimed, to "80,000 people being disenfranchised for [trading] apples."[78]

Beginning in 1930, the numbers of the disenfranchised began to decline in the registries of local state authorities. The figures on the disenfranchised as a percentage of voters revealed a sharp increase in the 1926–1927 campaign, a marginal increase with the campaign of 1928–1929, and then a sharp decline with the 1930–1931 campaign. For example, Moscow registered nearly 50,000 disenfranchised people in 1930, but by the 1931 campaign, rehabilitations, arrests, and deportations, as well as flight and relocation had cut the figure by as much as half.[79] Some members of the CEC refused to accept such declining figures. When he heard that the numbers of the disenfranchised in the North Caucasus krai dropped in the election campaign of 1931, Kutuzov had his doubts. It was more likely, he believed, that marked people were fleeing and changing residence in order to avoid being identified.

> The North Caucasus regional soviet executive committee will say that presently [their] number of disenfranchised is declining. But how is it declining? Do you take into account those who have fled from [your krai]? That's interesting. . . . If he has skipped out of the village then may he have a pleasant journey [*skatert'iu emu doroga*]. You record on the list [of the disenfranchised] the one who is present and disenfranchised. And so it's highly questionable [*sporno*] that the numbers of disenfranchised people are declining.[80]

In the 1930s, the declining figures in the numbers of disenfranchised people was due in part to the fact that many outcasts came under the supervision of the secret police (*OGPU-NKVD*) following arrest and deportation; still others suffered execution as dangerous kulaks.[81] Yet many members of the Central Electoral Commission did not attribute the decline to executions, arrests, and deportations but rather to the failure of state officials to unmask the enemy in their midst. With regard to the numbers of people without rights in Leningrad, one official reported to the CEC in 1929 that the figure of 1.5 percent of voters or 16,836 people did not reflect the actual number of people without rights in the city, which he maintained was closer to 5.6 percent of Leningraders or nearly 65,000 residents.[82] At a meeting of the Central Electoral Commission Plenum in 1931, another official argued that the declining figures on the disenfranchised merely demonstrated that outcasts had become more adept at concealing their identity: "The drop can be observed everywhere . . . throughout the country. . . . There was a very big outpouring [*uchechka*] of disenfranchised people who went from their place of residence to another. That isn't an actual drop in the number of disenfranchised, but [they're] just avoiding our glance."[83]

As Sheila Fitzpatrick describes, the disenfranchised hurried to establish new identities by changing their place of residence, place of work, relationships, and acquaintances.[84] Officials rather hopelessly acknowledged that people who had been disenfranchised or who would otherwise qualify for disenfranchisement were simply fleeing to other regions and starting new lives. At a meeting of a subcommittee of the Central Electoral Commission in 1929, one member lamented, "It was a big mistake that thus far we have not carried out an accounting of the disenfranchised who move. A disenfranchised person moves to another city and there becomes a citizen with full rights [*polnopravnyi grazhdanin*]."[85] Soviet authorities believed that their difficulty identifying members of the outcast categories was due in part to this crafty group's ability to avoid detection by moving frequently from one region to the next. Expressing his frustration over the absence of any uniform method of accounting for the disenfranchised, particularly when so many constantly changed residence, one Moscow official complained that "if a disenfranchised person leaves Moscow for Rostov, then they can't know there that he's disenfranchised, just as if he leaves Rostov for Moscow."[86] Officials distrusted data gathered on the numbers of people without rights because they believed so many had escaped detection by moving constantly.

The locally reported numbers of people disenfranchised in the 1930–1931 electoral campaign declined, probably the combined result of a mild policy retreat, an increase in rehabilitations, and the disappearance of people as the result of flights, arrests, and deportations. The disenfranchised comprised 3.9 percent of the voting-age population in the RSFSR in 1929, yet this declined to 3.2 percent in the 1930 campaign. A similar decline was recorded in the oblast and krai regions: In the North Caucasus, 3.8 percent in 1930 compared with 5.6 percent in 1929; in the Ivanovo Industrial oblast, 2.7 percent compared with 4.2 percent in 1929; in the Moscow oblast 2.1 percent in 1930 compared with 3.4 percent in 1929. N. F. Novikov, a member of VTsIK, offered two explanations for the decline in these numbers. On the one hand, the 1930 decrees that were aimed at reducing excesses in disenfranchisement had been implemented. On the other hand, local officials were failing to keep accurate track of people without rights. As he put it, "this decline in the overall numbers of the disenfranchised can be explained largely by the implementation of a series of measures to correct the excesses in disenfranchisement and the inadequate accounting [*nedouchet*] of people in a series of places because of weak class vigilance on the part of local soviets."[87] The ambivalence of Novikov's remark reveals a tension that emerged in the course of a policy to disenfranchise and rehabilitate aliens. According to the lists managed by the local state governing councils or soviets, the numbers of people without rights was falling, and this decline could be interpreted as either a success or a failure. Either abuses were being curtailed, or outcasts more skillfully masked their true identity. The dominant perception that eventually prevailed was the most alarmist, as shrinking lists of people without rights fueled suspicion concerning the presence of hidden enemies.

The Alien Is a Pretender

The official picture of Soviet aliens consistently portrayed them as masters of deception. Aliens routinely manipulated and tricked Soviet citizens and officials. Entrepreneurs or Nepmen circumvented the laws against private trade by simply closing their former enterprises and resuming capitalist activities under the false guise of officially sanctioned artisan cooperatives or artels. In December 1927, Stalin was highly critical of "exploiting elements" who "cunningly and ably . . . hide behind the flag of the industrial cooperatives and the flag of certain state trading bodies." The state's enemies were also peasants who resisted the requisitioning authorities by concealing their grain underground and in hidden storage. In April 1928, Stalin warned of severe measures against speculators and hoarders of grain, dishonest capitalist elements who "play tricks" with the state.[88] Following dekulakization and collectivization, Stalin remarked that the kulak enemy was now primarily characterized by his enmity toward Soviet power, which he conceals "under the mask of obedience and loyalty."[89]

Scare stories about undetected alien elements typically described how these enemies had infiltrated the organs of state power in order to subvert Soviet authority from within. In January 1929, Kiselev expressed concern over "alien elements" who were discovered working in the soviets: "former gendarmes, traders and even a former prince."[90] In Tomsk, a psalmodist worked in the rural soviet; in the Leningrad oblast, the daughter of a priest served in an electoral commission; and "the former [tsarist] vice governor of the Western krai [sic], Stavin-Gagine, works in Gosplan."[91] In 1931, Kutuzov claimed that this unexposed population of "sharks" harmed Soviet power.[92] Members of ethnic minority groups were frequently cast as aliens, and their communities were criticized for not punishing anti-Soviet elements. A report on the North Caucasus krai in 1931 noted that electoral commissions ("mainly" in Chechnia) were "contaminated by alien elements";[93] the "contamination [*zasorennost'*] of the electoral commissions by class alien elements" was believed to be common in the Caucasus region.[94]

Unexposed enemies not only infiltrated local government organs but consumed valuable and scarce resources to which they were not entitled. In the 1928–1929 campaign, Moscow officials were charged with failing to disenfranchise the former landowner from the Voronezh province, Prince V. S. Volkonskii, who was then collecting unemployment compensation.[95] Kutuzov also expressed anger at how the disenfranchised on the sly appropriated all the good Moscow apartments, leaving the worst for the working class. "They gave the disenfranchised the best accommodations . . . but workers from the factories were sent to very bad [ones] . . . the best apartments [go to] a group [*publika*] that concealed its past and now uses every possible means to undermine Soviet power."[96] Officials continued to reproduce the old epithets for the enemy classes. Aliens represented thieves who, through deception, robbed the public of necessary resources such as social welfare assistance and housing.

The disenfranchised who petitioned for the reinstatement of rights were viewed as manipulators, tricksters, and pretenders. Since cases relied heavily upon written materials, forgeries and the manipulation of official documents were common. One official pamphlet emphasized how letters required special vigilance (*osobaia bditel'nost'*), because the class enemy frequently provided false information, turning to forgery in an attempt to deceive Soviet power.[97] In 1929, the fact that nearly half of the disenfranchised in Moscow were reinstated in rights demonstrated to some that violations of disenfranchisement policy had occurred, while others simply accused the disenfranchised of being disingenuous in their petitions, and taking advantage of the rehabilitation mechanism.[98] In 1929, the city of Krasnodar catalogued such manipulative practices: "[T]hey all turn to [the city soviet] for rehabilitation, demonstrating that they're Soviet workers. . . . The disenfranchised now have become more active than before. It's not rare for them to appear as though they're for Soviet power only in order to be reinstated in rights. There were even cases in which certain disenfranchised people went to the trade unions and also to certain members of the union for documents [attesting to] their loyalty, and some of them even managed to secure a petition [on their behalf] from certain organizations."[99]

Many shared the view that crafty and sinister people had managed to acquire rights.[100] In 1930, the rate of rehabilitations accelerated as the Commission reinstated rights in nearly 60 percent of the cases which it reviewed. By 1931, Kutuzov expressed the typical anxieties: "I fear that they've begun to rehabilitate those who are actually kulaks, who really should be disenfranchised."[101] Some officials even wondered whether the effects of disenfranchisement were being offset entirely by the reinstatement of rights. In a number of cases, the reinstatement of rights seemed to follow disenfranchisement automatically. In 1929, one official described how "there are cases in which they disenfranchise [someone] seven times and they reinstate [his] rights seven times."[102] In the Chechen province in 1931, some rural electoral commissions rehabilitated every single person who had been disenfranchised in the previous campaign.[103] At a 1931 meeting of the Central Electoral Commission Plenum, Kutuzov expressed

the "fear that rehabilitation now is such that there won't be even one disenfranchised person [left]."[104]

Soviet officials often declined to interpret the reinstatement of rights as
an indication that alien elements became sovietized, and instead many believed that rehabilitations had been excessive or unwarranted. At a 1930
meeting of the Commission, one official protested when he learned that a
third of all the disenfranchised in the Central Black Earth region had been
reinstated in rights.[105] At a meeting of the Central Electoral Commission
plenum in 1931, Kutuzov complained that some members of the Industrial
Party (*Prompartiia*) had not been disenfranchised, even though they "had
their big-time land holdings [*pomest'ia*]."[106] Someone present turned the
complaint against Kutuzov when he interjected: "You reinstated rights for
several of them!"[107] Despite their own doubts and suspicions, Soviet officials continued to process and approve an increasing number of petitions
for the reinstatement of rights. However, the more people were reinstated
in rights, the more Soviet officials feared the presence of hidden enemies.
Few seemed convinced that a policy of exclusion and inclusion was helping to effectively engineer a new citizenry.

Soviet officials constantly doubted the sincerity of the petitioners' appeals. In a 1932 secret memo to the secretary of VTsIK and head of the
Central Electoral Commission, A. S. Kiselev, the secretary of the
Leningrad Soviet's commission for the rehabilitation of the disenfranchised, illustrated how people manipulated the rehabilitation mechanism
for their own advantage: "In most cases in the Leningrad oblast, one meets
with and will encounter in the future such cases: as soon as the rural soviet
disenfranchises someone, he goes to Leningrad, works at a factory, and
after a while goes to the district soviet or the Leningrad city soviet with a
petition "from a worker" even with a shock worker's award [*gramota*]
and asks that his petition for the reinstatement of rights be reviewed."[108]
Many Soviet officials believed that they were simply being outsmarted by
concealed enemies. A Sovnarkom official visited the North Caucasus krai
and reported on his visit to Kiselev at the end of 1928, describing how the
disenfranchised there had certain strategies for getting reinstated in rights,
such as selling off their property and calling off their agreements to hire
poor, landless laborers. "Extraordinarily active in acquiring voting rights,
90 percent of the disenfranchised on the Don filed petitions [*zaiavleniia*]
for the reinstatement of voting rights."[109] Frustrated authorities watched
in alarm as their policy appeared to be managed by its subjects.

Moreover, the increasing volume of petitions for rehabilitation appeared as subversion and generated criticism of aliens who deliberately
bombarded officials with their appeals. In one 1929 report, Kutuzov di-

rectly attributed the "constant stream" of petitions at least partly to the fact that obvious kulaks and other enemy elements were fighting stubbornly to assert their rights by hiring lawyers and petitioning repeatedly.[110] That same year he reiterated his belief that the rehabilitation mechanism was being abused and exploited by the "crafty" practices of the disenfranchised and their hired, savvy scribes.

> Why was there such a huge stream of people filing complaints in the last campaign? Why did many people turn up in the last campaign in the Soviet Union who found the address: Subcommission, VTsIK, Kremlin? They say that there was great activity [*aktivnost'*], people woke up—including those whom we call kulak elements, anti-soviet elements. And look, they've tried with all their might [*fibrami dushi*] to get rehabilitated; they write a petition to the subcommission [thinking that] maybe it will take pity. But here, of course, [there] was much craftiness [*khitrost'*]. Members of the college of defenders also played a large role here, working a lot in this matter. We received many petitions written in script, which, of course, is something of their doing [*delo ikh ruk*].[111]

The volume of petitions was unrelenting and excessive, as many wrote repeatedly until they received a positive decision. Bogged down with appeals for rights, officials grew even more suspicious of the people who overwhelmed them with letters. The practice of constantly writing for the reinstatement of rights was viewed rather cynically by many who believed that outcasts are cunning and manipulative, "masquerade as loyal to Soviet power," overload the system with petitions, and run it amok.[112] An instructional book published for rural soviets and electoral commissions in 1930 warned of insincere petitions from hidden enemies of the regime.

> Of course, it's impossible to assume that all petitions from former class enemies about granting them political rights are based on a sincere, honest desire to march in step with the working class. Reality shows that most of them masquerade as loyal to Soviet power and walk in our midst "with a stone in their bosom" [*s kamnem za pazukhoi*]. They try to acquire political rights only in order to worm into state organs and . . . harm socialist construction. . . . That's why in reviewing such petitions there must not be humane trust nor carelessness . . . [but] maximum vigilance toward the efforts of class enemies to be reinstated in voting rights.[113]

A number of factors convinced Soviet officials that their system of exclusion and inclusion was failing. It appeared that the wrong people routinely lost rights, while the true enemies remained unexposed, avoiding Soviet authorities by changing residence or deceiving them through effective petitions for rights. Enemy aliens were always criticized for concealing their true identity, but by the 1930s the act of concealing one's past became the most pronounced indicator of the alien, even more salient than former status. It appears that a shift had occurred in the early 1930s, as aliens who once possessed any number of negative characteristics became increasingly vilified for what now seemed to be their fundamental trait— that of a pretender. The mere act of concealing one's past proved more damaging than the nonlaboring activity or bourgeois past for which one was originally disenfranchised. Persons suspected of "masking" a former life were simply not reinstated in rights.

Conclusion

"WHO AM I?" one petitioner wrote in bold, "A wolf in sheep's clothing, or a man who is in an unfortunate situation?"[114] Indeed, Soviet officials often wondered precisely that. As early as 1929, the year when the greatest number of people lost all rights, Bolshevik leaders deeply distrusted their ability to track what they believed was an elusive and deceptive enemy. It did not take long for members of the Central Electoral Commission to express concern about the breakdown of policy and alarm about how officials were being manipulated by their own victims. It appeared that disenfranchisement caused a broad diversity of ordinary people to lose their rights, and rehabilitation often favored those with the most compelling story. Many people without rights moved from one city to another to avoid repression, exploring all avenues to social inclusion. Social engineering proved irregular, uneven, and often ineffectual as people reacquired rights through a variety of strategies and discovered many possible points of entry back into the society that excluded them.

The actions of outcasts were only partly responsible for the alarm felt within the party, for there was scarcely a movement from the disenfranchised that failed to generate official suspicion. Aliens were believed to be masked, deceptive and elusive, and this understanding of the Soviet enemy effectively ensured its perpetual existence. By definition, the danger could never diminish, and, in fact, it quickly grew more ominous. Those who successfully adapted to Soviet life seemed to be the true aliens who misled the authorities by their mobility and pretenses, while the lot of disenfranchised people appeared as pitiful creatures with bad luck. By 1930, rather than diminish fears concerning the threat of anti-Soviet elements, this policy of exclusion and inclusion had effectively accentuated them.

Adding to the anxieties of Kremlin officials was the fact that the process of re-entry into Soviet society proved neither predictable nor uniform. Outcasts managed to earn the full rights of citizens in a variety of ways, and not necessarily by performing socially useful labor and demonstrating loyalty to Soviet power.

Nikolai Dormidontov, *Street Musicians*. 1931–1934. © State Russian Museum, St. Peters-burg, 2001. From *Soviet Art: 1920s–1930s, Russian Museum, Leningrad*. New York: Harry N. Abrams, Inc., 1988. By permission of the Museum.

4

Hardship and Citizenship

The published narratives of class aliens have largely been authored by members of the old regime elites, as in the case of the memoir of S. M. Golitsyn, the disenfranchised descendant of a famous nobleman.[1] The fact that a more educated segment of the disenfranchised population chronicled its persecution reinforced party ideology, which described disenfranchisement as an assault against the old privileged classes. The present study uses recently available archival records to shift the balance of the written record in favor of ordinary and underprivileged people who, in fact, comprised the majority of Soviet aliens. Their handwritten appeals for rights are highly unusual because they represent the voice of Stalin's victims at the time of persecution as they directly addressed state agents, formulated appeals, and offered testimonies of defense.

In her memoirs, Nadezhda Mandelstam illustrated the importance of letters to Soviet authorities: "Which one of us had never written letters to the supreme powers. . . . If they are preserved, these mountains of letters will be a veritable treasure trove for historians: the life of our times is recorded in them far more faithfully than in any other form of writing."[2] People without rights wrote such letters in the hundreds of thousands. In their written appeals for the reinstatement of rights the disenfranchised explained their behavior, redefined themselves, and rewrote their personal history, often presenting new lives as well.

The task of discerning a petitioner's voice is complicated by the presence of a powerful audience that dictated certain formulas and of the scribes who sometimes reproduced them. Many of the disenfranchised were illiterate or semiliterate and had to have someone else write their petitions for them. In the 1920s, literacy in the RSFSR was roughly 40 percent overall and around 50 percent in the regions surrounding Moscow and Leningrad, although higher for young men and much lower for women and the elderly.[3] Literacy rates rose sharply in the course of the decade such that even rural women, whose rate of literacy remained among the lowest in the 1920s, reached around 70 percent by the end of the 1930s.[4] Although scribes often mediated life stories and included particular formulas for address and appeal, they largely used these devices as a frame for a story whose substance the disenfranchised person provided. The voice of the petitioner is present even in those cases where someone else wrote the text on the person's behalf. It appears that when people sought help, they more frequently turned to a literate relative to transcribe their appeals. For example, one woman closed her narrative with the following: "I ask that you excuse me for the poor handwriting; my granddaughter wrote from my dictation."[5]

If one's goal was rehabilitation, discursive embellishments reminiscent of the "cunning intelligentsia" or privileged classes proved less convincing than the clumsy words of ordinary folk. The less stylized the testimony and the more inarticulate the petitioner, the more authentic or sincere the testimony appeared. As Svetlana Boym notes, "inarticulateness and social clumsiness are read as true and sincere," as in Dostoevsky's novels where "tongue-tied characters devoid of rhetorical and oratorical skills often appear as spokesmen for the authorial Russian truth."[6] In Russian life as well, defendants acted ignorant before a powerful judge and presented themselves as sincere and well-meaning, such as the man charged with killing a Red Army soldier with his truck who concealed his literacy and "in court acts like a simpleton, an illiterate, dark man."[7] Stalin's outcasts often emphasized their ignorance and inarticulateness. "I don't even have the means to hire a jurist who would be able to beautifully draft my whole biography, so I must, of course, write myself," one appellant wrote, "Perhaps I don't put everything in quite the right way [*ne tak vse eto izlogaiu* (*sic*)], but what can I do?"[8]

The testimonies presented in the following pages are from petitions for the reinstatement of rights that were submitted by the disenfranchised between 1923 and 1937, although most of these letters originated in the years 1928–1931. The majority of narratives in this study represent a formal sample of five hundred letters that were systematically selected from over 100,000 cases of the RSFSR's disenfranchised. The cases are contained in the file of the VTsIK Central Electoral Commission, which is located in a closed archive in the remote Western Siberian town of Ialutorovsk. This distant warehouse stores the entire CEC file as well as various other state records, including films and recordings.[9] The enormous volume of cases in the CEC file span the entire decade that this state entity managed class enemies' disenfranchisement and reinstatement of rights, from 1926 to 1936. The systematic sample was constructed as follows: Beginning with the number of petitions filed for each year, I calculated 0.05 percent, divided this into the total number of cases stored for that year, then carefully selected every, say, twentieth or thirtieth case so as to compile a sample that spanned the catalog of cases for that particular year. I repeated this method for each of the ten years. Thus, from the total number of 100,000 cases stored in the Central Electoral Commission file, I generated a systematic sample of five hundred. For each case file in the sample I recorded the following information: petitioner's name, gender, date of birth, place, classification, date deprived of rights, TsIK decision on rehabilitation and date, lower-level administrative decisions on rehabilitation and dates. I also recorded nationality when given, transcribed the complete text of at least one petition from each case file, and assessed whether petitioners penned their own letters.

The five hundred cases from 1926 to 1936 exhibit a number of important characteristics. First, a comparison of the handwriting in personal letters and other official papers in each case file indicates that the disenfranchised largely wrote their own petitions, as just over a third (36 percent) of the letters include evidence (such as typing) that indicates the petitioner solicited the assistance of a scribe. Outcasts directed their appeals to various addressees, but roughly half of all sampled letters were addressed to the Central Electoral Commission. Other addressees included the local soviet executive committees, the peasant newspaper *Krest'ianskaia gazeta*, Lenin's wife N.K. Krupskaia, and institutions such as the TsIK Amnesty Commission, the complaints bureau of the Commissariat of Justice, the Commissariat of Finance, the NKVD, the TsIK chairman M.I. Kalinin, the military leader K.E. Voroshilov, and, of course, Stalin.

The Central Electoral Commission reinstated rights in all but thirty-four of the 500 cases in this sample (or 93 percent), and of the remaining thirty-four cases, nine were denied and the others included no decision. This exceptionally high rate of success might be misleading, however, as it only reflects success with the CEC and not with local officials. Indeed, if some narratives succeeded in persuading members of the Central Electoral Commission to reinstate rights, others had already failed with local officials. Half of the letters in this sample were addressed to district (*raion*) and provincial (*krai, oblast'*) electoral commissions, where they were rejected. The letters were then submitted up the state hierarchy for further consideration, as was the procedure. Therefore, these narratives reflect the preferences of party authorities in Moscow who found them compelling.

At the same time, the discursive strategies exhibited here cannot be understood as a mere catalog of "what worked," because so many of the same types of narratives failed to persuade local officials. Rather, these narratives more accurately reflect the preferences of the Kremlin authorities in the CEC, who considered the letters persuasive. The language of these petitions reflects not only the personal constraints and calculations of outcasts themselves but the preferences of central authorities.

The sample represents a broad diversity of outcasts from many regions and classifications who petitioned for the reinstatement of rights. Men petitioned individually in over 82 percent of the cases, whereas 14 percent of the petitions came from women, and only 3 percent from couples or families (in sharp contrast to the sizeable number of group letters from peasants during collectivization).[10] Regions that reported the highest number of petitioners in the sample include the cities of Moscow and Leningrad, the Moscow province, Leningrad province, and the Western Siberia province (*krai*). Many petitioners also identified the Ivanovo Industrial province and the Central Black Earth province as their home. The disenfranchised of these regions submitted over half of the petitions, but the remaining letters had their origin in more than 100 other regions represented by the sample. All the categories of the disenfranchised are represented in the sample, but some much more than others. By far, the largest category of disenfranchised people among the sampled cases are former traders (*torgovtsy*) who comprised nearly 40 percent of all cases. Others include: those who lived off unearned income (21 percent), used hired labor (15 percent), were financially dependent on someone disenfranchised (9 percent), former tsarist policemen (6 percent), clerics (5 percent), White Army officers (3 percent), and business owners (1 percent). The sample also included a couple of former land captains, an administrative exile, and a man sentenced as a counterrevolutionary. The age of petitioners varies widely, yet most were born between 1870 and 1900. The largest segment of petitioners lost their rights between 1926 and 1931, although they generally began to petition after 1930.

Personal petitions for the reinstatement of rights could be characterized by what James Scott would term "public transcripts," which are ritualistic, stereotyped, and largely shaped to appeal to the expectations of the powerful.[11] However, narrative patterns in the appeals of the disenfranchised demonstrate that despite an implicit imperative to speak the language of power, the disenfranchised produced effective narratives with considerable stylistic diversity. Outcasts did indeed follow certain conventions, but they also offered a range of testimony—from confessing their guilt, to vehemently condemning the charges against them, to admitting their action but denying any malicious intent. A variety of defense strategies appear in petitions but some more frequently than others. For example, few of the petitions included a flat denial of the charges, and when denials did appear, they often involved the assertion that the petitioner was denounced or that an obvious mistake was made. One man classified as a former landlord insisted: "Not only was I never such a thing, but I never had any property anywhere."[12] An Armenian, deprived of rights in Moscow for serving in the White Army, flatly denied his classification: "I never was and could never be [a "cornet" (*khorunzhii*)] because I'm an Armenian and only Cossacks can be cornets and moreover I, as an Armenian national at the time the White Army existed, was entirely demobilized."[13] A woman deprived of rights because of her husband repudiated the charge that he had traded timber before the revolution: "My husband was born in 1909 and before the revolution was 8 years old. Naturally, he couldn't trade timber."[14] Another wondered "how the rural soviet arrived [at this notion that] my mother is a trader. My natural mother died 25 years ago."[15]

The disenfranchised also rarely provided any acknowledgment of wrongdoing. Party culture of the late 1920s and 1930s required wrongdoers to confess their errors and miscalculations, renounce their past actions, and declare their commitment to the party.[16] However, the disenfranchised offered conspicuously different appeals, despite what they might have learned from the newspapers about the repentant behavior of party members. A stylized, confessional narrative seldom appears in these petitions, particularly those from commercial traders. However, confessions do arise in letters from religious servitors and White Army officers and in appeals drafted by scribes.[17] The following 1935 petition from a former officer of the White Army reveals a language that was common to those of his classification: "I have been working all this time, with complete awareness of my former guilt before the Soviet government and laboring people. I have made and [continue to] make every effort to expiate my guilt."[18] By sharp contrast, most of the other outcasts failed to acknowledge that they behaved improperly and refused confessions of guilt. Moreover, they very rarely identify themselves as former kulaks. Disenfranchised petitioners more closely resembled the peasant complainants in the trials of local officials from the 1930s who neither bowed to Soviet authority nor praised Stalin.[19] Typically, people without rights admitted the charges against them but denied any wrongdoing.[20] The stylized confession of one's mistakes, so common in the show trials and party purges of the 1930s, appears here as a language of educated Russian society. White Army officers and priests used such language. Judging from the kind of appeals made by traders, the ritualized confession of errors cannot be characterized as a popular discourse.

The sample of petitions from the Siberian warehouse reveals a range of narrative strategies. The appeals presented in these petitions can be classified into the six basic styles of argument that appear with the greatest frequency in the sample. Most petitions included more than one of the following strategies of appeal: a flat denial of the charges (13 percent); an accusation against or denunciation of another who was responsible for the petitioner's classification (16 percent);[21] an excuse that the activity was performed accidentally and temporarily and does not reflect the petitioner's true occupation or inclinations (24 percent); a lament that the petitioner is desperate and deserving of the reader's sympathy (39 percent); a claim of wrongful classification (for example, one is only a trader of rank one, or not really a dependent) (39 percent); the presentation of a Soviet self, boasts of loyalty, service, and work achievements (55 percent).

The six arguments were offered by outcasts and accepted by the CEC at a fairly constant rate from 1926 to 1936. Surprisingly, in the course of a decade, each strategy of appeal appears with the same regularity as a percentage of total petitions in the sample. Given that over 90 percent of the petitions in this sample proved successful, the consistency in the kinds of arguments represented demonstrates that the preferences of Kremlin officials remained largely unchanged. The Central Electoral Commission did not grow more favorable toward petitions in which the writer asserted a reformed Soviet self, despite the dramatic transformation in the political landscape with Stalin's promethean program for building socialism and its emphasis on productive labor, public demonstrations of loyalty, and iron faith in the power of human agency. The excuses of the disenfranchised reveal that, for years, just as many defended themselves, offered emotional pleas, explained their behavior, and challenged their classification, as made assertions of socially useful labor and loyalty.[22] Petitions for rights reflect a variety of habits of explanation, habits that a turbulent decade did not manage to break. The language used when addressing high-level Soviet authorities and the language that resonated with these officials reveals a striking degree of consistency over time. The experiences of a tumultuous decade, the severe dislocation and disruption, as well as a Stalin cult and massive re-education campaigns produced relatively few changes in the narrative styles of petitions for the reinstatement of rights. Only certain categories of outcasts re-entered Soviet society after having undergone the requisite personal transformation. Many others discovered different and no less legitimate paths to social membership. Party leaders sanctioned diverse and often divergent narratives when they granted full rights to these outcasts.

Aliens in the Construction of Citizens

Those who sought the reinstatement of their rights described themselves as sharply unlike the bourgeoisie, and their petitions reveal what the disenfranchised considered to be the main attributes of the bourgeois classes. For example, petitioners insisted that they were poor and laboring, unlike the rich and idle bourgeois classes. "I don't deserve to be among the ranks of the disenfranchised," one man argued; "[M]ine is a poor peasant household."[23] "Need pushed me into the category Nepman for seven months, but I myself am a poor peasant."[24] "I don't belong to the group of kulaks and exploiters, but was always and am a laboring peasant."[25] Petitioners also identified the class aliens as bandits and counterrevolutionaries, a group with which they have nothing in common. In his letter to the peasant newspaper, *Krest'ianskaia gazeta,* a man insisted that he was wrongly placed "on the black list together with priests and bandits."[26] An exiled group of self-proclaimed "Bolshevik-Leninist oppositionists" claimed that they should not be grouped "with the gendarme, White Army officers, kulaks and other counterrevolutionary swine."[27] As further evidence of how certain ethnic groups were identified with the bourgeois classes, one petitioner remarked, "I consider it radically incorrect and a violation of state and party directives to take the same approach to me as to an urban Jew."[28]

Appeals for the reinstatement of rights indicate what the main attributes of the bourgeois classes were understood to be, as well as how citizen identities emerged in contrast to the image of alien classes. From the hands of the disenfranchised, a picture of the bourgeois classes emerges that is thoroughly consistent with the party's characterizations. The exploiting classes do not work but live rich off the labor of others, as one outcast wrote: "What kind of exploiter am I? Is there anything in common between me, who spent his whole life in heavy manual labor and real, large-scale exploiters, factory-owners, landowners, shopkeepers like kulaks who live rich and satiated on account of others, while I survive on bread and water?"[29] According to the disenfranchised, the bourgeois classes "don't want to do productive work."[30]

Petitioners often described their personal enemies as wholly alike the state's bourgeois enemies, that is, as "parasites" who "engaged in trade but managed to penetrate the ranks of the party."[31] Similarly reproducing the official image of the masked, parasitic foe, one man described his family's personal enemies in strikingly familiar terms: "the secretary of the rural soviet Pavel Mikhailovo Smirnov (a former psalmodist and the son of a priest), the schoolteacher . . . Peter Vasilevich Dromino (the son of a priest) . . . and the chairman or the rural soviet Kurdiukov, who concealed his real name . . . Smirnov (the son of a priest) has land but he does not work [the land] himself at all, only his hired help does."[32] Petitioners also described their personal enemies as masked deviants who have gone "completely unpunished."[33] Appeals for rights reveal how people constructed individual citizen identities in opposition to the standard profile of the bourgeoisie. Therefore, they accentuated distinctly non-bourgeois, or proletarian, attributes such as productive labor, sincerity, the experience of exploitation, and poverty. In petitions, the disenfranchised reproduced the official image of the bourgeois alien and used this portrait to construct an opposing identity for themselves, one entirely distinct from the rich, idle, parasitic, and hidden enemy.

Petitioners asserted that they were essentially different from the nonlaboring and parasitic group that the state had targeted for disenfranchisement. Some denied that they should be disenfranchised by virtue of social origin. A woman from Novosibirsk who listed her social origin as petty bourgeois claimed that "as a Jewish woman, I could not and cannot in any way be an enemy of the Soviets."[34] A Jewish man from Leningrad argued "I'm the son of a Novgorod petty bourgeois man [*meshchanin*] and so by social origin I can't be an enemy of the current order."[35] Others insisted that they were not class enemies by nature. "I don't consider myself a trader by nature [*prirodnyi torgovets*]";[36] "I'm not a real [*nastoiashchii*] trader";[37] "Essentially, I'm a worker."[38] A woman deprived of rights for trading with her husband insisted: "Naturally, psychologically, in lifestyle and in origin, I have nothing in common with traders."[39] A former land captain (*zemskii nachal'nik*), deprived of rights in 1927, described himself as someone politically benign who never committed repressive acts. To demonstrate this, he noted that local peasants took no hostile action against him; he remained in the town where he had served as land captain from the February revolution until late 1919.[40] Self-constructions were submitted to authorities as a challenge, a counter-narrative to the accuser's story about them. Autobiographical narratives of the disenfranchised demonstrate, as George Steiner wrote, that self-portraiture can be the most adversarial form of creation.[41]

The Soviet regime required transparency from petitioners which is why so many of them spoke of their "true" self or essential nature, just as the man who wrote, "In essence, I want to explain to you who I am."[42] Party policy targeted the so-called exploiting, privileged classes for disenfranchisement, and petitioners rejected any likeness between them and these old regime elites. "I am not the son of a merchant or landlord," one man wrote, "but of a young woman farm laborer."[43] A woman deprived of rights for being a nun insisted that she went to the monastery because she was poor and worked there as an employee but did not take part in monastic life.[44] A man deprived of rights for being a Baptist reader (*nachetnik baptistov*) insisted: "I did not receive any compensation from the society of Baptists, either in money or in kind; I didn't use [my service] as a means of existence as the Orthodox clergy does."[45] A Greek national was deprived of rights in 1926 as a cleric, although he never received payment for what he insisted was his minor role of "singing [in the choir] as a believer and enthusiast [*liubitel'*]."[46] To dispute any affinity with such bourgeois elements, petitioners consistently presented themselves as minor figures who held unassuming jobs, entirely uninvolved in money-making or politics.

Outcasts presented themselves as petty figures, so inconsequential that they do not even warrant the attention of Soviet officials. A former landowner and military judge wondered why the state would even bother with a person as insignificant as he: "What danger or harm is eliminated by [depriving me of rights]? I live and work in a remote province. Not only in central administrative institutions but even in provincial ones—they don't know me."[47] A man deprived of rights for serving in the tsarist police argued that he never fulfilled any police function but rather worked in the Justice of the Peace's chamber delivering packets of documents between institutions and the post office.[48] Another former tsarist policeman also described his duties as those of a bureaucratic messenger of papers and notices claimed he "never played a significant, active role" in the police.[49]

Legislation on disenfranchisement was based on the principle that class enemies had malicious intent, that traders were out for profit, that those who hired labor intended to exploit others, and that those who served in the tsarist police did so out of political conviction. In order to challenge these official assumptions, petitioners portrayed themselves as apolitical or naive at best, desperate and unfortunate, or subject to the bad influences or manipulations of others. The disenfranchised portrayed themselves as essentially common people, in no way exceptional, and certainly not motivated to act contrary to the wishes of Soviet authorities. A man deprived of rights for buying and selling bricks wrote that he was just doing what every person did: "I like other citizens sold [things] at the market and in this way supported my household."[50] One writer argued that if the law were applied consistently, then workers and many communists would have to be considered exploiters too for hiring domestic help.[51] Denying that he had actively supported the Old Regime, one former tsarist policeman insisted: "I, like many others, was a simple worker who did what was instructed."[52] By their own accounts, these outcasts actually represented ordinary folk, and not Russia's bourgeois classes.

Diminished Selves

Referring to himself as a "small person" (*malen'kii chelovek*),[53] one petitioner expressed in two words an identity that many other disenfranchised people described in detail. Accused of being enemies and socially harmful, outcasts challenged this image by presenting themselves as the opposite. They were benign and innocuous, small and insignificant. In many petitions, people without rights explained and diminished their actions by describing them as temporary, minor, petty, unprofitable, or otherwise contrary to those of a big-time trader or political enemy. These outcasts diminished almost every indicator of their identity in some way—their capacity for work (as they were sick, handicapped); their knowledge (as they were illiterate, politically in the dark); their actions (as they were petty, unprofitable traders or simple monastery employees); even their motivations (as they were naive or compelled by unfortunate circumstances).

The party identified several categories of people who should be protected from the loss of rights, and petitioners referred to these legal exceptions when they argued for their wrongful disenfranchisement. The 1926 Instructions on Elections to the Soviets excluded the following groups of people from disenfranchisement: (1) peasants who hired one laborer because of illness, mobilization, the presence of seasonal or factory work or who hired no more than two laborers for a short time during harvest; (2) craftsmen (*kustari i remeslenniki*) who hired one adult worker or two apprentices; (3) workers, peasants, Cossacks, and craftsmen mobilized into the White Army; (4) persons who received interest from savings accounts and from government bonds or from communal and cooperative credit if such income did not constitute one's primary source of support; (5) people who temporarily engaged in petty trade for special reasons, such as invalidity or unemployment, or who held a rank-one license;[54] (6) those hired or elected by a religious community to serve an administrative or technical function such as guard, janitor, singer, and so on; (7) people of the free professions (such as doctors and lawyers) who engaged in socially useful labor; (8) family members who were not materially dependent on persons disenfranchised but had an independent source of socially useful labor.

Two additional exceptions were added to the 1930 Instructions on Elections to the Soviets that did not appear in the 1926 Instructions: (1) former White Army officers, bureaucrats, and leaders of counterrevolutionary bands who then enlisted in the Red Army and took active part in the armed defense of Soviet power during the civil war; (2) farmers and craftsmen who sold the products of their own labor on the open market.

Kremlin officials often emphasized the need to protect the weakest segments of society from disenfranchisement. For example, in September 1925, Kalinin encouraged officials to consider some of the constraints on the "rank-and-file peasant policeman," namely, that he sometimes joined in 1914 to avoid military service. In 1929, the Presidium of the Central Electoral Commission urged the review of lists of disenfranchised people for those "who engaged in trade temporarily as a consequence of acute need."[55] Consistent with this message, petitioners argued, for example, that they only used hired labor because of illness or served as a mere janitor in the church and nothing more or temporarily engaged in petty trade when unemployed or enlisted in the White Army due to compulsory mobilization. Petitioners presented almost every activity, be it trade, police work, or church service, as incidental and innocuous. They argued that their actions were "completely accidental,"[56] "for an insignificant period of time,"[57] "an insignificant, accidental episode,"[58] a minor transgression in an otherwise proletarian or peasant life. The following insistence from one former tsarist policeman was typical: "I served as a watchman [*strazhnik*][59] for only one month in 1906, over 20 years ago."[60] Similarly, those accused of trading described the activity as unprofitable and short-lived. "I traded in a kiosk, on a street corner; it was a petty trade," one petitioner claimed.[61] A young man, deprived of rights in 1925 as the son of a trader, insisted that his father's trading was small and ceased as early as 1914.[62] A man disenfranchised for being dependent on a wife who traded, argued: "My wife's profits from trading produce [*bakaleinye tovary*] weren't so great . . . that I could be considered dependent on her."[63] One woman testified, "I had a license of rank one and I traded only one bag of potatoes a day and in this way fed my family and I traded for only one season."[64] A man who traded meats in the Moscow province said he only traded in the winter months when there was dire need.[65] "Really," one woman insisted, "I traded pastries for only eight months, trade was very small. . . ."[66] "Except for that one time, I was never a trader."[67]

Many women, in particular, were disenfranchised because of income they received from renting out space in their homes. It appears that the "unearned income" category disproportionately condemned women. In their appeals, women diminished the profitability of their actions and insisted that the income they derived from the home was minimal, at least in comparison to the home's expenses. Two sisters, deprived of rights as home owners, claimed that they were "mistakenly" placed on the list of the disenfranchised since they enjoyed "no material benefit" from a home whose "insignificant profit" was offset by expenses in maintenance and renovation.[68] Another woman deprived of rights as a home owner made the same argument and provided extensive accounting and detail of the expenses she incurred on the house such as taxes, security, cleaning, maintenance, garbage collection, painting, and renovation. In light of these expenses, she argued, "nothing remains from the profits on the house."[69] A woman from Voronezh, deprived of rights in 1928, discounted the 35 ruble income she derived from her home: "With five people dependent on me and three small children . . . there is no 35 rubles and it's impossible to survive."[70]

Compelled by Circumstances, Motivated by Ignorance

Я поступил в быв. полиции-- как и многие другие-- как говорит пословица-- "не ради исуса, а ради хлеба куса."[71]

In his book on the Small Peoples of the North, Yuri Slezkine quotes a group of Mansi who in 1598 sent a petition to Moscow in which they made the following plea: "It is impossible for us, your orphans, to plough your, sovereign, field, because, sovereign, we have lost all our property, sold our wives and children, and are now starving to death."[72] Such stylized explanations of behavior that include mention of poverty and starvation were regularly produced by Russia's subjects. People without rights offered similarly vivid accounts of their unfortunate life circumstances. A trader from Moscow wrote: "From 1925 to 1927 I was without work and had no means to feed my family. Petty trade was for me accidental and temporary, due to unemployment and influenced by acute need and difficult circumstances in my family life."[73] "I came to trade only through an unfortunate circumstance."[74] "I'm a refugee from Poland . . . who under complicated circumstances was forced to trade temporarily."[75] Difficult life circumstances could mean any number of things, from old age and declining health, to injury, handicap, the physical inability to work, a large family of dependents, unemployment, illiteracy, and the need to supplement income. A trader from Borisoglebsk wrote: "I became a trader under the pressure of need because of my family and my being an invalid."[76] Besides trading, one man wrote, there was no other source of income, because on his small plot of land "it is impossible to feed a family."[77] An Old Believer priest claimed he was compelled to serve "out of extreme necessity."[78] A former tsarist policeman from 1913 to 1916 argued that he took the job out of necessity and kept it to avoid being drafted to the front.[79] When the Whites occupied his village, another man insisted, he had no choice but to join their ranks "in order to save myself and my family and my young children from execution."[80] A poor musician described how his art did not support him so he turned to trade: "From 1923 to 1925 I worked as a musician but later my income became inconsistent, and I quickly stopped. Without an income to live on, I was drawn to the nonlaboring path."[81] One trader explained his activities by describing his father's mental illness, psychiatric institutionalization, and inability to find and keep decent work, all of which resulted in insufficient income for his family of six.[82]

Many of the disenfranchised argued that necessity motivated them more than any anti-soviet sentiment or political conviction. A former church worker insisted, "circumstances of life, and not religion, forced me to become a psalmodist."[83] A former trader from Ufa said that the need for survival and not a desire for profit motivated his commercial activities.[84] A former member of the tsarist police wrote: "I served not in defense of the bourgeois order, but only for a crumb of bread since I was burdened with five small children."[85] A former tsarist watchman argued that he served because he was hungry and needed a job and that his act was actually for the good of society since he could have chosen to be a thief instead, "I think that worker-peasant power insults me [*menia pozorit*] because I served as a watchman. At that time, I wanted to eat and drink. Hunger and need forced me into it. I didn't want to be a thief or a brigand [*razboinik*] and that's why I fell into that group [of tsarist watchmen]."[86]

People also cited illness or death in the family to explain their activities. A Siberian man disenfranchised for using hired labor argued in a petition to the rural soviet that he needed domestic help while his wife was ill.[87] "As always, I was helping my widowed mother," another argued.[88] A man claimed that his wife's mental illness compelled him to serve as a gendarme.[89] A Leningrad man deprived of rights described how the death of his eldest son forced him to engage in trade. Assisted by his son before the young man perished in the civil war, the petitioner explained how he lost his "last support" (*poslednaia opora*) and had to resort to commerce for some income.[90] A man from the Western province provided a long description of his ailments and insisted that doctor's orders kept him from work in agriculture. "I'm sixty years old and have a hernia [*gryzhevaia bolezn'*]. In 1928, the medical commission acknowledged a 50 percent reduction in my health. Besides the hernia, I've had an ulcer since 1919, which I managed to cure with the help of an operation in December, 1924. After the operation, the doctor would not allow me to work in the fields for two years."[91] He refrained from physical labor on doctor's orders and started to trade but then abandoned "damn trading" and returned, once again, to agricultural work. Similarly, a man with a severe case of tuberculosis claimed he started trading after his doctor forbade him to work because of his illness.[92] "And so," one former trader lamented, "I came upon this path due to illness and that's why I'm now tormented."[93]

Emotional descriptions of illnesses, physical handicaps, and poverty fill many of these letters. "Without any land or wages, my father was in no position to feed eight small children, which is why I had to work from the age of eleven," a petitioner wrote from Moscow.[94] "To my great misfortune, I have a mild case of tuberculosis; I worry and I burst into tears."[95] A former trader gave an extensive account of his own illnesses as well as the illness of his son: "I, Radionov, am a poverty-stricken, hunchbacked man . . . an invalid. . . . At the present time, because of my weak health, I'm unemployed. My only hope and support in life was my son, Anatolii, the eldest . . . at work, mining gravel, he got sick with influenza [*gripp*] in the quarry and from complications . . . he's been in a psychiatric hospital for eleven months already." Another wrote, "I ask you to pay attention to my old age; I'm already 75 years old so I can't do anything harmful to the government."[96]

Petitioners attributed their decision to trade on the chronic problem of unemployment in the 1920s.[97] The unemployment crisis affected millions of people, but especially the weakest segments of society such as peasant migrants to the cities and female workers, as women were often the first fired.[98] One man argued, "From a very young age, I worked as a wage laborer [*po naimu*] and only under accidental circumstances in connection with unemployment and a horrible material condition, with my wife, child and mother dependent on me, I was forced to turn to work that was unpleasant for me, that is, trade in meats, in order to save my family from hunger."[99] A Moscow man made a similar argument, "I was a co-proprietor in trade only by accident [*sluchaino*] because I couldn't find any work [*sluzhba*] for myself."[100] Another lamented, "because of severe unemployment I was forced to start a small trade in produce."[101] The problem of unemployment inspired one man to speak frankly about difficult times, "It's well-known that in 1927 a peasant who wasn't a trade union member and had no defined specialization had a hard time finding work."[102] Two Greek brothers also attributed their trading to unemployment. Deprived of rights in Leningrad in 1929 for trading during NEP, Khristofor and Kharlampii had come to Leningrad from Bessarabia. After "hopeless" efforts to find work, they decided to open a booth and sell sausage. "Because of unemployment," one of the brothers argued, "I was forced for a short time to make use of a nonlaboring means of existence." At the same time, he assured Soviet officials that with the first opportunity for work in a cooperative organization, he quickly abandoned his "nonlaboring occupation."[103] Many of the disenfranchised explained their commercial activities in the light of the country's acute economic crisis and unemployment.

Invalids, the sick, and the elderly also detailed how a physical impairment severely restricted their choice of work, as in the case of a Leningrad man who severed his right leg after falling under a tram. As a result of the accident, he lost his ability to work and turned instead to repairing watches, a profession that led to his disenfranchisement.[104] A man explained how the bone in his left foot was mangled in the war when he fought in the Red Army, and, therefore, he traded because as an invalid he could not perform any other kind of work.[105] Another trader wrote: "I'm not fit for difficult labor; I'm an invalid without a bone in my right leg; they did an operation in which they cut the bone."[106] A man deprived of rights as a trader lamented that given his age and illness, he could not get a job with a state institution and thus was forced to trade. "Being elderly and sick, they won't accept me to work in an artel and I can't do manual labor either. So I must be a craftsman and sew hats on order . . . and sell them at the market."[107] Soviet officials found such claims persuasive because they knew that trade often served in place of regular work for the unskilled, invalid, or unemployed.

The disenfranchised rarely attributed their unacceptable behavior to a conscious choice but largely cited factors beyond their control, such as production imperatives, ignorance, or the bad influence of others. A man who opened a small printing office and was disenfranchised for using hired labor argued, "everyone knows that you can't do typographical work with one employee."[108] A man from the Caucasus wrote from Moscow where he was disenfranchised for hiring labor in the production of candy. His commodity was caramel with fillings, and, in his petition, he provided detail on the production of his confectionery to demonstrate the impossibility of his working alone. "The production of caramel requires the presence of three workers minimum. Production takes place as follows: (a) one worker must roll the caramel constantly over heat with the fruit juice filling; (b) another must roll it out and; (c) a third must press it and give it a certain shape. All these processes must take place simultaneously, otherwise the entire thing spoils: the caramel settles; the fruit juice spills over and turns into a formless mass. This shows that one person can't carry out the whole operation."[109]

Petitioners often attributed their behavior to ignorance, illiteracy, or naïveté, and used the Bolshevik image of the dark, backward, and unconscious peasant to their advantage.[110] A former trader argued that his actions were motivated "more from ignorance [*temnota*] and need than from profit."[111] Deprived of rights as a craftsman, a Moscow man argued, "as a man almost completely illiterate and therefore not prepared for any kind of work [*sluzhba*)], I was forced to return to my craft as a barber."[112] Another apologized to Kalinin for not coming to Moscow personally to offer his testimony but explained that "dark," insular village life made it difficult to travel to the central cities: "Of course, I am a dark village man, not very familiar with the situation."[113] In another case, an alleged kulak confessed to the party central committee: "I'm as ignorant as a pipe."[114]

Many people argued that they traded or registered a particular trading license out of sheer ignorance. One man characterized his activity as "trade out of misunderstanding *nedorazumenie*]."[115] Another explained, "I was temporarily associated with trade; this was my gross ignorance [*neponimanie*]."[116] A former trader insisted, "How could I have known then since I had completely no idea what NEP or trade was and besides, I am still semiliterate."[117] Another attributed his trading "mistake" to the fact that "I was not so politically developed."[118] Deprived of rights, a former tsarist policeman described himself as "a completely ignorant man [who] had no idea what the police were and why they existed."[119] A man accused of trading with a license of rank three described how it was ignorance, not the volume of his commercial activity, that caused him to register a trader's license of such high rank: "I had license three by accident. I understood nothing about it . . . and if they made me choose rank four, I would have taken that too."[120]

The peasant newspaper, *Krest'ianskaia gazeta,* heard from a former member of the tsarist police who asked whether one could be disenfranchised "if that person joined the watchmen not knowing what the deal was [*ne znaia v chem delo*]." The newspaper's legal consultant stated that even those who "did not understand the political significance" of their actions are to be disenfranchised, but the person could petition if he acted "out of a lack of consciousness."[121] Peasants probably received a lot of legal advice of this kind because pleas of ignorance pervaded these petitions. A member of the prerevolutionary intelligentsia who was subjected to hours of NKVD interrogation described afterward how a claim of ignorance could provide effective self-defense, "In general the best is to look dumb and completely self-confident."[122] A number of petitioners appreciated the efficacy of this approach. The son of a priest claimed that he did not know anything about the political significance of serving in the church and that he became a church regent out of ignorance. He maintained that the reason he took the job was to support himself in the village where he could study carpentry. "At the time, I wasn't able to consider the political importance of the issue since I was semiliterate."[123] A former tsarist policeman asserted, "I didn't know what politics was and what it came from."[124] In his letter to Stalin, a young man also feigned political ignorance: "I didn't see the old order. We [young people] don't even know anything about it."[125] Whatever they did, whoever they were, people deprived of rights argued that they were wholly unaware of the political meanings attached to these activities.

The Oppressed and Exploited

"I cannot exclude myself from the working class," one woman argued, "because my sufferings and deprivations are identical with theirs."[126] She was reproducing a central idea of Bolshevism—that the party of Lenin represented not only the working class but the underclass, the exploited, the poor. The regime's ideology dictated that victims of exploitation, the formerly poor and oppressed masses, were de facto Soviet citizens. From ethnic minorities in the Far North to Muslim women in Central Asia, the oppressed masses constituted a proletariat no less than the industrial worker.[127] An elderly former priest from the North Caucasus also made claims to membership in the proletariat because of his parents' history of oppression: "My parents lived under serfdom and, having experienced all the horrors of landlord oppression [*pomeshchichii gnet*], they passed along to me as well a deep hatred for the bourgeois order."[128] Another man from the Western province argued that a past of capitalist oppression earned him rights under Soviet rule: "As a poor Jew before the revolution who experienced all the oppression of capitalism, I must now have the rights of the proletariat by law."[129] One man stressed that his father "worked as a wage laborer for landlords until his death, and my mother was a serf. . . . From the age of thirteen I've been exploited."[130] Identifying herself as poor and exploited, one woman lamented that "from a young age, I worked for others for a crumb of bread."[131] The disenfranchised presented themselves as citizens by virtue of their oppression, exploitation, or suffering.

In their petitions, outcasts often appear as the victims of another's manipulation. "Everyone knows," wrote one former member of the tsarist police, "that low-ranking policemen didn't have any rights; they themselves were oppressed people."[132] A man from Sevastopol deprived of rights for trading produce said that he, the son of a farm laborer, was in fact just an assistant for the real, big-time traders. Although he did trade, he pointed out that essentially he was exploited by more powerful traders. "Rather, I was a shop-assistant in this petty trade and not the proprietor. Since I had no capital, I went to help big-time traders who supplied me with a small amount of petty goods and took a profit from me, while I had . . . a pitiful existence."[133] Many described how they suffered in an exploitative relationship. A former psalmodist from Tomsk maintained that the priest, Melentev, took advantage of his weak character and manipulated him, turning him away from the "right path."[134] A woman whose husband was deprived of rights as a psalmodist explained that he was a victim: "being a psalmodist means being a servant for a priest and receiving one fourth of all profits."[135] A man disenfranchised for working in the church as a psalmodist also described himself as a victim. The real wrongdoers were the priests who took advantage of him. "In the course of my service in the church, I mechanically fulfilled my duties and was rather in the situation of a farm laborer because the priests tried in every way to exploit me, using me as a psalmodist, regent, secretary and also registrar, while giving me only a paltry portion of the church's profits."[136]

Petitioners repeatedly testified that the bad influence of others caused them to digress from the Soviet path. One man said that his former coworkers "suggested that I trade and obtain goods from them on credit."[137] "It must be openly acknowledged," insisted a former Leningrad trader, "that the advice of my former employers and their agreement to lend me goods for petty trade played a fatal role in my decision [to trade]."[138] Another trader from Leningrad gave the following testimony that placed the blame for his trading squarely on his business partners: "They convinced me that the law allowed the opening of a booth [*lavka*] . . . and that [Soviet] power allows several people to participate together in a small deal with equal shares, especially the unemployed and invalids, if the partners labor themselves. Forced by unemployment to trust these people's assurances, I accepted the offer and joined the company. . . ."[139] One woman also maintained that the people who gave her a license to trade at a higher rank were to blame: "Why they gave me a license of rank two I don't know since my trading was so petty."[140] A former Land Captain also placed responsibility on others: "I, mechanically, like many Justices of the Peace, was transferred to the position of Land Captain."[141]

Stalin's outcasts insisted that they did not trade or serve in the church or tsarist police because of political or religious conviction or a desire for profit. Rather, they were weak and vulnerable, manipulated by persons as well as circumstances. Time and again, the disenfranchised present themselves as powerless individuals trying desperately to cope with life's tragedies. They portrayed diminished selves, compelled by unfortunate life circumstances and manipulated and exploited by others more educated than they. At times, the emotional content of these letters, the element of desperation, and the appeal for sympathy were highly formulaic, and they therefore lend themselves to a comparison with the traditional Russian folk lament.

The Ritual Lament

"I decided to describe to you," wrote one woman, "who Silicheva was and by what unhappy road she reached the point of trading."[142] Having assumed the role of tragic storyteller, she referred to herself in the third person and began to explain her behavior. The disenfranchised very often positioned themselves, like Silicheva, along an "unhappy road." People deprived of rights told a tragic story, a kind of ritual lament, in which they consistently mourned their fate and expressed sorrow for themselves. Many tragic narratives were highly stylized, and their rhetorical form and emotional content give them the characteristics of a ritual lament.[143] The lament employed distinct formulas and patterns. For example, phrases such as "deprived a crumb of bread" or "lacking any means of subsistence" or descriptions of the petitioner as barefoot, begging, desperate, and humiliated are invoked repeatedly. A formulaic lament appears in many petitions and with such frequency, consistency and linguistic uniformity that this genre deserves separate treatment.

The laments of the disenfranchised appealed to a reader who shared certain moral assumptions with the petitioner.[144] This genre of petition can be generally characterized as a traditional lament because it bears an important resemblance to the Russian *plach*—a crying of one's fate. Similarly, laments from the disenfranchised represent life stories offered as part of a ritual of passage, in this case, from outcast to citizen. Laments were a popular genre in the Soviet period, and people composed such poetry for the death of both Lenin and Kirov, for soldiers who went off to fight in the civil war, and for Stalin too. Yuri Sokolov, whose study of Russian folklore analyzes the lament in great detail, quotes one poem in which Lenin's "zealous heart is troubled" and the Bolshevik leader *himself* laments the presence of enemies of the revolution.[145] Although a biblical genre, scholars have spotted this narrative form in various places, from nineteenth-century Russian literature to everyday conversation just before the collapse of the Soviet Union.[146]

Petitions of the disenfranchised share a number of important stylistic

and functional similarities with traditional Russian laments. So many petition narratives resemble a lament because of the centrality of fate and sentiment; they were indeed a crying of one's fate. Lament poetry was offered
at times of symbolic or social death, on occasions when soldiers were recruited for the tsar's army or, as Natalie Kononenko describes, when
women married. At her wedding, the woman traditionally asked "her parents how she has displeased them that they should want to be rid of her"
and "begs her parents for mercy," in much the same way as the disenfranchised lament their abandonment and seek the sympathy of Soviet officials.[147] The *plachi*, poetic songs for the dead, were performed in the name
of those left behind (such as the widow, the orphaned children, the
mother, the siblings), and expressed certain attitudes toward the deceased,
namely, that he is to be feared and implored to take pity on and defend the
abandoned family. Similarly, when petitioners from the 1920s and 1930s
appealed for rights, they spoke of their hardship to state authorities whom
they both feared and hoped would defend them. Lament poetry also re-
counted the life of the deceased and the condition of those left behind and
was, in this way, historical or autobiographical, much like the petitions of
the disenfranchised.

Moreover, popular laments addressed the injustices of social life, as did
the petitions of the disenfranchised that chronicle abandonment by one's
family (many called themselves orphans) and community (as social outcasts). Sokolov described how the traditional laments "passionately expressed feeling of popular protest against the tsarist regime itself, which
kept the countryside in poverty and injustice, degrading the human dignity
of the peasant." Lamenters would use the life of the deceased and the family left behind in order to tell a larger story of social injustice, destitution,
and humiliation, much like the disenfranchised. Indeed, Lenin "considered
laments for departing soldiers a most valuable record for the history of
popular life and popular moods" especially "popular wrath and hatred
toward the enslavers."[148]

The tragic tales of Soviet outcasts were often set against a backdrop of
relative comfort in the past, thereby forming an indictment of the current
Soviet order. In the following, a former trader recounts his difficulties
growing up under tsarist rule, yet these hardships pale in comparison to
what he has endured as someone without rights. "From a young age, I
didn't know power or luxury. Food was bitter bread, potatoes and milk;
there was always some beef . . . nonetheless it was possible to exist. . . . At
the present time, there isn't even any chicken and not a kopek."[149] Not entirely benign or devoid of political content, laments suggested that author-

ities who claimed to defend social justice were obligated to alleviate the petitioner's suffering. When they crafted petitions in the form of a lament, the disenfranchised challenged Soviet officials to conform to their own self-image, to act more benevolent and compassionate than their tsarist predecessors, and to truly behave as new bureaucrats presiding over an improved social order.

A Cycle of Misfortune

A dominant theme of the lament was powerlessness. Petitioners described a highly stylized pattern of continuous misfortune in which the principal characters (petitioners, their parents) confronted by unfortunate circumstances (unemployment, illness, death in the family) acted out of desperation (turning to trade, hired labor, police service) only to find themselves faced with yet another misfortune (disenfranchisement). This cycle of adversity also appeared in the petitions of children who spoke of having inherited their parents' life of exploitation, ignorance or illiteracy, and poverty. Caught within a seemingly inevitable pattern of hardship, the disenfranchised presented themselves as completely powerless, entirely without agency or the ability to break out of this cycle themselves.

Laments told a tragic tale of poverty and abandonment that extended from the petitioner's childhood into the present. Far from privileged, the petitioner was born into a poor family,[150] and the parents essentially served as slaves.[151] A man detailed how his family "in the winter walked around barefoot and hungry, in the summer ate exclusively greens."[152] "My mother walked around begging for charity in order to feed her family."[153] A former trader mentioned his difficult upbringing and equated the hardship he endured as a child to his present difficulties as someone disenfranchised, marking a life of continuous disadvantage and suffering: "From childhood, I was homeless since I had no parents. I encountered many difficulties in the course of my life. . . . From the age of 12 I went to the city to work in the factory. . . . My family is poor . . . and since November I've been unemployed. Living like I did in childhood has been difficult for me and now it's simply impossible; I have no means whatsoever [*net nikakikh sredstv*]."[154] A similar lament on a life of continuous suffering came in the following letter from a former watchman in the tsarist police. His autobiography of early childhood is a classic lament from the disenfranchised that touches on illness, poverty, and the difficulties of being an orphan: "By origin, I am a complete orphan, an infant taken into an orphanage"; "From a young age, I was an orphan; I was raised in need."[155] "I was abandoned by my mother at the age of three. . . . She was the maid of a lord [*gospodin*] and she gave birth to me there, at the time of the infectious disease cholera. She died and left me in an orphanage. Then my uncle took me from the orphanage and raised me as his son and fed me. My uncle was completely poor and walked around begging [*khodil po miru i prosil milostyniu*]. . . . When I turned 17 I began to leave my uncle . . . for work to feed myself and my uncle, who had no land. . . . I endured a lot of misfortune and need. From a young age I walked around begging for food together with my uncle and later was a farm laborer."[156] People presented lives characterized by abandonment, humiliation, and misfortune.

The lament style of appeal was especially common in the letters of Russia's traditional social outcasts such as the elderly and invalids, ethnic minorities and women. The lament provided a common poetic form for those who told stories of suffering and oppression. Language similar in style to the lament very frequently appeared in the petitions of disenfranchised Jews. Specifically, of those petitioners in the systematic sample who identified themselves as Jewish, nearly 80 percent made their appeal for rights in the form of a lament. They described the life of oppression, disadvantage, and misfortune that was so common for Jewish members of the Imperial Russian empire. One trader offered the following appeal: "I ask the Central Electoral Commission to take into account that I am from a poor Jewish family; give me an appropriate education; I'm completely illiterate and have poor command of the Russian language."[157] Another petitioner explained, "I was born in 1903 . . . in a poor Jewish family. . . . As a result of the pogroms . . . my whole family was left without . . . a crumb of bread and because of complete impoverishment I wasn't even able to study."[158] The most marginal groups in Russian society, such as ethnic minorities, women, and the poor underclass, described a life of suffering, poverty and oppression in a similar style. Their biographical narratives frequently appear in the form of a lament, and nowhere are these tragic personal stories more vivid than in the letters of women.

The Woman's Lament

After hearing the performance of a woman's lament, the Soviet writer Maxim Gorky wrote that the "wails of a Russian woman, weeping over her bitter fate . . . chanting the woe of life in the old Russian songs . . . *is* a Russian history."[159] According to this study's sample of more than five hundred petitions, nearly two-thirds of the letters from women included a lament. Although more than half of the men's petitions also reproduced this genre, the woman's lament appears distinctive in that it provided an emotional narrative concerning abusive husbands, starving children, female poverty, and illiteracy. The themes in a woman's lament focused on hardships that were particularly common to women in this period, such as coping with a drunken husband, being left a widow, raising small children alone, managing a living while illiterate and unemployed, caring for sick or handicapped family members.[160] Like other laments, these testimonies provided social commentary on Soviet life, and their sincerity can hardly be doubted given the overwhelming evidence of Soviet women's particular hardships.

Women describe the family circumstances that compelled them to accept undesirable work, such as trading. In particular, women attributed their trading to an abusive, sick, deceased, or deadbeat husband. A Penza woman, who identified herself as a housewife, described her activity as petty trade that began only because her husband was ill.[161] A woman from Ialta, disenfranchised for trading, offered the following lament in which a "drunken husband" featured prominently and she described herself as a "sick orphan and widow." "[My husband] became an alcoholic and unable to keep a steady job. I had to endure the beating of a drunken husband and help him. I was forced to engage in trade, in tea and cold appetizers, at the bazaar. . . . [One cannot] lay great blame on a sick orphan and widow . . . forced by circumstances to temporarily engage in petty trade."[162] A woman deprived of rights for trading knits, silks, and textiles, offered the following lament on her alcoholic husband who led her to trade.

> He couldn't always work; he was sick from alcoholism. He often took to drinking and lost his job after which he started trading. I was, against my own wishes, his helper. . . . [After 1926] he worked no more and drank without mercy, walking around barefoot begging for vodka, and I got tired of taking loans to support such a husband. It was hard. . . . I started to trade needles on the open market in the cold. . . . My poverty dragged on, and I supported a drunken husband [*na moiu doliu dostalsia muzh pianitsa*] who led me to trade.[163]

A woman from Samara, deprived of rights for being dependent on her husband, a trader, painfully described how she had to bear not only her husband's illness but also the fact that he left her disenfranchised: "I married a man who was ill, and I didn't see one bright day. He began to trade [on a license of] rank three, and the whole time was sick from consumption. He died in 1929, and I was left alone. I couldn't get work because I was disenfranchised. I can't sell myself, and I haven't done any trading."[164]

Trading potatoes during what she referred to as her "nightmarish life," one woman described what she endured from her husband, a freight worker for more than twenty-five years on the banks of the Volga. "I don't think it's necessary to describe the life of a docker [*gruzchik*]; everyone knows it well. Every day there is drunkenness. He was no help [*negodnyi*] to his family, started fights and scandals. He threw me out on the street in the middle of winter together with my children. . . . My entire nightmarish life I saved [*sic*] them only on my own shoulders."[165]

Husbands featured prominently in these tragic life stories, but Russian women had more to lament than their spouses. They described themselves as "semiliterate, incapable,"[166] and lamented their inability to find work and the need to support children. "Because of my illiteracy, I didn't know that trade was harmful to the government," one woman wrote.[167] Another argued that she traded "because of my inexperience, lack of understanding, and young age."[168] "I'm an illiterate and dark woman," wrote one outcast who hired labor. While it was true that women were less literate than men in Russia, it also appears that disenfranchised women, like peasant women during collectivization and women activists in the 1920s, invoked the standard image of the backward, easily manipulated, highly emotional *baba* as a way of effectively asserting their interests before Soviet authorities.[169]

Women often spoke of themselves as the sole providers for starving and needy children. One described her disabled children at length and how she was "forced" to trade because she had "two deaf-mute [*glukhonemnye*] children who needed to be fed."[170] An ethnic Armenian wrote of how "being a former Turkish national compelled me at the time to trade" especially given "the presence of three small children and the absence of a husband."[171] Some defended their earlier state of dependency by arguing that the rearing of young children made work outside the home impossible, as in the following case: "I was not able to assume individual and independent labor because I was burdened with four young children. Presently I am self-sufficient and independent of my husband, having acquired my means of sustenance through physical labor. Moreover, I support my four young children. . . . [But earlier] I was unable to free myself from dependence on my husband because I was burdened with young children."[172] Finally, a woman from Arkhangelsk expressed several themes of a typical woman's lament. In a highly emotional appeal, this former trader described herself as ignorant and her life as a series of misfortunes:

I traded for three years, 1925–1928, but it must be considered that I am practically illiterate and have never seen joy in my life. . . . I had an entire childhood of difficult deprivations and acute need. . . . my whole life was one complete torture, a struggle for a crumb of bread. . . . As a result of trading, I have been completely ruined. I am left by a broken carriage [sic] with the difficult awareness of being outcast from a society of workers, a person deprived of rights. . . . I ask the regional soviet executive committee [*kraiispolkom*] to give the right to be a useful worker to me, a woman semi-literate but taught by the bitter experience of life.[173]

The lament style of petitions from disenfranchised women is especially apparent when compared with Russian lament poetry. The following lament from the popular poet I. A. Fedosova was published by a folklorist in 1872, yet it includes the same sentiments of despair and humiliation that one finds in the laments of disenfranchised women decades later, plus many of the same themes. Speaking as a woman married to a drunkard, she describes how this husband ruined her, and the shame of being a social outcast.

I have gone through the licensed taverns,
I have stood around by the public houses;
Looking at his spending, I have trembled,
I have called upon him who should be my hope, I have humiliated myself,
I, miserable one, have heard enough of humiliation,
I have endured heavy beating;
He shamed me, he dishonored me before good people.[174]

Similar in style to the traditional Russian lament, the stylized and emotional appeals of the disenfranchised appear as a distinctly un-Soviet narrative. Petitioners often argued their innocence not by repudiating past actions but by placing them in context, a context of misfortune, as one expression of a wholly tragic life. In the foreground of these stories stand the difficult circumstances of life, the mishaps and struggles, while individuals themselves appear utterly powerless. Writers proclaimed their innocence in the form of a lament that appealed to a certain notion of innocence before fate and misfortune, grounded on the assumption that an individual caught in a life tragedy cannot be culpable. As one petitioner wrote, "I'm sure that you will be sympathetic to my critical situation and be lenient towards me."[175]

The disenfranchised offered personal narratives that often departed from the formal guidelines for the reinstatement of rights. Laments did not conform with the official requirements for rehabilitation, as petitioners failed to mention their socially useful labor or loyalty to Soviet power. Nor did they offer any confession to Bolshevik authorities.

Laments did not involve assertions of an empowered, useful Soviet self, but of a disempowered, incapable self—ignorant, pitiful, manipulated by others, impoverished, and frail. In this genre, there is no redemptive act, no demonstration of worthiness, no display of loyalty. And yet the success of these appeals demonstrates that poverty, suffering, and exploitation often entitled one to social inclusion in the years of Stalin's revolution.

Weak Subject, Powerful Plea

In her work on letters of remission in early modern France, Natalie Zemon Davis argues that the official pardon enhanced the king's sovereignty by displaying his capacity for mercy and reminding supplicants where power resided.[176] It appears that the Soviet practice of granting amnesty and rehabilitation was analogous to the French example. But the issue of "where power resided" is not so clear in the Soviet case. For when laments were offered and accepted, it was not the disenfranchised who were conforming to their reader's instruction. Rather, it was the other way around. What makes the lament such a compelling and effective strategy for rehabilitation is the way that it challenged the reader to act. The more powerless the disenfranchised presented themselves, the more they intensified the obligation of Soviet officials to respond.[177] In the lament, the burden of proof was not on the petitioner, as when one offered demonstrations of worthiness and displays of loyalty. Instead, laments place a burden of conscience squarely on the reader who is implored to respond sympathetically. As one writer made explicit, "I do not doubt that TsIK will rehabilitate my mother and not refuse her a crumb of bread."[178]

Often outcasts simply made a desperate and moving appeal and begged the reader to reinstate rights immediately. "At the present time, I'm in a critical situation. . . . My family of five young children is doomed to death from starvation."[179] A woman who was left without a husband and forced to raise three children alone, begged for rights if only for the sake of her children: "I turn to you, comrade Kalinin, with a petition for the reinstatement of my voting rights. Keep in mind that at the present time I am left with three orphan children who will suffer because of their parents. . . . if only for the sake of the children . . . don't let us perish . . . for the sake of the children, don't refuse me."[180] The wife of a trader wrote: "I've grown weak, and I feel my strength declining."[181] A man deprived of rights for trading asked the county soviet executive committee to "turn attention to my dire circumstances [*bezvykhodnoe polozhenie*]." He continued, "In such a situation, to express it simply, I am doomed to perish. . . . How will my family live—my mother, 67 and an invalid . . . my wife and two children. One must assume that their situation will be this bad until I receive the title of citizen who is allowed to work in state and cooperative institutions."[182] In addition, the disenfranchised often wrote about how their rehabilitation was necessary for the sake of those on whom they relied or who relied on them. "I have my family in my own hands. . . . disenfranchised, I'm deprived the opportunity to raise my family."[183] "Don't let [my] innocent children die from the horrors of disenfranchisement with all its consequences."[184] The unjust suffering of innocent children was often mentioned in desperate appeals, as though echoing Ivan Karamazov's famous declaration that children who are "innocent must not suffer for another's sins."[185] One former tsarist policeman asserted, "My children aren't guilty for my . . . service," and implored his reader: "At the present time, I'm in a critical situation. . . . I have no means of existence and my children are starving."[186]

In addition, children described the financial burden to them of supporting a disenfranchised parent, or argued that the family urgently needed an adult with full rights. In one instance, the children of a disenfranchised woman wrote a petition for the reinstatement of their mother's rights, since she was a "necessary member of our family." One of the woman's sons lost his wife and was left with two small children. "The two children, ages nine and fourteen, need to be watched by [our mother]."[187] The appeal was addressed to Kalinin, who personally scribbled his decision on the corner of the petition: "reinstate in voting rights." Helpless children surely inspired the sympathy of Soviet leaders like Kalinin, but what about helpless adult males? Two brothers, deprived of rights because their sister baked bread for church services and received a minor fee, insisted that they could not, as the law prescribed, live separately from her. "It's impossible for us to live completely separate from our sister since we are both single and no longer young. We have no money to hire a servant since we do not get wages."[188] The Soviet officials who reinstated rights agreed that these single men needed a woman's help.

Some writers warned state authorities of the negative social consequences if they failed to be reinstated in rights. The disenfranchised would include comments like: "Don't throw me over the edge."[189] Some young petitioners even made threats of suicide. Expelled from school in 1929 as the daughter of a priest, a young woman wrote to Nadezhda Krupskaia, Lenin's widow: "I must now sit in my apartment without bread or do something to myself, that is, poison myself."[190] A young man desperately appealed to Kalinin: "I now walk around Sevastopol without even a kopek. They won't hire me to work anywhere. So look, I'm asking you for advice—what should I do? Rob or murder or throw myself into the sea? What can I do?"[191] A similar plea came from the son of a Moscow woman disenfranchised as a former landowner who petitioned for the reinstatement of his mother's rights. A former priest in the church of Old Believers wrote that his family was starving: "In the end, they expect very sad results if you don't take their difficult situation into account."[192]

The young often warned that living as outcasts, they would turn into thieves and other socially dangerous elements. As one put it, "If I am fired from my job in industry, I must either perish or resort to stealing the necessary means of subsistence. I ask you to grant my rights back to me so that at my young age I do not get messed up in such unspeakable things."[193] After an unsuccessful search for employment in the major industrial cities, the son of a disenfranchised man wrote Stalin in 1930, warning that "the young have their whole lives ahead of them and you shouldn't turn them into . . . renegades, people embittered, unfortunate tramps, and hooligans."[194] A woman who was deprived of rights in Ialta for trading cold appetizers claimed that her daughter and dependent, who was also disenfranchised, would resort to prostitution, like many of Russia's poor and unemployed women in the 1920s. "Thus [my daughter], without rights, is forced to become a woman of the street, that is, engage in prostitution. Since the aim of the government is not to increase prostitution but to wage a battle against it . . . I ask, once again, the city soviet to reinstate my rights."[195]

The lament proved effective in persuading Soviet officials to reinstate rights, in particular, because of the way in which these desperate appeals affected their audience. The lament was not only about self, the writer, but about audience, the reader. It might be unclear who these official Soviet readers were, but it is apparent from petitions who the disenfranchised wanted them to be. For just as people shaped a particular kind of self through lamentation, they also constructed an image of the audience for their narratives and challenged their powerful reader to conform to this image. Evidently some officials, self-fashioned as new Soviet patrons, could not behave like the notorious "heartless bureaucrats" of the old tsarist power structure. Petitioners assume that the just reader would reinstate rights, yet what if this audience did not? Outcasts presented their readers with some stark and unpleasant alternatives, perhaps even ultimatums. A woman claimed that her children would starve or turn to prostitution; a man threatened that he would rob or murder. Having constructed the audience as the sole agent who can reverse the fate of the writer, lamenting petitioners shifted the focus of judgment from themselves to their reader. And whose fault would this be if children starved? Surely, *yours* (the reader's) for failing to act. Implicit in the claim "I might starve" is the charge "you might kill me." In this way, laments had a sharp edge. Not simply tales of woe, these narratives made the writer the judge of how the reader should act (rather than the other way around) and practically compelled a sympathetic judgment.

Conclusion

The revolutionary poet Vladimir Mayakovsky wrote that "If a museum exhibited a Bolshevik in tears, Night and day that museum would be visited.—You couldn't see such in a hundred years!"[196] In marked contrast to the lament, Bolshevism signified happiness, and in 1935, Stalin asserted that life was indeed "becoming more joyous." In the 1930s, children thanked Stalin for their happy childhood, and adults recalled the hardship of their childhood as compared with their present happiness.[197] In the public discourse of high Stalinism, the popular lament served as part of a larger narrative that emphasized the successful personal journey of the petitioner and the great accomplishments of Soviet power. Individual biographies captured the meaning of the revolution—lives turned around, new worlds remade, happiness secured. In his study of the Nivkhi of Sakhalin Island, Bruce Grant quotes the February 1930 testimony of Nivkh Primka at the first District Clan Congress of Sakhalin Nivkhi, Oroki, and Evenki: "We—we are a dark and uneducated people. Before Soviet power, people thought of the natives as there to be trod upon [podmetka] and said, why not let them die off? The Japanese gave us vodka and little else. Under the Japanese, everyone died off because the Japanese didn't pay us. The Soviet authorities prohibited the sale of vodka and paid us. We are grateful. . . . We have become farmers."[198] An old woman from the Stalin District of the city of Moscow offered a similar lament on a difficult life in the past coupled with gratitude for a new life. She grew up in the tsarist countryside but later worked in a Soviet factory, and in December 1937, she combined a traditional lament on her past life with praise for the Soviet present: "I had a bad life before. I lived in the country. My father died, leaving my mother with five children on her hands. No one bothered to educate us. We wandered around barefoot and hungry. When I was eleven my mother hired me out as a nanny. . . . But now I live well. I've been given a little room of my own, I have an easy life, and for that I thank Comrade Stalin from the bottom of my heart."[199] By the late 1930s, emotional appeals and laments that failed to include the happy twist at the end (the result of Soviet achievements) constituted a counternarrative.

In the decade under examination, laments represented ambivalent discourses that could be interpreted as both Soviet and un-Soviet in style. Outcasts' laments and Soviet officials' responses to them illustrate the persistence of a customary law that valued pity and humility as well as informality, one that called attention to the particularities of people's lives and activities.[200] The dominant presence of laments in the petitions of the disenfranchised reflects the inability or unwillingness of some people to embrace the values of the new Soviet regime, and to adopt for themselves the identity of New Soviet Person.[201] The fact that these appeals succeeded demonstrates that Soviet officials acknowledged their subjects' genuine hardship, as well as the limited ability of the regime to inculcate entirely new values and a new way of thinking.

At the same time, the presence and acceptance of the lament reveals the multiple meanings made possible by Bolshevik revolutionary ideology. One cannot simply say that people chose to offer a stylized lamentation in place of a formulaic declaration of loyalty to Soviet power, and did so as a conscious act of resistance, an overt refusal to speak the public language of the regime, or offer a few words of praise to Stalin and the revolution (although who could exclude the possibility that some did precisely that?). A more plausible conclusion would take into account the enormous burden of social life in Russia. If one accepts that petitions for the reinstatement of rights were not simply fiction, then life circumstances did indeed dictate people's choice of narrative and the form of appeal that they would compose. Social and demographic realities and not Bolshevism alone shaped citizen identities. In many ways, Russia in the 1920s and 1930s was a crippled, sick, and starving country, populated by many humiliated and oppressed people. Just as Maxim Gorky claimed, these wails represented more than creative oral verse; they were Russian history itself. Certainly, people lived in Russia who would not, indeed could not, provide years of socially useful labor in a factory for heavy industry. Instead they were forced to engage Soviet officials about the difficulties of their lives. For the lamenting disenfranchised, there existed few other avenues to social membership than the back door for the downtrodden.

Given this fact, what remains most striking is that social life did not make ideology irrelevant. Lamenters were far from the model Stalinist citizen who performed productive labor and actively participated in political life, yet laments proved perfectly consistent with a Marxist theory that identified the proletariat as the oppressed and exploited class. In an impoverished yet revolutionary state that defined itself according to class, the unprivileged masses acquired the status of a privileged class. Bolshevik leaders probably did not expect so many of the disenfranchised to remind them that inclusion was reserved for the exploited masses, and that one could acquire a proletarian identity by making a claim of hardship. But how could they be surprised? There remained a corner of Bolshevik ideology that accommodated the oppressed masses. However, under Stalin the legitimacy of this narrative would not last long. Popular songs such as the "March of the Happy-Go-Lucky Guys" asserted that Russians "can sing and laugh like children, amid our constant struggle and toil," while others describing the hardship of Russian life were officially banned.[202] Stalin sought to wage an emotional revolution. No less utopian than the leader's other endeavors, this project to transform popular sentiment dictated that joy and gratitude should replace Russia's tears and suffering.

Piotr Osolodkov, *A Miner*. 1933–1934. © State Russian Museum, St. Petersburg, 2001. From *Soviet Art: 1920s–1930s, Russian Museum, Leningrad*. New York: Harry N. Abrams, Inc., 1988. By permission of the Museum.

5

The Talents and Traits of Soviet Citizens

Some of Stalin's outcasts reacquired rights by offering a lament narrative, but others re-entered the society that excluded them by fulfilling the requirements of Soviet law on rehabilitation—demonstrating loyalty to Soviet power and performing socially useful labor. However, people complied with these requirements for inclusion in different ways and to varying degrees. The process of becoming Soviet was far from uniform. Broad guidelines for rehabilitation and a mix of people interpreting and applying them proved only partly responsible for the range of Soviet selves that emerged from the rehabilitation process. Many assessed the relative risks involved in either petitioning before officials or concealing oneself from them and decided in favor of the latter. Still others avoided personal transformations entirely, preferring instead a rhetorical reframing of their damaging past. The process of acquiring rights provided the new citizenry with certain lessons on the construction of Soviet identity. The bureaucratic nature of rehabilitation led many to pay attention to making the proper political claims and finding neighbors and officials who would vouch for their credibility in writing. Moreover, people who sought to regain their rights learned how to conceal a damaging past, effectively engage state agents, and present a convincing and plausible Soviet self, and they also learned to demand and expect certain rewards for their labors. In the end, the social engineering function of disenfranchisement and the reinstatement of rights did produce a new Soviet citizenry, but one comprised of a variety of citizen selves who often had opposing talents and traits.

Managing on the Margins

For those who hoped to re-enter Soviet society, the act of demonstrating loyalty to Soviet power and a record of socially useful labor before an official of state was often neither easy nor desirable. The deprivation of rights affected lives differently depending on people's private resources, past activities, and personal luck, and the disenfranchised coped with the loss of rights in disparate ways. Sometimes they lived with family members who tried to assist them, but as one petitioner described, "without a ration card [*produktovoi kartochki*)], I naturally am a significant burden on my brother, who has a . . . wife and two children."[1] In the least, people without rights lived lives of great uncertainty and instability, moving from one odd job and region to the next, always vulnerable to severe discrimination. The following short biography illustrates the kind of existence that was shared by many. Deported by the OGPU in 1925 for having traded in the years 1922–1925, one man was barred from living in the country's six major cities. After returning from deportation in 1928, he found work as a canteen worker in an artel. In 1928–1929, he was disenfranchised and immediately petitioned for the reinstatement of rights, all the while continuing to work as a waiter. In 1930, he stopped working and became dependent on his wife for a couple of years before he again found a job, this time in sanitation. He was then fired in 1933 "as a disenfranchised person" and stayed home caring for his child while his wife worked.[2]

If they were fortunate enough to avoid arrest or deportation, the disenfranchised managed a living in temporary and odd jobs. A woman from Voronezh province, deprived of rights in 1927 for trading in knits and buttons, worked as a domestic laborer following her disenfranchisement.[3] A man from Kamensk, deprived of rights in 1926 as a trader, found employment as a courier (*izvoznichestvo*).[4] Another from Chembar in the Central Volga krai worked by day as a roofer and painter at the city soviet and the office of roads.[5] A man from the Western Siberia oblast was a wage laborer and mechanic, and others found employment at the Leningrad port and on a steamship in Omsk.[6] After losing his rights, one man turned his attention to a plot of land he kept in order to feed himself and later worked in a park and as a carpenter in a collective farm. For almost a year he labored as a foreman in a sawmill factory and afterward took a couple of jobs in construction and one cutting firewood.[7] A number of outcasts earned money as hairdressers and barbers. Several monks from the city of Sergiev petitioned while working in the State Historical Art Museum as gallery assistants and guards.[8]

People deprived of voting rights often found short-term employment, but it was much harder for them to secure more stable and preferable work. Soviet institutions, such as trade unions, schools, and factories required that individuals demonstrate their status as citizens with full rights. Although VTsIK explicitly forbid the practice in 1931, state institutions continued to require that people present a document (*spravka*) proving that they had voting rights and, thereby, the right to employment, a pension, insurance, and so on. Those who went before a complaints bureau or a people's court would also be asked about their "material position" and voting-rights status. This prompted the public to bombard their local soviets with requests for documents confirming that they had rights. In the meantime, the disenfranchised often resorted to forgery to obtain documents and trade union cards because they faced the impossible situation of not being allowed to work yet needing a history of work in order to petition for the reinstatement of rights. This quandary prompted an insolent remark by a woman disenfranchised for trading, "As for my not having demonstrated loyalty to Soviet power, it's true, yes. And there's nowhere for me to demonstrate [loyalty] since they don't give work to the disenfranchised."[9]

To get around the problem, many took the gamble of concealing their stigma although they faced even further sanction if discovered. On August 13, 1928, the RSFSR Supreme Court issued a decree that whoever exercises "rights not belonging to this category of persons" would be criminally prosecuted.[10] Nonetheless, the disenfranchised often risked it and just hoped to avoid any suspicion that might prompt an inquiry into their past. A man who was disenfranchised, dekulakized, and deported to the Urals in 1931 returned to the Smolensk area in 1933, at which time he presented false documents to the effect that he had been working for a year in various jobs and even held a position in the workers' committee and membership in the trade union.[11] The son of a landowner worked as an accountant at a construction site from 1932–1935, accumulating proletarian credentials while hiding the fact that he was disenfranchised.[12] A desire to conceal their stigma led others to take advantage of the black market in cooperative membership cards and hide their economic activities by listing themselves as dependent on their proletarian children.[13] Such activities involved no small risk. Forgeries of protocols confirming someone's rehabilitation and other official documents, such as attestations regarding work history or other identity papers, were considered a criminal offense.[14] Any manipulation of official protocols on the reinstatement of rights could result in arrest and severe punishment. Nonetheless, many took the risk anyway.

Although some concealed their identity by keeping a low profile, others did the opposite. The most vulnerable to political attack, the "masked" outcasts tried to protect themselves by being model Soviet activists, even informers for the secret police. For example, the son of a dekulakized, wealthy Ukrainian peasant, who was stripped of much of his land after the October revolution, moved to Moscow on forged, working class documents and struggled to overcome his spoiled identity by becoming the head of a shock-worker brigade, editor of a wall newspaper, member of the komsomol and factory board, and even an informer for State Security.[15] Such behavior was not uncommon. During the Great Purges of 1936–1938, Vadim Rogovin describes how N. V. Krylenko denounced enemies of the people with exceptional zeal because he felt vulnerable himself, since his sister lived abroad and was married to the famous American Trotskyist, Max Eastman. Vasily Grossman also portrayed a voluntary police informer with a class alien background who "helped to destroy many people" because he so badly wanted to be accepted in the new society.[16] Similar cases appear in East Germany where Stasi informers collaborated with the regime in order to disarm suspicion regarding their political loyalties.[17] One wonders how many of the regime's ardent activists were motivated in part by simple self-defense and the desire to deflect attention from their own damaging biographies.

In a region other than one's own it was easiest to hide the fact of having been disenfranchised and to adopt a new identity. People without rights moved around in this period like almost everyone else, in search of jobs and a place in the new Soviet order. Indeed, by the early 1930s, Russia had become what Moshe Lewin called "a country of vagrants" with millions moving permanently from the countryside to the towns in the late 1920s and early 1930s, taking new jobs, and also changing jobs continuously.[18] Peasants who moved to Moscow in the early and mid-1930s apparently acquired false documents and forged passports with ease.[19] The regime's class enemies were probably the first among vagrants. They had a history of movement from the period of the revolution and civil war, when many fled central Russia in the hope of finding safe refuge not only abroad but also in Siberia, the Far East, and the Crimea.[20]

Although concealing one's past was a dangerous strategy, those who chose to confront Soviet officials with an appeal for the reinstatement of rights also made themselves vulnerable to the unpredictable scrutiny of neighbors and officials. For example, some cases went to the Commissariat of Justice for an investigation or confirmation (*proverka*) of materials, and investigators from the Worker-Peasant Inspectorate and district procurators often conducted verifications of the charges and claims made in letters. Certain circumstances might cause officials to initiate an investigation if they believed that there was not enough case material to warrant a judgment or if certain allegations in the petition needed to be confirmed. In one case, a Tambov peasant was disenfranchised for taking part in the Antonov uprising and robberies of state farms. He insisted in his petition that he was forced into joining the group of insurgents and that the actual cause of his disenfranchisement was the fact that he exposed cases of the abuse of power (*zloupotreblenie*) by local officials in the township soviet executive committee, so they had "personal scores" to settle with him.[21] In light of his assertion, the Central Electoral Commission requested an investigation.

The outcome of a case often relied on the personal testimony of those whom investigators happened to approach for an opinion. In the case of N. M. Egorov from the Serpukhov district, the investigator relied greatly on citizen testimony to support Egorov's reinstatement of rights. Egorov was apparently of the third category of "less dangerous" kulaks, those who escaped the worst punishment of arrest or exile and instead served, like many others, "as a disenfranchised labor force in the collective farms until they could prove themselves *worthy* of membership."[22] During his visit to the man's village, the investigator determined certain facts of the case at "a general meeting of citizens." The issue of whether Egorov had been wrongly disenfranchised was discussed with a "group of poor peasants and all the poor peasants were in favor of Egorov's reinstatement of voting rights and accepting him into the kolkhoz."[23] In Egorov's case and others, officials conducted investigations and solicited additional information when deciding whether to reinstate rights. Petitions were frequently passed from VTsIK to the regional soviet executive committee and various other state organs for additional information on the appellant. Any number of people could potentially offer the decisive opinion in a given case.

Whether or not to publicly declare oneself disenfranchised and formally appeal for rights constituted a personal dilemma, and outcasts decided this differently. Non-Russian minorities were apparently among the least likely to expose themselves to state authorities by filing formal appeals, while Muscovites, by contrast, appeared among the most active petitioners. For example, in the 1928–1929 campaign there were 219,084 disenfranchised in the Moscow oblast, and a striking 85 percent, or 185,700, submitted petitions for the reinstatement of rights. In sharp contrast, in 1929 only about 5 percent of the nearly 3,000 disenfranchised in the city of Krasnoiarsk and about 16 percent in the city of Iaroslavl filed petitions for the reinstatement of rights with their local electoral commissions.[24] In particular, many autonomous oblasts or ethnic enclaves reported conspicuously low numbers of appeals for rights. In 1929, a representative of the

Ingush oblast executive committee disclosed that there is "practically nothing to do" with respect to petitions from the disenfranchised because "our disenfranchised don't try to get rehabilitated since reports say that they will not be rehabilitated." With 2,500 persons deprived of rights in the oblast, the oblast soviet executive committee received only 120 petitions, and it did not pass the petitions to local authorities, arguing that "personal vendettas [*lichnye schety*] are firmly in place in our low-level bureaucracy."[25] Kutuzov lamented the trickle of petitions sent to the Central Electoral Commission from the North Caucasus krai during the 1930–1931 campaign:

> Look at what's going on in the oblasts. This is typical. Take any autonomous oblast: In Adygei there are 4,080 disenfranchised but only 10 petitions [*khodataistva*] sent to us. In Osetia there are 2,593 disenfranchised but only one complaint was filed with us and he, incidentally, was reinstated. In Kabardino-Balkarsk there are 5,861 disenfranchised and not one person filed a complaint with us. In Karachai there are 3,157 disenfranchised but three filed petitions and of them two were reinstated and they didn't file [the complaint] themselves, but others did for them. In North Osetia there are 5,626 disenfranchised but two filed complaints. In the Cherkessk oblast there are 1,750 disenfranchised and one filed a complaint. In Chechnia there are 11,274 disenfranchised and five filed a complaint. The North Caucasus krai should pay the most serious attention to this because [the disenfranchised] are probably not turning to them [with complaints] either. Unfortunately, even in Rostov on Don these complaints come in trickles [*postupaiut kak kot naplakal*].[26]

Although some chose not to make a formal appeal for rights, others who had an especially damaging past refused to be discouraged, and a few even proved surprisingly successful. In 1928, the case of a petitioner from Tambov described him as a leader of a counterrevolutionary band, a former kulak, an ardent counterrevolutionary who commanded a detachment during the Antonov uprising (a 1921 peasant revolt in Tambov against Soviet power) and who also had a hostile attitude toward Soviet power.[27] Another 1927 case from the Smolensk gubernia described the supplicant as a former member of the nationalist Union of the Russian People (*soiuz Russkogo naroda*), twice arrested for active counterrevolutionary work, repeatedly recognized for anti-Soviet activity and who, at the time of his petition, was serving a sentence because he was convicted under article 58 of the Criminal Code for counterrevolutionary activity.[28] The Central Electoral Commission rejected these appeals, but others with similar backgrounds were successful. Those reinstated in rights included people who led counterrevolutionary bands or participated in local uprisings, were sentenced to deprivation of rights by a revolutionary tribunal for counterrevolution, or were described as "a former big-time landowner, a nobleman . . . father owned an estate."[29]

What determined one's success or failure in regaining rights as persons reformed? Why were some prompted to conceal their identities and others to confront Soviet authorities with demonstrations of loyalty and socially useful labor? Each of the disenfranchised weighed the likelihood of formal rehabilitation against the risks of concealment. Whether the petitioner could compile a dossier in the appropriate language and with the requisite local support significantly affected one's chances for reacquiring rights. It appears that the mechanism for formal reinstatement of rights favored the better connected, the literate, and those who, according to one petitioner, "have the means to go to the oblast and even to TsIK and make a fuss [*khlopotat'*]."[30]

The Gatekeepers of the Soviet Polity

"I am no kind of alien element [but] completely reformed," wrote one petitioner.[31] Yet central authorities wanted others to vouch for such assertions. The party demanded that people make a life transition in order to earn the reinstatement of rights, but authorities expected corroboration of a person's own transformation. From the policy's inception, party leaders stressed the importance of testimony on behalf of petitioners, from local officials, co-workers, and others. In September 1925, the chairman of the All-Russian Central Executive Committee (*VTsIK*) drafted a letter to the chairmen of all the krai, oblast, and gubernia soviet executive committees (that later formed the basis of a February 1926 secret circular) on the rehabilitation of former tsarist police, prison guards, and others of their category. Kalinin urged local officials to gather a variety of materials in the form of public opinion and character references:

> It's necessary to try, whenever possible, to obtain detailed information through the rural soviets, township soviet executive committee, raion soviet executive committee, in the form of decrees and recommendations from the population of those places where the person held their position. . . . [Also to be taken into account are] character references and recommendations from social and local professional organizations, civil and military institutions and, in exceptional cases, from individuals testifying to the person's actual participation in work after the revolution—service

in the Red Army, active participation in social work in institutions and organizations.[32]

As with disenfranchisement, a degree of irregularity characterized the reinstatement of rights because a multitude of neighbors, co-workers, and local officials served as the actual gatekeepers of Soviet society. The disenfranchised submitted not only a petition, but also testimonials (*otzyvy*) from officials and employers, the opinions of the neighbors, as well as character references and recommendations from local trade unions, social organizations, and civil and military institutions. They included various official documents and attestations (*udostoverenie*) to confirm the assertions in their petition. These papers were intended to corroborate a variety of claims, for example, that the petitioner was a veteran of the Red Army, a Red partisan, or a shock worker; an invalid or otherwise unable to work; a poor peasant or conscientious in the payment of taxes. Documents attached to written appeals confirmed the petitioner's economic position (for example, a listing of personal possessions) and work record (specifying place and length of employment, as well as position and title). Trading licenses were also included when petitioners wanted to demonstrate the petty nature of their trading. One appellant enclosed a series of receipts verifying his payment of taxes.[33] Deportees (*trudposelentsy*) attached recommendations confirming that they deserved to be reinstated in rights, character references (*kharakteristika*) from the NKVD commanders attesting to their record of work and attitude toward work, status as a shock worker, and loyalty to the regime.[34] Some even enclosed pictures of their humble dwellings to demonstrate that they were not members of a privileged class.

When they carefully compiled a personal case file in preparation for their appeal, outcasts knew that Soviet identity did not exist apart from the bureaucratic documents that made it legal. Citizen and alien identities depended on whether individuals possessed the proper official papers. People were stripped of their identity cards after disenfranchisement, and they needed official documents that confirmed the reinstatement of their rights if they wanted to enter the party or acquire legitimate state employment. At the same time, failure to possess the right papers sometimes provided the pretext for disenfranchisement. For example, a young man complained about the rural soviet's refusal to issue him an act of separation (*razdelnoi akt*) from his disenfranchised father or his military card (*voinskii bilet*), arguing that the absence of these documents led to his own loss of rights. Others lost rights for failing to demonstrate that they lived on earned income or were not a former landowner (*pomeshchik*).[35] Documents proved critical in the entire process of constructing identity, which is why rehabilitation favored those who could secure the proper papers. The new Soviet citizen became especially adept at what Michael Herzfeld described as the bureaucratic management of identity.[36]

Petitioners who were successful in their appeals for the reinstatement of rights often had positive character references in their case file. These came from a variety of sources, such as party members, a group of poor peasants, the housing management, the collective farm, rural soviet, local procurator, workers and factory committees (*zavkomy*), participants in the civil war and the excursion to Iakutia,[37] and the editors of the peasant newspaper, *Krest'ianskaia gazeta*.[38] In the 1920s, outcasts often included references from co-villagers who confirmed a petitioner's "good relations with the local peasant population," and in the 1930s, references typically came from co-workers and housing officials who noted a petitioner's respect for neighbors.[39] One young man included with his petition a protocol from a general meeting of his local villagers in 1929 at which those present vouched for his economic independence from a disenfranchised father.[40] Work references generally noted certain key elements: participation in the social life of the factory, shock work (*udarnik* or *stakhanovite* status), awards or promotions (*premirovaniia*), attention to one's duties and responsibilities.[41] A good work reference often mentioned the fact that co-workers had not issued any complaints about the petitioner.[42] These testimonies proved so important to one's chances for rehabilitation that the wife of a kulak reportedly went "around to schools, gave [the children] 20 kopeks each, and collected signatures for [her husband's] character reference."[43]

Local opinion may have been more significant for the reinstatement of rights than one's own personal transformation. Some of the disenfranchised who had particularly damaging biographies managed to be rehabilitated because of others' positive testimony on their behalf. Zhukov, a resident of the Penza gubernia, attached numerous supporting documents to his petition. Disenfranchised as a former nobleman and large landowner, he served in Soviet institutions following the revolution and was a trade union member since 1921. After being disenfranchised in 1925, his rights were reinstated, but he was then stripped of rights again in the 1926–1927 electoral campaign. The Central Electoral Commission reinstated Zhukov's rights shortly thereafter, since he submitted the proper documents, namely, recommendations from party members, attestations from the rural soviet, and a document from 1909 in which local peasants expressed their gratitude toward him.[44] Zhukov seemed quite adept at gathering the appropriate documents, and he was not

alone. A member of the princely landowning family, Golitsin, was reinstated in rights in 1930 because he had good references.[45] The granddaughter of the novelist Leo Tolstoy also reacquired her rights in 1930.[46]
Some petitioners had influential party members supporting their appeals.
The successful appeal of one Novgorod man included an official note
that "Comrade Solts supports the petition."[47]

In rehabilitation cases involving counterrevolutionaries and "former
classes," the most critical opinion came from the offices of the secret police
(*GPU-OGPU-NKVD*). The Central Electoral Commission typically asked
the security organs for a determination (*zakliuchenie*) in the cases of former police, religious clerics, prison guards, counterrevolutionaries, and
certain criminals, such as thieves. For example, the Commission looked to
the secret police in the 1924 for an opinion on the case of a trade union
member who was deprived of rights and exiled "on the suspicion of stealing logs."[48] Similarly, in a 1935 case, the chairman of the Stalingrad regional soviet executive committee wrote the NKVD about a petitioner, a
former cleric, asking the NKVD to provide information on the petitioner's
attitude toward Soviet power, length of religious service, social origin, and
activities during the civil war.[49] Appeals for rights faced sure rejection if
the security organs disapproved of someone's rehabilitation or, as in the
case of one former White Army officer, described a person as "politically
unreliable."[50] The Procuracy also weighed in on these important matters,
such as when it opposed the reinstatement of rights for a former counterrevolutionary leader from 1919, a man from the Orenburg gubernia who
was sentenced to five years deprivation of freedom.[51] The NKVD also received letters from disenfranchised people requesting the reinstatement of
rights, as deportees sometimes wrote directly to their Gulag administra-
tors.[52] Petitions and requests for information traveled back and forth between the Soviet secret police and the Central Electoral Commission. For
example, in 1935 the NKVD received petitions for the reinstatement of
rights, which it passed along to the Commission for a decision or confirmation that the petitioner from its camps, who was requesting to be returned to his homeland (*rodina*), had indeed been rehabilitated by the
Commission. In turn, the Commission would send the NKVD petitions it
received as well, asking for the latter's decision on a case plus information
on the petitioner's social origin, past activities, parents, and political mood
(*nastroenie*).[53]

Just as the community excluded individuals, it played a key role in their
social reintegration. In the vast majority of cases, central authorities went
along with the views of local officials, and local opinion itself often proved
cause for rejection. For example, the position of local officials prompted

the Commission to reject the appeal of a woman from Orel who served as a nun from 1894 to 1916, even though "since the first days of the revolution to the present she lives in the village and engages in agriculture."[54] An appeal for rights by Perstiagin, who traded before the revolution but served in the Red Army since 1921, was rejected by the CEC after local soviet officials expressed opposition to his reinstatement.[55] The important role of personal connections demonstrates that more was required of aspiring citizens than claims of personal transformation. In the dossiers of those who were unsuccessful in their petition for the reinstatement of rights, one finds various references to local official opinion. For example, rejected cases included comments that the local trade union committee had not supported a petition or the provincial soviet executive committee insisted that a man's voting rights be denied despite his service in Soviet institutions since 1918.[56] The Central Electoral Commission was not the only authority that deferred to local opinion when deciding cases of inclusion. In 1929, in the Riazan gubernia, officials "rubber-stamped the decrees of the rural and volost electoral commissions."[57] In 1933, the secretary of the Central Electoral Commission, Raab, described how raion and krai officials simply confirmed the decisions of the rural soviets even in the absence of supporting documentation.[58] Local authorities not only chose whom to disenfranchise, but they largely had the authority to decide rehabilitation cases as well.

Like disenfranchisement, the reinstatement of rights involved the broad participation of many institutions. The media, finance organs, secret police, Procuracy and investigative bodies, even Stalin and Kalinin confronted the appeals of noncitizens. Although the Central Executive Committee and the secret police were involved in hearing appeals and deciding cases, much of the authority over this process rested with local soviet officials. The disenfranchised certainly wrote to Stalin and Kalinin in great numbers, but these letters were often simply directed to the local soviets, and even the NKVD urged that local officials shoulder most of the burden in processing petitions, particularly as the volume of these letters grew over the years. Each level of the soviet state bureaucracy processed the cases of disenfranchised people and decided whether to reinstate rights, but these officials all relied on information generated from below. Cases were often decided by the written words of petitioners and the people who vouched for them.

Often forced to rehabilitate themselves, people without rights labored to construct an effective appeal with the requisite supporting documentation and testimony. Those who submitted petitions for the reinstatement of rights assumed responsibility for compiling the essential elements of the all-important case file: the personal narrative, character references, and official attestations. The reinstatement of rights was itself a bureaucratic process that required documentation, so life changes had not only to be declared in petitions but also validated or substantiated by others. Often more important than the substance of one's personal transformation were the people who could document or vouch for it. Rehabilitation taught new Soviet citizens to be just as aware of the need to change behavior as of the obligation to verify the conversion in official documents and attestations. Too often, identity papers and recommendations became surrogates for personal transformation and thereby subverted the goal of social engineering.

Asserting Soviet Selves

Authoritarian regimes insisted on public expressions of political loyalty, and this included the demonstration of proper language proficiency, the practice of what Stephen Kotkin calls "Speaking Bolshevik" in Stalin's Russia or what Simonetta Falasca-Zamponi describes as "Speaking Fascist" in Mussolini's Italy.[59] Language, especially new words and rhetorical styles, served as a key indicator of one's political education and allegiance. Not surprisingly, many of the disenfranchised knew to invoke the dominant idiom when they made appeals before powerful Soviet officials. Assertions of a Soviet self were markedly different from the ritual lament, because they involved an appeal to political values rather than to sentiment.

Soviet officials looked for evidence of personal transformation in these dossiers as well. In order to be reinstated in rights, the disenfranchised had to change their lives, abandon past activities, demonstrate loyalty to Soviet power, and engage in socially useful labor. They noted everything they could in their petitions, from their high rates of productivity, to children in the communist youth league or komsomol, to their significant inventions. In order to become citizens, they assembled documents and performed new roles—such as those of shock worker, atheist, or wife of a proletarian. Successful petitioners for rights fulfilled the requirements of loyalty and socially useful labor in a variety of ways and exposed multiple points of entry back into Soviet society. Seeing no single route to reinstatement, people chose the path that appeared to them both safe and available. For example, not everyone could hope to make a major life transformation in a short time, so many of the disenfranchised used the

Soviet lives of family members to rehabilitate themselves. In their petitions for rights, some of the disenfranchised referred to family members who had a good Soviet profile and listed the socially useful activities of relatives. Those who lagged behind in making a personal transformation looked to politically precocious family members for a boost and demonstrated loyalty and socially useful labor through husbands, parents, and children. Family relationships were often stigmatizing, but they could be rehabilitative as well.

People disenfranchised as family dependents needed to renounce their former relationship of dependency. For example, women condemned for being economically dependent on their husbands emphasized that they divorced their discrediting spouses or became financially independent. More surprisingly, if women lost their rights for reasons unrelated to their spouse, rehabilitation nonetheless took account of the husband's identity. Disenfranchised women almost without exception discussed husbands in their petitions for rights, because decisions on whether to rehabilitate them considered the husband's identity as well. In the following letter from the husband of a kulak's daughter, the man acknowledged his responsibility for the woman's political education, a view that Soviet officials apparently shared: "From the day I married her, I concerned myself with her re-education. That proved to be quite easy since she was still young. My hopes were entirely justified, so I decided to courageously turn to the electoral commission [for her reinstatement of rights]."[60] Women understood the significance of their husband's identities for their own rehabilitation effort and regularly referred to spouses regardless of the man's role in their disenfranchisement. A woman from the North Caucasus, deprived of rights in 1925 for maintaining a cafeteria, touted the Soviet identity of her deceased husband who fought in the civil war. Rather than proclaim herself to be reformed or worthy because of her own actions, she specifically requested rehabilitation as the wife of a good Soviet man: "From the first days of the October revolution, my husband was on the side of the working class and together with Red partisans took part in the battle with the White Army. . . . [I request] the reinstatement of rights as the wife of a former partisan who fought against White Army bands."[61]

Spouses played a critical role in rehabilitation, whether or not they were responsible for the person's loss of rights. Women always mentioned their husbands in petitions, and husbands occasionally made useful reference to their wives as well. In his petition, a Urals man noted the favorable identity of his spouse even though he was disenfranchised for his activities during the civil war—collaborating with the White Army, carrying out searches of communists, and insulting their families and wives. To counter these charges, he used the example of his wife in order to prove his high regard for communists. How could she, the former wife of a communist killed in the civil war, agree to marry him if he had earlier been so abusive to communists' wives? "[My wife] is also the former wife of the executed communist Nekrasov. If I mocked or humiliated communists and their wives, then she could not have become my own wife."[62]

Parents and children disenfranchised as dependents naturally emphasized acts of separation. A woman who lost her rights after her son was exiled to Solovki for counterrevolutionary activity also included the standard declaration of independence in her appeal. "[My son's] exile," she wrote, "can in no way concern me because I was not involved or judged by a court in this case. I was never materially dependent on my son."[63] Similarly, one man included in his petition evidence of "separation from my son."[64] The following petition from a young man, deprived of rights because he was dependent on his mother who used hired help, also illustrates this point. "Presently, I have separated from my mother's home [*khoziastva*] and entered a legal marriage with M. I. Vdovina. . . . I broke off all material ties with my mother's home and live temporarily (until I acquire my own place) in the home of my wife's mother."[65]

Besides these mandatory declarations that directly addressed the substance of the charge against them, the disenfranchised used family ties as evidence of loyalty and socially useful labor. People presented new Soviet identities vis-à-vis other members of their family. For example, the military service of family members during the civil war and the revolution were frequently mentioned as evidence of political loyalty. A Jewish man from the city of Uman in the Kiev oblast could not claim service in the Red Army, but he told the following war tale instead about his brother's military sacrifice and his own suffering at the hands of the enemy: "I suffered at the hands of the White bandits materially (from the pogroms) and my brother was killed by the Whites as a Red partisan. I myself was forced to flee the city since I was being chased by White bandits for actively assisting the Red Army."[66] The social origin of someone's parents also served as evidence of loyalty. "I am the son of a worker. My father was illiterate and worked as a wage laborer for more than forty years as a factory worker."[67] People rehabilitated themselves through their family members thus demonstrating that, like exclusion, inclusion was not simply a matter of personal identity but of social relationships as well.

Parents often stressed the achievements of their sons and daughters as testimony to their fine Soviet upbringing. The father of four sons who served in the Red Army catalogued their sacrifices in his petition: the two youngest never returned from the front, another became an invalid, and the oldest was awarded military honors.[68] Another petitioner declared, "I have seven children whom I have raised to work [*kotorym ia dal trudovoe vospitanie*]. . . . Four of them are active participants in socialist construction. My oldest son was in the Red Army and now works as an engineer."[69] Another heralded "two daughters . . . who were accepted into the ranks of young pioneers."[70] A similar appeal boasted: "I put all my children on their feet, made them useful citizens of the Soviet state. They all work conscientiously."[71] Parents used the achievements of their children as evidence that they kept good Soviet households. One man, deprived of rights for trading, argued confidently that if he were indeed a kulak his children could not have turned out so well. "My second son at 17 volunteered for the Red Army, served in a partisan brigade [*osnovtsik*] and fought against Kolchak. . . . My daughter worked for several years (8–9) as a schoolteacher and joined the party. . . . If I were a kulak, then my children would have to have an ideology that was hostile to [Soviet] power."[72]

Petitioners' emphasis on their good Soviet parenting was an appropriate strategy of appeal, for Stalin maintained that women who sympathize with Soviet power will provide a healthy upbringing for the next generation.[73] Outcasts effectively invoked this notion when they argued that proper Soviet parenting constituted a kind of socially useful labor. When children wrote petitions on behalf of their parents, they described parenting as a form of state service, as one young man wrote: "Our mother raised us—worthy members and sons of our communist, socialist country."[74] Writing for the rehabilitation of his mother, another young man focused on his own Soviet identity because it would reflect well on his mother. "I am a scientist, an inventor, with honors and awards. I have a series of published works. I worked out an entire chemistry theory which was applied in practice and led to greater efficiency in alkaloid factories."[75] For the reinstatement of rights, people had to demonstrate loyalty and socially useful labor. The case files of the disenfranchised reveal that outcasts successfully met these requirements in various ways.

Moreover, the disenfranchised often assumed a Soviet identity through a rewriting of their past rather than through an actual change in behavior. A man from the Ivanovo Industrial gubernia was disenfranchised as a former landowner who came from a landowning noble family. In 1929, the Central Electoral Commission reinstated his rights, describing him as a former member of the Union of Struggle (*soiuza bor'by*)[76] who had served several prison sentences, including one in the Peter and Paul Fortress, plus a term of exile with the chairman of the RSFSR Supreme Court, P.I. Stuchka.[77] This former landowner did not acquire Soviet credentials; rather his Sovietization involved a rewriting of personal history. For many, it was preferable and easier to acquire a Soviet identity rhetorically, as it were, by reframing the past or by emphasizing what one had *not* done. "I never participated in banditry, or joined Kolchak," one Siberian earnestly declared.[78] A Ukrainian described how he did not join the Whites: "Although I was in an extremely difficult situation, without a kopek; I was literally starving; despite the exhortations and promises of the voluntary [military] agents, I decided that I would in no way join an army that was alien to the class interests of the proletariat."[79]

Not everyone became Soviet indirectly, through relatives or a rewriting of the past. Many adopted a Soviet lifestyle, although their biographical narratives were not entirely formulaic. Others presented a Soviet self in assorted and surprising ways. Petitioners reproduced various elements of what Katerina Clark describes as the Bolshevik grand narrative or master plot, and they chronicled how they overcame obstacles (such as poverty or a parental stigma), performed exceptionally at work, and experienced a personal transformation in the service of Soviet power.[80] The dominant themes that recurred in these letters included productive work, loyalty, sacrifice, and risk to advance the goals of the party. One man described his work in the timber industry as "connected with great risk to life no less than on the military front," since many of those who worked in timber perished in the line of duty.[81] A woman deprived of rights as the daughter of a kulak professed her unyielding loyalty to Bolshevism despite her father's cruel rejection. "At the end of 1926, I myself wanted to know how and why there was a revolution and I began to look for people who could tell me. With another woman, I organized a youth circle and, in the beginning of 1927 began to organize a komsomol cell. Since my father was strict, I worked in secret. When he learned what I was doing, my father threw me out of the house without anything."[82] Outcasts also listed the physical injuries they endured in the revolution and civil war, emphasizing in particular the shedding of blood for the Bolshevik cause.[83]

In the petitions of the 1930s, people began to identify themselves with the heroes of the day, as shock workers and inventors. Yet loyalty and conscientious labor were not the only essential characteristics of the citizen, for citizens also had to avoid arrest and pay their taxes too. These diligent taxpayers were no robbers of public funds. Many outcasts stressed the lack of any criminal record or involvement in counterrevolutionary activity and their prompt payment of all taxes and fees.[84]

I have never been sentenced by a court or investigated. I was never involved in any counterrevolutionary parties or acts [*vystupleniia*]. On the contrary, I was in the Red Army and always stood on the side of strengthening the worker-peasant government. . . . I consider myself completely loyal to Soviet power and to its initiatives [*meropriiatiia*]. . . . I paid all taxes and fees. . . . [85]

My attitude toward Soviet power has always been and still is loyal. I always pay my taxes promptly. I have been responsive to all of the initiatives of Soviet power.[86]

Volunteerism and acts of social service also demonstrated loyalty to Soviet power, so outcasts donated their time at the firefighters club (*pozharnyi klub*) or for the promotion of literacy.[87] Peasants in certain areas of Samara gave out their surplus bread and participated in Red brigades in order to avoid disenfranchisement.[88] One petitioner, a former trader, mentioned how he and his wife had adopted two orphaned children, following the 1926 party decree "On Measures to Combat Child Homelessness" which, he claimed, urged peasants to accept and raise homeless children.[89] This couple had no children before the adoption, but they did have a record of trading. Although peasants were granted a tax break for taking in homeless children, the couple's desire to compensate for a history of trade might have influenced their decision to adopt. They were able to request rights for the sake of the children. "My wife and I adopted [a three-year old boy and a two-year old girl] and they live with us as our own [*rodnye*] children. Now we send them to school. We feel and understand that to create normal conditions for the further upbringing of these children it would be effective and useful if my wife and I were reinstated in rights."[90]

The disenfranchised became the inventors of their own Soviet selves, emphasizing various aspects of their biography, profiling parents and children, and choosing volunteer work. People discovered many ways to compile a Soviet profile, as demonstrated by the remarkable case of a Leningrad woman, Serafima Lazarevna Vinogradova. In 1929, she was deprived of rights for using hired labor (two workers and two apprentices) during a six-month period in her workshop for "the production of the game 'ping-pong,' of which she is the inventor."[91] Serafima was first employed as a gym teacher but then turned to handicrafts and made women's hats. Later, she developed an interest in inventing and, in particular, in the production of celluloid objects and ping-pong balls. She described her work proudly:

> I was the first in the USSR to organize the production of celluloid balls for ping-pong. I invented the method of production; I also invented the means of producing celluloid handles for bicycles. The exceedingly high demand of my customers grew exceptionally. . . . [92]
>
> Earlier, [the game of ping-pong and ping-pong balls] were only produced abroad. I initiated this production in Leningrad.[93]

As the demand from consumers and cooperative enterprises for Serafima's ping-pong balls grew, she expanded production, acquired a craftsman's patent, and hired two workers and two apprentices. This marked the beginning of her troubles. Realizing that she risked disenfranchisement for employing hired labor, Serafima returned her patent and tried to hand over her successful production to a producer's cooperative. With the help of the Manufacturing Union and the All-Russian Society of the Blind, she organized a producer-cooperative artel. Her contract with the Society for the Blind stipulated that she would act as director of production, while the Society would supply the labor. This arrangement resulted in the successful production of bicycle handles in addition to the ping-pong balls.

Serafima was only disenfranchised after she approached Soviet authorities. Thinking she had already been deprived of rights, she wasted no time and petitioned immediately for rehabilitation. Local records indicated that she was not disenfranchised, but the authorities took notice of her premature petition and disenfranchised her. Serafima extolled the successes of her workshop and thereby generated suspicion among Soviet officials, but this simply encouraged her to petition again for the reinstatement of rights. Serafima had no shortage of socially useful labor and other achievements about which to boast: her artel generated hard currency and offered employment to invalids, and she involved herself in the club "Avtodor" as the first woman motorcyclist, for which she was photographed in the press.[94] She simply lived according to plan, and for this re-acquired rights less than two years after her disenfranchisement. As Serafima's case illustrates, Soviet traits appeared in unusual and highly individual configurations. This pioneer in ping-pong ball production was also the manager of a workshop that accommodated blind laborers and a woman motorcyclist.

The proletarian state might have championed Serafima as an exemplary citizen, but neither she nor the model Soviet parent or volunteer petitioned for rights with the same confidence and authority as the industrial worker.

Those who faced the toughest sanctions after disenfranchisement petitioned with the greatest sense of entitlement.

Compulsory and Redemptive Employment

By the early 1930s, a rewriting of the laws on rehabilitation allowed a new category of disenfranchised people, deported kulaks, to regain their rights. During the 1929–1930 campaign to "liquidate the kulaks as a class," many people who had been disenfranchised were automatically labeled kulaks and deported to work as forced laborers on the country's monumental construction projects in places including the Far North, Siberia, the Urals, and Kazakhstan. By January 1932, nearly 1.5 million deportees or special settlers (*spetspereselentsy*) lived in forced labor under the command of the OGPU. The Politburo Central Committee was very reluctant to reinstate the rights of these deported kulaks in the early 1930s, and the party leadership's instructions in 1931 and 1934 only cautiously allowed for their reinstatement in rights under certain specified conditions.[95] Like other disenfranchised people, deportees had the choice of either petitioning for the reinstatement of rights or complaining about wrongful disenfranchisement, yet the odds of having one's complaint vindicated were slim. In the period 1932–1940, only 33,055 (or less than 2 percent) of the over two million deportees were freed "as wrongly deported."[96] A far more common approach for deportees was the petition, an appeal that one had earned rights through socially useful labor.

In a 1931 OGPU directive, deported kulaks had the right to obtain full reinstatement of all civil rights (*pravo na polnoe vosstanovlenie*) after five years from the date of their deportation.[97] A TsIK decree of July 3, 1931, made it possible for deported kulaks to be reinstated in rights under certain conditions.[98] Entitled "The Procedure for Reinstating the Civil [*grazhdanskie*] Rights of Deported Kulaks," the decree promised the following:

> Kulaks, deprived of voting rights on the basis of the USSR Constitution and the Instructions on Elections to the Soviets . . . for anti-Soviet and anti-kolkhoz actions—arson, banditry, etc.—are reinstated in all civil rights after five years from the date of the their deportation and receive voting rights under the following conditions: (1) if in the course of this [five year] period they demonstrate that they have ceased their battle against . . . the policies of Soviet power. . . . (2) if they demonstrate that they are honest and conscientious laborers at work.[99]

As with other petitioners, deported kulaks could regain their rights through socially useful labor. At a time when the party was rapidly expanding the industrial base of the country and, in this way, "building socialism," party leaders were quite explicit about the need to employ all labor, even that of aliens. Speaking in 1932, a peak year in the reinstatement of rights, I. I. Kutuzov, head of the Central Electoral Commission's subcommission on reviewing complaints of wrongful disenfranchisement, defended the use of "all productive resources," even the disenfranchised, for the purpose of socialist construction: "All productive resources [*sily*] must be used—first and foremost cadres, who are capable, willing and worthy to be conscious participants in the building of socialism. This should refer also to the infamous [*izvestnye*] categories of people who, for one reason or another, have been disenfranchised."[100]

Work seemed to hold the most promise for those seeking the restoration of their civil rights. Officially, deported kulaks who demonstrated that they had "undoubtedly" engaged in honest work and supported the policies of Soviet power could be reinstated in rights by local administrative organs after five years and only on explicit instruction of the OGPU administration. A Sovnarkom decree of July 16, 1932, allowed krai and oblast executive committees to reinstate the rights of those who worked in gold mines for three years rather than the usual five years if they were recommended by the gold-mine administration for their exceptional work and for overfulfilling work norms.[101] Specialists who were sentenced by a court or by the OGPU and who worked for two years in the gold and platinum industries could also be reinstated in rights if they had good recommendations from the administration at their place of employment.[102] Stalin and others in the party leadership must have agreed with M. I. Kalinin's public statement that "children of the disenfranchised, raised and educated under Soviet conditions, are unwittingly infected by the mood (*nastroenie*) that our political, economic, and social life inspires." That segment of the disenfranchised population whose rehabilitation had the most support from Kremlin authorities consisted of the young and able-bodied, those who could still perform years of labor for Soviet power. By March 1933, children of deported kulaks could be reinstated in rights if they engaged in socially useful labor, and they were not required to have a minimum five-year work record.[103]

In a 1934 secret memo to the Central Electoral Commission secretary I. G. Raab, the head of the OGPU Gulag, Matvei Berman, outlined the procedure for reinstating the civil rights of deportees.[104] The groups which were eligible for the reinstatement of rights included: people recommended for their honest labor, loyalty, and support for Soviet power; the "best part" of the group of deportees (*pereselentsy*), in particular, the young who were shock workers in industry and actively participated in social work; children of deportees who had come of age, engaged in socially useful labor and worked conscientiously. In such cases, the settlement's commander and the enterprises' administration selected those worthy of rehabilitation. The OGPU then submitted the files (which consisted of the petition, character references, and recommendations from the person's place of work) to the krai or oblast executive committee for the appropriate documents supporting the person's reinstatement of rights. Thus, the OGPU from the Urals oblast, Western Siberia krai, and so on sent lists with the names of hundreds of deportees to TsIK for a stamp of approval. The names would be listed along with reasons for the reinstatement of rights, for example, "has a good attitude toward work, takes part in cultural and social work."[105] With respect to the rehabilitation of deportees, Berman gave the soviet executive committees no decision-making authority; they could merely issue documents confirming rehabilitation upon notice from the OGPU. The only instance where the district (*raion*) soviet executive committee had authority to reinstate the voting rights of deportees was in the case of children of deportees.

A key consideration for reinstating the rights of deportees was whether or not the individual or family had adopted a Soviet way of life. In this 1934 secret memo to the Central Electoral Commission, Berman listed the criteria for reinstating the rights of deportees as follows: (1) evidence of work in industry and participation in the social life of the settlement (*poselka*); (2) the extent to which the given family of deportees had established itself economically as indicated by membership in a collective farm,[106] the purchase of a house in installments from an agricultural organization, or the presence of a garden, a building, or livestock. In this letter, Berman uses the terms "civil rights" (*grazhdanskie prava*) and "citizenship" (*grazhdanstvo*), rather than voting rights.[107]

Also among the ranks of the country's forced laborers were young men, the children of the disenfranchised, who had reached draft age. Barred from enlisting in the Red Army because the disenfranchised were not trusted to carry guns, the state drafted these military conscripts without rights into the rear militia, and sent them to construction sites where they worked as forced laborers on large-scale projects throughout the country. Once assigned to the rear militia, these young men could be eligible for the reinstatement of rights and a transfer to the Red Army, provided they met certain conditions similar to those for deported kulaks. In March 1932, following an inquiry from the People's Commissariat of Labor, the Central Electoral Commission issued a decree which specified that, like deported kulaks, rear militiamen too could be reinstated in rights. They needed to meet a number of criteria, that is, demonstrate a record of having worked conscientiously, an attestation from the leader of their unit (*chasti*), the fulfillment of their work output (*vyrabotka*), and a five-year work record.[108] A September 27, 1933, TsIK and Sovnarkom decree "On the Rear Militia" stated that the rear militia commander had the right to petition TsIK for the rehabilitation of those rear militiamen who in a two-year period of service demonstrated that they were disciplined, honest, and model workers.[109]

Over the next three years, the party would relax the procedure governing the reinstatement of rights for rear militiamen. According to the 1933 decree, these aliens could be reinstated in rights only by TsIK upon petition from their commander and unit commissar. Local executive committees and rural soviets did not have this right except in "indisputable cases" in which people were enlisted in the rear militia after being wrongly disenfranchised. However, the 1934 TsIK Instructions stated that the local executive committee had no restrictions in reinstating the rights of rear militiamen. Another contradiction emerged in a VTsIK circular of July 1, 1935, which asserted that TsIK was the sole authority that could reinstate the voting rights of rear militiamen and only when their commanders petitioned on their behalf.[110] Noting this inconsistency, a TsIK official urged that local officials be granted the right to rehabilitate rear militiamen. "I think that it's necessary to clarify to the People's Commissariat of Defense [*Narkomoborony*] that a decision of the local executive committee on reinstating the voting rights of citizens in the rear militia is sufficient grounds for discharging them from the rear militia. One must decide the issue in this way because many rear militiamen were wrongly disenfranchised."[111]

The Soviet prosecutor's office articulated a similar position in 1936, when it urged VTsIK to have its July 1935 circular changed because it was opposed to TsIK legislation. The People's Chief Prosecutor, A. Ia. Vyshinskii, believed that two categories of persons should be discharged from the rear militia—those who enlisted because they were wrongly disenfranchised by a local soviet executive committee and those disenfranchised for being dependent on someone who had since been reinstated in voting rights. The latter should be "automatically reinstated in voting rights."[112] The 1936 law on military service incorporated Vyshinskii's suggestions, and the reinstatement of rights provided an incentive that motivated militiamen in their work.[113] According to the head of the political department (*politotdel*) of the Red Army's Rear Militia Administration, "The struggle for the right to be reinstated by TsIK prior to the end of one's sentence [*dosrochno*] is the primary incentive [*osnovnyi stimul*] in the productive and other activities of our regiments."[114]

The New Proletariat of Forced Labor Camps

Forcibly removed from their villages and cities, deportees made the journey to special settlements with great difficulty. The deportees described being alienated and cut off from the world (*otrezany ot vsego mira*), living in conditions unfit even for animals. For many in such circumstances, writing provided a connection with the outside world and gave voice to those who were silenced and out of view. One writer described himself as an eyewitness (*ochevidets*) who helps others by drawing attention to their suffering and connecting them to a community that did not see or hear them. "Living in exile, I look around me at all the horrors of this massive deportation of entire families. Not able to help these suffering people in any other way, I decided to write to you. . . . Here is a picture of this camp." "We are no longer peasants," one wrote. "Here [people] are transformed completely into wild beasts. A person cannot remain a human being in such conditions."[115]

Eventually, deportees writing from work sites and construction projects of the White Sea Canal, the Siberian timber camps, the Far North, and the industrial regions of the Urals and Kuzbass, composed joint petitions that asserted a strong, collective, proletarian identity. Almost no other group of disenfranchised people wrote joint petitions or demanded rights so forcefully. If Soviet identity was rooted in one's work, one's socially useful labor, none of the disenfranchised had a greater claim to inclusion than those compelled to work on the nation's various construction projects. Here, people without rights made claims against the state after they performed meritorious service in the military or in industry. In their appeals, deportees echoed a view shared by many petitioners, namely, that state service conferred benefits or entitled one to certain rights.

Working as they did in industry and construction, forced laborers made the most legitimate claim to proletarian identity. Petitions from forced-labor camps demanded, among other things, equal rights with other workers, passports, stakhanovite documents in recognition of their above-average work record, even hardship pay for living in the polar regions.[116] The following note from a deportee to the USSR Supreme Soviet included a request for a passport that he believed he had earned through meritorious labor. "I am a deportee [*pereselenets*] from the B[elorussian] SSR to Kazakhstan ASSR and have worked in construction. From August 16, 1935 to November 1936 I have worked as an udarnik and now I work as a stakhanovite, fulfilling many norms in construction three times over."[117] When they petitioned for rights, they did not invoke parents and children or rewrite their personal histories because the state had compelled their Soviet transformation through compulsory work and resettlement. These men spoke confidently about their socially useful labor, the fact that they overfulfilled production norms and worked honestly and conscientiously. A young man from Kostroma, deprived of rights as a psalmodist, described his exceptional work record: "I do physical labor in production at the factory . . . already two years and I haven't missed even a day's work. I fulfill all the norms 100 percent and more."[118] In 1935, a petitioner made the remarkable claim that "Since 1930 I have worked consistently and without interruption; I haven't skipped a day nor have I been late to work."[119] "I am a shock worker [*udarnik*] and have repeatedly been given awards."[120] People without rights who worked in Soviet factories noted their achievements with the conviction that the reinstatement of their rights was due to them. "In my six years of working, I fully demonstrated that I am genuinely of the working class. By my work I have corrected for my temporary absence from a laboring path and have rehabilitated myself. Thus I can be sure that Soviet power has trust in me."[121] One man, deprived of rights in 1926 and sent to a concentration camp in 1930, touted his early release and claimed that his good work while in forced labor was recognized with "expressions of gratitude and money."[122] The son of a kulak, deported with his father to Western Siberia in 1933, used his work as evidence that he deserved full rights: "I was in a labor camp in Western Siberia for one and a half years. I'm disciplined. When I came to the labor camp I was immediately directed by the political section of the OGPU to the coal mines . . . where I have good references and overfulfilled the technical norms. . . . I deserve the full reinstatement of rights."[123] Another man, deported in 1931, touted his achievements while in forced labor. "In exile in Magnitogorsk I showed myself there to be a real son of the laboring people of the USSR."[124] These individuals did not request rights with the humility of a supplicant. Rather, they demanded what they believed the government owed them.

Men who served in the rear militia also emphasized their labor on the nation's construction projects. Like other deportees, they referred to their period of forced labor as proof of proletarian identity. The son of a priest expressed the meaning of militia service in a form that he completed for the reinstatement of rights. The question read: "Did you serve in the Red Army? What years? Were you drafted or did you volunteer?" The young man wrote the following reply: "I served in the labor army from 1931–1934."[125] He continued to equate forced labor with national service in his petition for the reinstatement of rights. "I think I have enough useful labor . . . I worked in the coal mines on the Donbass . . . I was drafted [*zabran*] to serve in the rear militia army where I served for 3 years. During the time of my service, I showed myself to be a disciplined and conscientious worker. I was often given awards and thanks for my service. . . . Surely our labor army is considered social [*sic*] labor?"[126]

Another young man touted his militia service as evidence of his political re-education. The rear militia, like a correctional facility, had reformed him. "Presently, I finished my term in the rear militia where I was under the leadership of the Political Command for three years (1930–1933). I passed the school of moral re-education. I have in hand good recommendations . . . from the commander and political leadership."[127] John Scott described meeting a young disenfranchised man at Magnitogorsk, the son of a kulak, who admitted that he was "trying to expiate his crimes in honest labor." Scott expressed a certain bewilderment at the young man's commitment to his work: "Shabkov was one of the best brigadiers in the whole outfit. He spared neither himself nor those under him, and he used his head. And yet he was a kulak, serving a sentence, living in a section of town under the surveillance of the GPU, a class enemy. Funny business, that." Shabkov was not unusual, for Scott admits that the "specials," those under GPU surveillance, "worked better than the average." Shapkov himself claimed that he was trying to overcome a damaging past, like so many other class enemies, through exceptional acts of service. It appears likely that among the more energetic workers at these construction sites were the disenfranchised who had a greater need to be outstanding workers in order to regain their rights.[128]

A proletarian state can define its citizens as workers and its outcasts as parasites, but when it forced outcasts to labor on the nation's most prized construction projects it faced a dilemma. Surely, they are proletarians too. These forced laborers certainly thought so. For them, the experience of deportation and forced labor represented a rite of passage that made it possible for them to re-enter the society that discarded them. They used their proletarian experience to adamantly affirm their place within Soviet society. The most severely stigmatized aliens, those who had been deported and worked in forced labor, demanded their rights due with a great sense of entitlement. Writing from forced labor camps, prisoners insisted that through years of compulsory labor they earned the full rights of citizens. What emerged in Russia from these labor camps of enemies were self-proclaimed citizens with a vengeance.

Engineering a New Dialogue

More than socially engineer a new citizenry, the rehabilitation mechanism shaped a particular dialogue between citizens and the state in the Stalin era. The newly enfranchised citizenry developed certain understandings and expectations of Soviet power. For example, the process of granting rights encouraged some petitioners to appeal to a notion of fairness under the Soviet system. In his letter to Kalinin, a former trader wrote: "There isn't another country on earth with such freedom to address the highest authorities. . . . Only you can judge impartially, according to law and truth."[129] The son of a trader who was deprived of rights as a dependent claimed to be incredulous. Could the workers' state really be so harsh? "There can hardly be a directive from our Soviet power that children who are independent of their relatives who are alien elements must perish because of a speculator-father."[130] Also, by praising the compassion and justice of the Soviet regime, the disenfranchised challenged Soviet officials to uphold their own standard, to satisfy the petitioner's request or risk hypocrisy. In his 1935 letter to Stalin, a man expressed his hope for rehabilitation because "I know that comrade Stalin is so just."[131] A young, deported Uzbek man declared: "I'm amazed at the difference between the old tsarist order and the magnificent USSR."[132] In addition, petitioners argued that they were treated unjustly according to the regime's own standards of fairness. A young man considered it offensive that he, who was exploited by the bourgeoisie before the revolution and worked for Soviet power, was deprived of rights.[133] Another expressed his indignation with the way he was being treated by a government that claimed to value service. "I've given half my life to the komsomol for [the task of] reforming agriculture. To then politically shoot a man I think is not right."[134]

The disenfranchised also understood that the requirements for rehabilitation were highly practical and served the interests of a regime that wanted productive and loyal subjects. Here too, petitioners used an underlying principle of policy to their own advantage and argued that it was hardly expedient to disenfranchise people during this important period of socialist construction. With so many talented individuals deprived of the right to engage fully in productive labor, surely the country had much to lose. A former landowner and military judge asked the rhetorical question: "Whom would it serve, who would benefit if a useful worker, desiring and able to work, were turned into a parasite, a pauper?"[135] Others emphasized the particular contribution they could make if reinstated in rights. A Urals woman, deprived of rights as the wife of a psalmodist, emphasized her current occupation as a teacher among deportees and, in her words, a shock worker (*udarnitsa*) in teaching. She asked for her rights, as well as rights for her husband, so that she would no longer be constrained in her pedagogical work by the epithet (*klichka*), "wife of a disenfranchised man." The reinstatement of rights would give her "strong weaponry in the battle on the cultural front," she concluded.[136] A Leningrad man, deprived of rights as a former factory-owner, stressed his service to Soviet power and his many credentials—"engineer, mechanic and chief mechanic" at various factories. He argued that the country could really use well-educated people like him: "I can't imagine how I will live knowing that the USSR doesn't have enough specialists."[137] Another man from Kursk took a similar approach: "I feel healthy [and yet] I am unable, since I'm disenfranchised, to be useful to the proletarian government where I would be able to serve and work in my specialty area . . . in which I have great experience."[138] Young people who could promise years of service to Soviet power made pragmatic appeals that emphasized their talents and usefulness. As one put it, "I am young, 33 years old . . . [and] I want to work and put my young strength in the use of building socialism but the stigma of the disenfranchised torments me."[139]

One particular feature of the state-society relationship under Stalin became especially pronounced by the rehabilitation system, namely, that labor and other public service entitled one to make demands on the state. A deportee turned shock worker expressed this expectation when he asked the USSR Supreme Soviet for "the stakhanovite document I deserve."[140] Soviet practice encouraged such claims by granting various incentives and rewards for service to the state, including the reinstatement of rights. Once the state secured its monopoly over the country's resources, rights took on the character of a reward to be earned. This expectation was nothing new in Russian politics. Imperial and Soviet power fixated on the duties and obligations of subjects before the state, granting rights selectively in exchange for loyalty and service. In turn, Russian subjects expected that those who served the state should correspondingly receive certain concessions and rights. For example, serfs who fought against Napoleon in 1812 and in the Crimean War expected that the tsar would emancipate them after years of loyal military service, and women activists in the 1920s believed that if they supported labor conscription, then the government would grant them child care and dining facilities in return.[141] Similarly, in their appeals for rehabilitation, Stalin's outcasts expressed confidence that they earned or deserved rights because of their service to the state.

The act of reclaiming rights or insisting on one's due was based in part on a particular understanding of the relationship between citizens and the state, namely, that the state granted rights to the subjects who earned them. The mechanism for the reinstatement of rights communicated the fact that the Soviet state was not prepared to give rights gratis. But neither were Soviet subjects willing to squander their labor and service without some payback.

Conclusion

According to official rehabilitation policy, in order to become citizens people had to perform redemptive acts of service for Soviet power. In particular, the disenfranchised were required to abandon their exploitative, parasitic, and nonlaboring ways in favor of socially useful labor. Yet this forced transition proved highly irregular and uneven, and the process of rehabilitation exposed the many ways that people could make themselves Soviet. Local control over decisions and the often unfavorable odds of being reinstated in rights discouraged many from petitioning and prompted some to conceal their disenfranchisement, seek forgeries of identity papers, adopt a Soviet lifestyle, and try to avoid any suspicion or scrutiny. Others chose to conform in some way with the requirements for reinstatement, document their proletarian activities and relationships, and compile a dossier that illustrated loyalty to Soviet power and socially useful labor. Those who could not secure proletarian labor managed to find other avenues of service, such as Soviet parenting, adoption, and volunteer work, and in doing so, they exposed the many possible points of re-entry into Soviet society.

Not only did petitioners choose numerous ways of performing socially useful labor, but productive work itself proved neither necessary nor sufficient for earning rights. Some asserted a Soviet self by soliciting positive character references from employers and neighbors and the support of local authorities. In many cases, those who could work the system and document their identities most effectively represented the redeemed citizens of Soviet power. A rehabilitation process that often made the bureaucratic construction of identity tantamount to identity itself only subverted the goal of social engineering. Nonetheless, the process of restoring rights to persons who documented a life of loyalty and labor was itself productive. The rehabilitation mechanism forged a certain relationship between citizens and the Soviet state. The reinstatement of rights articulated and reinforced terms of inclusion in which the regime granted rights in exchange for state service or productive labor. Apparently, no one understood this better than those who labored on the monumental construction projects of the First Five-Year Plan, the pride of Stalinist industrialization. Deported aliens and rear militiamen compelled to work in NKVD labor camps became de facto proletarian laborers and demanded rights due with an acute sense of entitlement. Thus the significance of rehabilitation consists in the terms of inclusion that the system institutionalized as well as the behaviors and practices that this rite of passage encouraged.

Boris Ermolaev, *Family Portrait*. 1930s. © State Russian Museum, St. Petersburg, 2001.

6

Endings and Enduring Legacies

Disenfranchisement, a dual policy of exclusion and inclusion managed by the soviets, slowed considerably in the first half of the 1930s. Elections to the soviets were held every year in the Russian Republic from 1926 to 1931, but this schedule of annual local campaigns changed abruptly. Several years passed before the next election of 1934, and, in 1936, the new Stalin Constitution ended the practice of denying voting rights to traders, clerics, tsarist policemen, and other former bourgeois classes. In the 1931 and 1934 elections, the numbers of people on the soviets' lists of the disenfranchised declined sharply as compared with previous campaigns, and official concerns about the presence of masked enemies continued to intensify. Party leaders sharply criticized local disenfranchisement practices as ineffectual, at the same time that a burgeoning volume of petitions for the reinstatement of rights simply overwhelmed state officials.

In 1936, party leaders publicly justified the final abandonment of disenfranchisement on grounds that the class enemies had been liquidated. Yet when one returns to the initial rationale behind the policy, other reasons for ending the practice of depriving and reinstating rights appear more plausible. Through its policy of disenfranchisement and rehabilitation, the party forced people to transform their identities, change their economic practices and dependencies, and become productive and loyal laborers of the Soviet state—this in exchange for the full rights of citizens. The Kremlin leadership also created a class of outcasts as a way of minimizing the number of citizen claims on shortage state resources such as housing, pensions, and staple goods. By the early 1930s, it appeared that the policy had accomplished these goals as much as it could. Now, more effective means of purging, social engineering, and population control would be necessary to shape the

159

political and economic behavior of Soviet subjects. In the early 1930s, police and security organs extended their authority and absorbed the soviets' task of identifying hidden alien elements. As a result, the punishment of class enemies turned more severe, and victims' opportunities for appeal and official redemption became increasingly remote. An older policy of exclusion and inclusion might have formally ended with Stalin's 1936 Constitution, but the assault against bourgeois, nonlaboring elements was far from over.

The Authority of Law and Policing

Social engineering and the purging of alien elements remained priorities even after the "victory of socialism," but in the 1930s these goals would be pursued without reliance on the soviets. In the 1930s, a number of party initiatives transferred powers away from the soviets in an attempt to check the authority that local officials had amassed during the decentralization trend of the 1920s.[1] Responsibility for identifying, punishing, and managing aliens or "hostile class elements" shifted gradually from the soviets to the courts, police (*militsiia*), and secret police (*OGPU-NKVD*) as Stalin promoted the authority of law. Pressure to expose hidden class enemies remained high, but as the act of concealing one's disenfranchisement became a criminal offense, the Procuracy rather than the soviets assumed jurisdiction over masked enemies. Procuracy and investigative organs were urged to prosecute those who lied about their voting-rights status, especially in those cases "where hostile class elements [*klassovo-vrazhdebnye elementy*] penetrate the state apparatus and social organizations for the purpose of receiving material advantages [*vygody*], by providing false information about their having voting rights. . . ."[2] As in earlier years, the party focused its attacks on deceptive class aliens who illicitly consumed the public's resources.

Two laws, in particular, demonstrate the increased powers of the police. Stalin intensified his assault against the robbers of public funds when he passed his draconian Law of August 7, 1932. This measure to brutally punish acts of theft against state property targeted kulaks and class-hostile elements in particular. The law classified all thieves and illegal traders according to the more threatening category "enemies of the people" and punished them with death or no less than ten years incarceration.[3] If the August 7th law condemned the state's thieves, the passport system targeted nonlaboring and anti-soviet elements. Instituted in December 1932, the internal passport system for urban residents required that all those who did not qualify for a residence permit be evicted from their apartments and denied the right to live within city limits.[4] Since policing organs issued these personal documents, they would determine the status and rights of urban residents. No longer marked by soviet officials at election time, urban citizens and aliens became identified by the police in the course of issuing passports. The stated purpose of the new passport system was to relieve the urban population of persons not engaged in socially useful labor, as well as "hidden kulak, criminal and other anti-societal elements." By 1935, the majority of those prosecuted by the police for passport violations in Moscow and Leningrad reflected the face of the disenfranchised with striking similarity. These nonlaboring elements included kulaks, criminals, beggars, and prostitutes.[5] After internal passports were fully introduced in 1933, attempts to "clean up" the cities and remove these alien elements probably resulted in the eviction of hundreds of thousands of people from the cities. Instead of neighbors and communities, the gatekeepers of the Soviet polity were now in passport control.

Like disenfranchisement, the passport system provided a method of screening people before they gained access to state goods and services. The passport law was instituted in large part because the urban rationing and supply systems were on the verge of collapse after the 1932–1933 famine provoked a massive urban migration. Newspaper commentaries spoke of how the eviction of parasitic elements would have the effect of preserving the housing fund.[6] Throughout the 1930s, housing was one of the resources in high demand and short supply. In Leningrad alone, housing space per resident fell from 8.5 square meters in 1927 to 5.8 square meters in 1934–1935.[7] Passportization did, in fact, reduce the state's ever-increasing social-welfare expenses. For example, the number of people who received bread from the state declined slightly from 40.3 to 39 million following the introduction of internal passports.[8] The excluded shared a familiar profile. Newspaper commentaries on the passport law described the necessary eviction of "kulaks, thieves, speculators, and swindlers."[9]

As with disenfranchisement, the enforcement of passportization was irregular and erratic. In some cases, those refused passports in Leningrad formed large crowds of people "wandering along roads out of the city searching for food and shelter," and elsewhere people deprived of rights, seeing that they were at risk of expulsion, left the cities voluntarily after the policy of passportization became official.[10] Nonetheless, reports persisted throughout the mid-1930s of people who lacked passports or residence permits working in Moscow factories and living in workers' barracks. After implementation of the passport system in Moscow in January 1933, no huge exodus of people denied passports followed. Rather, Moscow's population rose rapidly in 1934 as managers were eager to hire laborers in their expanding industries.[11]

In the 1930s, the role of the local soviets in depriving rights diminished, as the occasion for identifying anti-Soviet elements shifted from electoral campaigns to the criminal process, the selective distribution of internal passports, as well as state and party purges. A. Ia. Vyshinskii, who promoted iron discipline and the strict observance of law, became deputy Procurator-General of a newly formed USSR Procuracy in June 1933, an indication of Stalin's heightened emphasis on stability and order.[12] Responsibility for depriving rights shifted increasingly to the courts, as in the case of people who had been taxed individually and failed to pay their taxes.[13] If soviet officials once disenfranchised people for drunkenness, now the courts punished such deviants as "petty-bourgeois undisciplined types" and people with "alien social origin."[14]

Although the Politburo wanted to minimize social tensions after a year of famine and strikes, commitment remained to hunting down and punishing enemies.[15] In January 1933, Lazar Kaganovich announced the creation of political departments of the MTS whose task it was, among other things, to purge the collective farms of "alien" members, "kulaks" and their "associates" (*podkulachniki*). Repression during the first few months of 1933 was directed at "class alien and anti-kolkhoz elements."[16] Purges were also conducted in the party and the Soviet bureaucracy where "alien elements" were believed to have entered during the years of economic expansion.[17] At the Central Committee Plenum in January 1933, the leadership renewed its campaign against anti-soviet elements by initiating a party purge. In a letter to Kalinin, one man claimed that the Leningrad Party Control Commission disenfranchised his father in 1934. For concealing this fact, he found himself "at the verge of a life catastrophe," purged from the party, and "suffocating in the clutches of slander and prejudice because of my father's prerevolutionary past."[18] When such victims of the party purge appealed for reinstatement, their chances were slim. In 1934–1935, an appeals body established under the Commission of Soviet Control heard requests of purge victims for reinstatement in their jobs, to the party, and so on. Lenin's sister, Maria I. Ulianova, chaired this appeals body as head of the Commission's complaints bureau (*biuro zhalob*). Appeals for reinstatement were uniformly rejected in the cases of those people identified as having "hidden their social origin."[19]

Failures, Inefficiencies, and Breakdowns

Warnings about hidden enemies continued and even intensified in the 1930s, and the standard characterizations of alien elements also persisted.

At a 1934 meeting of the VTsIK Presidium, A. S. Kiselev, the Chairman of the Central Electoral Commission, described how concealed aliens had infiltrated "a rural electoral commission [in the Bashkir ASSR]" and "they included two people who served in the White Army, the son of a mullah, and a drunk sentenced for embezzlement, and one former counterfeiter.[20] Consistent with the usual descriptions of a policy turned upside down and backward, that year Kiselev also complained of how lists of the disenfranchised included "persons who received a letter from a former kulak" but omitted former clerics and traders.[21] In a 1934 report of the Soviet Control Commission, one official expressed outrage at how purges were being conducted in state institutions: "The label [alien element] is attached so often and without grounds that often the result is that we turn a worker into someone who begins to harbor hatred [*vrazhda*] toward Soviet power."[22] Party leaders continued to worry about the threat of a deceptive, parasitic enemy and the dangers of a policy run amok.

Records on the numbers of people deprived of rights also remained grossly inefficient and unreliable. One worker in the Orenburg city soviet admitted in 1934 that their records on disenfranchisement had been "in chaotic condition," and in many places, including Orenburg, Tatar ASSR, and Western Siberia province (*krai*), people who had been reinstated in rights still appeared on the lists of the disenfranchised.[23] Central authorities complained more than usual about incomplete, sketchy, and even nonexistent lists of the disenfranchised. A 1934–1935 report by VTsIK described the problems in the Eastern Siberia province: "According to their lists, in the Irkutsk city soviet it is completely impossible to determine how many disenfranchised people there are in fact in the city. Lists are compiled on the basis of old data from past campaigns, beginning with 1923. These lists include several thousand names, without any indication of social origin or the reasons for disenfranchisement."[24] Some lists were made up mostly or entirely of people who had migrated out of the region or had been deported. In one district (*raion*) in 1934, according to an outside official, "the majority of those deprived of rights left the raion 2–3 years ago."[25] Another overseer reported that in a district of the Lower Volga krai the list of the disenfranchised was comprised of "dekulakized peasants exclusively, who had already been deported from the territory of the rural soviet, beyond the borders of the province or district. That is, they're dead souls; they have been deported beyond the borders of the Lower Volga krai and of the given raion. But . . . in order to show that they have disenfranchised people, [they] include them."[26]

While the familiar problems with disenfranchisement persisted into the 1930s, new troubles also emerged. The volume of petitions for the reinstatement of rights mounted steadily and thoroughly overwhelmed local soviet officials as well as members of the CEC. In the 1930s, the Central Electoral Commission in Moscow employed roughly twenty people just to process the nearly 350 petitions arriving daily from the disenfranchised, in addition to the thousands of complaints made in person at their office (*na lichnom prieme*). If the Commission received nearly 22,000 petitions for the reinstatement of rights over the two-year period from 1927 to 1929, the number jumped to over 36,000 in 1932, nearly doubled to 62,000 the following year, and increased again to 74,000 in 1934. In the Kalinin province in 1935, as many as half of the petitions received by the complaints bureau of the regional soviet executive committee (*oblispolkom*) in a six-month period concerned the reinstatement of voting rights. The North krai soviet executive committee received 4,810 complaints in the first eleven months of 1935, almost half of which concerned the reinstatement of voting rights and the improper classification of "kulak." Who was sending all these appeals? Although letters from urban residents peaked in 1932 and then declined in following years, petitions from rural dwellers increased steadily in the years following dekulakization, from 1932 to 1936. In 1931, traders comprised the largest group of petitioners, and their letters made up nearly half of all petitions received by the Central Electoral Commission. Those disenfranchised for receiving unearned income also composed a large proportion of these letters throughout the 1930s and nearly half of all petitions to the Commission by 1935.[27]

Local officials grew increasingly inefficient in handling the burgeoning volume of paperwork. The collection, assessment, and review of documentary information on the identities represented by this enormous population proved to be a daunting task. Keen to lighten their burden of citizen complaints, officials simply shuffled petitions through the bureaucracy, causing great delays and confusion. Often administrative organs claimed they needed additional information in order to decide a case, such as verification of the petitioner's marital status, the date of disenfranchisement, or even a letter from the health department regarding someone's mental illness.[28] Officials reported cases in which petitions and complaints were thrown on the floor, stored in a chaotic manner, and ignored for months. This only encouraged those without rights to stubbornly persist in their appeals and to send off multiple letters. In 1933, the Central Electoral Commission secretary, I. Raab, complained about the administrative organs' poor handling of petitions: "One can see the red-tape, complaints being passed to those organs about which the petitioner is complaining, constant inquiries to higher organs, including the Central Electoral Commission, decisions [*otvety*] on cases of the disenfranchised are delayed for months and even years." Letters from the disenfranchised got confused with other citizen letters and passed on to commissions for the review of peasant complaints, complaint bureaus, and secretariats. To urge action from this overburdened and confused bureaucratic apparatus, some petitioners wrote as many as four follow-up letters with threats (*napominaniia s ugrozami*).[29]

The rehabilitation mechanism had become more inefficient but also more lenient. Rates of rehabilitation increased sharply, particularly after 1933. In absolute numbers, however, rehabilitations did not offset disenfranchisements in places like Moscow, where the number of citizens being deprived of voting rights was more than double the number being rehabilitated in 1934.[30] One's chances of being reinstated in rights by the CEC fell after 1932 but then increased steadily from 1933 to 1936. Official data is inconsistent, but the Central Electoral Commission's overall approval rate on those petitions reviewed appears at between 42 and 52 percent in 1933 and between 46 and 61 percent in 1934. Rehabilitation rates varied by region, and people who lived on special settlements were apparently among the least likely to achieve success when they appealed for rights, probably because the secret police, or OGPU-NKVD, had the decisive voice in these decisions. In 1933–1934, only 24 to 27 percent of petitions reviewed from the Western Siberia krai received a favorable decision from the Central Electoral Commission to reinstate rights.[31] Nonetheless, the generally higher rates of rehabilitations proved disquieting for those party leaders who identified successful petitioners with masked enemies. Some officials believed that a lack of class vigilance was resulting in too many rehabilitations.[32]

Into the 1930s, petitioners for the reinstatement of rights continued to be characterized as skillful in the art of deception. A 1934 article described Kalinin's ability to detect the insincere petitioner: "Capitalist elements have hurried to paint themselves as loyal to Soviet power and are earnestly asking for help and defense. But you can't fool comrade Kalinin! With exceptional ability, he can detect the class enemy, even one masked behind loyalty to Soviet power. He has the ability to pick out the truly aggrieved from among the mass of complaints."[33] Although Kalinin could not be fooled, central authorities believed that local officials were repeatedly being "bought" by alien elements. Sometimes a single soviet executive committee secretary decided cases, granting rights freely in exchange for personal favors.[34] In a 1935 case from the Kursk province, a number of "kulaks" had their voting rights reinstated by a district party secretary and another clerk who forged a raikom presidium protocol attesting to their rehabilitation.[35] One official wrote Kiselev in order to confirm the reinstatement of rights for a number of rear militiamen, explaining that "because there were cases of forgeries of documents about rehabilitation, the documents which [we] have raise some doubt."[36] Many outcasts themselves shared officials' cynical view of rehabilitation and expressed outrage at how "exploiters and other nonlaboring elements are being reinstated in voting rights." As one petitioner noted, "I suffer for nothing and many who are better off than I have long since been reinstated in voting rights." A woman trader complained about "the former big-time traders we have in Kuznetsk and now they are all reinstated in rights."[37] From party leaders to the disenfranchised themselves, many people shared the same perception of a badly broken policy. Publicly, however, Kremlin officials offered a different message touting the elimination of class antagonism and the victory of socialist construction.

The End of Class War and the Rights of Deportees

The seventeenth party congress in 1934 or the "Congress of Victors" affirmed the triumph of socialism and thereby abandoned ideological justification for the disenfranchisement of class enemies. The 1934 electoral campaign, the first since 1930–1931, witnessed a sharp decline in the numbers of people listed as disenfranchised on the registers of the soviets. By 1935, the percentage of people without voting rights in the USSR had declined to 2.6 percent of eligible voters in the rural areas and 2.4 percent in the cities, significantly lower than for 1927 when these figures were at 3.6 percent and 7.7 percent respectively.[38] A number of factors help to explain the decline in these numbers. Many people were dropped from the soviets' lists of the disenfranchised following their arrest, deportation, flight, or rehabilitation. In one case from the Central Black Earth region in 1934, a man was disenfranchised by the rural soviet as a "class alien element" but then arrested and sentenced to five years deprivation of freedom.[39] In this way, his fate was decided by the authority of the courts and not the soviets. In Moscow alone, almost half of the people listed as disenfranchised in 1935 no longer lived at their original place of residence, either due to deportation or flight, and were eventually removed from the register of disenfranchised persons.[40] Moreover, rates of rehabilitations continued to rise as central authorities spoke of the need to reinstate rights in cases where people demonstrate "service on the labor front," exceptional productivity or shock work, and usefulness to socialist construction.[41] Party officials so often interpreted rehabilitations as a sign of weak class vigilance, but their laws on restoring rights to young and productive workers indicate much less ambivalence about granting rights to this particular segment of the disenfranchised population.

In the late 1920s, disenfranchisement disproportionately affected private traders and nonlaboring elements, people who lived off unearned income or were financially dependent on persons already deprived of rights. Just as these groups represented the principal targets of exclusion at the height of disenfranchisement under Stalin, they also provide the key to understanding the policy's abandonment in the mid-1930s. As the laments of the disenfranchised indicate, many people traded because of difficult circumstances and the inability to find other work. Invalidism, old age, and other factors made it hard for people to secure socially useful labor in state enterprises or bureaucracy. Official acceptance of these laments demonstrates that policymakers always acknowledged the limits of their efforts to stamp out private commercial activity. By the mid-1930s, the party became more tolerant of small-scale informal trade and even promoted "cultured" trade. Yet its policies remained as ambivalent as in earlier years, as the legalization of some market trade was combined with harsh criminal sentences for people who performed "speculative" sales.[42] This change in policy toward private trade coincided with greater leniency in granting the reinstatement of rights. In particular, the party's policy on rehabilitation was most accommodating in the case of young dependents. The 1930 and 1934 Instructions on Elections to the Soviets specified that children of disenfranchised persons who came of age in 1925 or thereafter could be reinstated in rights if they simply demonstrated an independent source of socially useful labor, and article 23 of the 1934 TsIK Instructions allowed the automatic reinstatement of rights for people disenfranchised as dependents when the head of household had been reinstated. The labor of the young proved to be a critical factor in the eventual abandonment of class discrimination. The state favored this group in its rehabilitation legislation.

The reinstatement of rights for productive laborers, presumably the young and able-bodied, followed the completion of major construction projects initiated in the First Five-Year Plan. For example, after the construction of the White Sea canal, TsIK issued a decree on August 4, 1933, that rehabilitated thousands of people and even promoted their re-entry into Soviet society by offering them privileged documents and employment assistance. Over twelve thousand people were freed as "completely rehabilitated [*ispravivshiesia*] and useful for socialist construction" and received labor awards (*udarnye ili pochetnye gramoty*), while nearly sixty thousands were released for being "energetic workers in construction."[43] The head of the OGPU Gulag indicated in a letter to the Central Electoral

Commission that those released should receive "all voting rights" and "every kind of assistance" in finding work within their area of specialization (*po spetsial'nosti*) at institutions and enterprises.[44] On September 27, 1933, the party allowed rear militiamen to be reinstated in rights in those cases where "by their labor, discipline and attitude toward socialist property they proved that they have become model workers."[45] However, as the party demonstrated a willingness to reinstate rights to productive laborers, questions remained regarding the meaning of rehabilitation for deportees (*pereselentsy*). On the one hand, the reward of rights for exceptional young laborers would presumably buy their continued loyalty and productivity. Yet state officials could not tolerate an enormous exodus from strategic industries and new settlements in the far regions of the country.

Soviet leaders embraced the idea of reinstating rights to deportees who proved their worthiness through productive labor, but the leadership was not willing to grant the right of mobility. A 1931 TsIK decree on the reinstatement of rights for deported kulaks did not address whether these newly reinstated citizens had freedom of mobility, but in May 1932, the TsIK Presidium indicated that special settlers who were reinstated in rights should be issued documents indicating that they had "voting rights and all other civil rights and that they are allowed freedom of residence [*svobodnoe prozhivanie*] in the USSR."[46] However, later that year, the party reversed its policy. At the end of 1932, the VTsIK Presidium agreed to allow the North krai soviet executive committee to rehabilitate young, deported kulaks whom the krai considered "good workers, shock workers, people trying to take part in the social life [of the krai]," but stated that "return to their place of former residence is difficult [*zatrudnitel'nyi*]." Only in exceptional cases, as when a deported kulak demonstrated that he served in the Red Army, was someone allowed to return to their former place of residence.[47] The right of mobility constituted a major caveat in the rehabilitation of deportees, as many people reinstated in rights could not leave their settlement (*spetsposelka*) after the restoration of rights.

The party leadership clearly worried that the reinstatement of rights would result in massive flight from these settlements. Rhetorically, officials like Matvei Berman, the head of the OGPU Gulag, claimed that "people who are reinstated in rights enjoy all the rights of citizens of the USSR; they have the right to leave the settlement and no restrictions can be applied to them," and argued that "our task is to create such conditions so that people who acquire citizenship won't have the desire to abandon the settlement."[48] In fact, rehabilitated deportees in the North krai did not enjoy the right of mobility because they were issued documents that stated that they were free to live wherever they wanted but only "within the boundaries of the North krai."[49] The OGPU Procuracy condemned that practice, saying that "no documents [*udostoverenii*] should be issued to these people which show that they have limited rights to reside only in the North krai," but this organ did not establish a right of mobility. Instead, it simply restated the importance of securing [*privesti k zakrepleniiu*] the residency of deportees in the North krai."[50] The explicit ban on all departures came in January 25, 1935, when the government declared that "the reinstatement of civil rights for deported kulaks does not give them the right to leave their place of settlement."[51] In 1935, roughly 1.2 million deported kulaks and family members lived in settlements without freedom of movement and under the guard of the NKVD. Only in 1938 were children of deported kulaks allowed to leave their settlements. Restrictions on the rights of deportees were gradually lifted after the war, from 1946 to 1954.[52]

Once the leadership decided the question of deportees' right to mobility, this two-pronged policy of exclusion and inclusion could be formally abolished. From now on, party leaders would no longer fear that rehabilitations might result in a large flight to the cities and strain the already overburdened urban distribution system for shortage resources such as housing and food. The government's moves to institute internal passports and deny the right of mobility to rehabilitated deportees enhanced its control over the distribution and allocation of state resources. If class discrimination was needed at an earlier time to restrict access to shortage goods, this was no longer the case, as the party now controlled the population more effectively by other means. The decision to end rationing in the cities in January 1935 appears as the first in a series of measures that signaled an end to class discrimination. Shortly thereafter, Molotov suggested at the seventh congress of soviets that it was time to abolish class restrictions, and later that year a central decree reversed the law that barred children of the disenfranchised from higher education, since "this restriction is not necessary in the present time." The Central Committee also issued an unpublicized decision that allowed former kulaks to enter the collective farm.[53]

By December 1935, class discrimination represented a policy of the past, especially after Stalin made his famous remark that "a son does not answer for his father."[54] This formulation was nothing new, as angry petitioners had been making the same point. In 1934, the son of a deported kulak and former landowner wrote: "I am no criminal; there's no law that says I have to answer for other people."[55] After Stalin legitimized this idea, the phrase appeared with greater frequency in petitions for the reinstatement of rights. The son of a White Army soldier, a Cossack, confidently declared, "I hardly am the embodiment of capitalism, that is, its deficiencies. . . . Answer for my father? I didn't choose him for myself."[56] These people, disenfranchised as dependents, represented the main beneficiaries of the party's change in policy and the leadership's principal target of inclusion. The state had a compelling interest to abandon class discrimination and extend rights to this new generation.

Stalin's Constitution of 1936

When he formulated a policy of discrimination against Russia's bourgeois classes or the exploiting and nonlaboring old regime elites, Vladimir Lenin defended this as a temporary measure and argued that sometime in the socialist future, once the possibility of counterrevolution had been eliminated, disenfranchisement would no longer be necessary.[57] The party leadership invoked Lenin's argument to justify the elimination of the outcast categories and proclaim universal suffrage in Stalin's USSR Constitution of 1936. According to Molotov, now that socialism was victorious and "all parasitic classes" liquidated, the working class had firmly established its leading role. It was possible to discard previous restrictions against the exploiting classes that were necessary at a time when these groups exerted influence, and counterrevolution was a real possibility. For this reason, the new Stalin Constitution "settles the question of the disenfranchised groups, for all citizens without exception receive the right to elect and be elected to the soviets."[58]

With the ban on all departures from forced settlements in January 1935, disenfranchisement policy could be formally abolished. Indeed, in that year, the earliest discussions on the new Stalin Constitution demonstrate that the electoral rights section was slated for fundamental revision. With respect to voting rights, Stalin's 1936 Constitution would represent a sharp departure from the constitution adopted under Lenin. In the summer of 1935, TsIK began working through various legal issues in order to produce the draft of a new constitution. In July 1935, an internal TsIK memo listed the issues that would be addressed in the upcoming discussions (*razrabotke*) on the new Soviet Constitution, and included among them were "electoral rights" and "the disenfranchised." In August, Karl Radek chaired a meeting of the subcommission on electoral rights that was attended by three representatives from TsIK and three from the Institute of Soviet Construction and Law. The Institute's E. B. Pashukanis had earlier offered the opinion that the disenfranchised be described simply under the broad heading of persons "who by their past activities have shown themselves to be enemies of the laboring population." In his formulation, Pashukanis captured in brief what earlier laws expressed in greater detail, namely, that the disenfranchised represented those who exhibited idle and parasitic behavior. The August meeting produced a draft of the electoral rights section of a new constitution that provided for the reinstatement of rights to those "who presently and in the course of a number of years had recommended themselves by their honest labor and loyalty to Soviet power."[59] This focus on the need to disenfranchise nonlaboring elements and rehabilitate those who engaged in honest labor suggests an underlying continuity with previous policy. Yet the changes appear more striking.

The draft constitution produced by Radek's subcommission sharply departed from previous Soviet constitutions. It eliminated private traders and middlemen from the categories of people who should be denied voting rights, and other changes followed just a few months later. On March 11, 1936, the subcommission in charge of drafting the electoral rights section of the constitution adopted a new draft that it circulated as "secret." Unlike the earlier version, the March draft did not specify that voting rights were reserved for "all citizens of the USSR who engage in socially useful labor," nor did it include any list of the disenfranchised.[60] It simply indicated, consistent with the August draft, that the mentally ill and those deprived of voting rights by a decision of the court should be disenfranchised.[61] Party officials had decided to abandon a policy that punished the bourgeois classes with disenfranchisement.

Moreover, several events pointed to the decline in the power and prestige of the Central Electoral Commission. The Soviet Control Commission strongly condemned the work of the CEC, describing numerous deficiencies in the handling of complaints.[62] Kiselev tried to defend his institution against such charges. He sent an angry letter to an NKVD agent charging that the security organ was taking too long with cases and "generates extraordinary difficulties in the work of the Central Electoral Commission."[63] Kiselev's accusation did little to slow the precipitous decline of his institution or to redirect the blame for inefficiencies. Kiselev hardly possessed the stature of years past, and already in 1934 he lost his post as candidate member of the Party Central Committee. Kiselev's name appears among the long list of party leaders who fell victim to the Stalinist purges in 1937.

Weeks before the draft constitution was made public, a decree of the Soviet Control Commission on May 30, 1936, all but dismantled disenfranchisement policy. The decree stated that certain discriminatory practices for reasons of social origin were inadmissible, including the "improper fir-

ing of a worker or the refusal to hire someone . . . because of social origin. . . . Such practices come from some heads of institutions in pursuit of
a false self-protection [*v tseliakh fal'shivoi samostrakhovki*)]. It is especially inadmissible to deprive young people of an education, to not admit
them or expel them, for such reasons. . . . It is necessary to stop firing
[people] or refusing [them] employment in Soviet, economic and other organizations for reasons such as social origin."[64] Finally, the draft constitution that formally removed the bourgeois classes from the categories of the
disenfranchised was published in the Soviet press in June 1936.[65] The constitution was more explicit than the Radek draft in that it proclaimed
"universal" suffrage for all citizens independent of "social origin, property
[*imushchestvennoe polozhenie*] and past activities." Article 135 of the
1936 Constitution stated that "elections of deputies are universal: all citizens of the USSR who are at least 18 years old, independent of racial or
national affiliation, religious conviction, education, settlement, social origin, property and past activities, have the right to participate in the election of deputies and to be elected, with the exception of the mentally ill
and persons sentenced by a court to deprivation of voting rights."[66]

The draft constitution was published prior to its formal adoption for
the purpose of generating a public discussion (*vsenarodnoe obsuzhdenie*)
on its contents. In the months that followed publication, it appeared that
the public greeted the removal of outcast categories from the constitution
with some hesitation, and many openly objected to the constitution's extension of suffrage to former class enemies. In an internal TsIK memoran-
dum of 15 November 1936, complaints about article 135 on the voting
system outnumbered those on all other points except the rights and benefits of citizens.[67] Reporting on popular discussion of the draft constitution,
the Moscow regional soviet executive committee (*oblispolkom*) noted that
"in almost all districts [*raiony*] there are suggestions made not to give voting rights to priests."[68] In his study of citizen letters to the Constitutional
Commission that offered opinions on the draft document, J. Arch Getty
concluded that people generally opposed the extension of voting rights to
priests and members of alien classes. Getty notes that "in rural regions like
Smolensk, and indeed across the Soviet Union, around 17 percent of all
suggestions represented a protest against allowing such persons to vote; it
was the second most popular suggestion in Smolensk."[69]

It appears that popular opposition to the lifting of sanctions against
class enemies was largely motivated by concerns about the availability and
distribution of shortage resources. For example, those who objected to
lifting the ban on discrimination against children of the disenfranchised in
higher education argued that children from traditionally better-educated

families would reduce the opportunities of other children. "The children of the disenfranchised will create competition, as they will study well and get high marks, while the factory worker will lag behind." This response was similar to objections that people raised at the end of rationing, namely, that the higher prices would only be accessible to White guards, kulaks, the bourgeoisie, and alien elements.[70] Much of the public believed that without the discriminatory distribution of resources in favor of the working class, shortage goods would be consumed largely by the former bourgeois classes. A policy of exclusion appeared benign to those concerned about the daily competition with fellow citizens over scarce goods.

Days after the new constitution was formally adopted on December 5, 1936, Kalinin issued a radio announcement that called for an end to all work on reviewing any kind of petition for the reinstatement of rights. He urged a suspension of all case reviews, the return of petitions and accompanying case materials to petitioners, and the storage of old lists of the disenfranchised in republic, krai, and oblast archives.[71] Kalinin's public announcement came at the end of a year in which officials had already dramatically altered their approach to petitions. In 1936, the subcommission on petitions of the disenfranchised reinstated rights in 70 percent of the cases it reviewed, a sharp increase over previous years, and the highest rate of rehabilitation ever.[72] It appears that the Central Electoral Commission had already altered its behavior with the drafts of the new constitution circulating, but changes at other institutions occurred more slowly. In July 1937, the government formally lifted the ban on pension assistance to persons previously disenfranchised except those deprived of voting rights by a court sentence.[73] The Russian Central Association of Trade Unions (*VTsSPS*) issued a decree on July 11, 1937, overturning the former policy of excluding the disenfranchised from membership in a trade union. It abolished restrictions barring blue- and white-collar workers (*rabochie i sluzhashchie*) in enterprises and institutions from becoming members of a trade union "for reasons of social origin and past activity."[74]

Stalin's Constitution required that Soviet institutions reform their old practices, but none found the new order as onerous as the People's Commissariat of Justice (*Narkomiust*). The tasks of keeping accurate records of the nation's disenfranchised and processing their petitions was not a welcome inheritance. In 1937, the Justice Commissar N. V. Krylenko instructed the courts that with every decision to deprive someone of voting rights a document to that effect had to be issued to the Commissariat of Justice in Moscow.[75] Narkomiust was supposed to compile an annual alphabetical listing of persons sentenced by a court to deprivation of rights, using data from the local courts; the list was supposed to be distributed to all electoral districts (*okuga*).[76] As for the burden of petitions, the people's court now assumed responsibility for handling complaints concerning exclusion from the voters' list.[77]

Recognizing the problems in store for his cadres, Krylenko made a bold attempt to protect justice officials from the impending bureaucratic nightmare. Krylenko explained in a top-secret memo that it was no easy matter for court officials to produce an accurate account (*uchet*) of persons disenfranchised by a sentence of the court. After conducting a review of how both the courts and the administrative organs kept records in the past on persons disenfranchised by a court decision, he described a "depressing result," a "sad picture." The courts kept no record of the disenfranchised sentenced to deprivation of rights by legal decision, and the administrative organs "as a rule" did not either. According to Krylenko, in order now to construct a list of persons disenfranchised by a court decision, one would have to go through archives of court cases for "a ten-year period at least" and not only record who was deprived of rights but also account for who was later amnestied as well. Simply, "an accurate record of persons deprived of voting rights by a court is extremely difficult to produce even for the last several years." Consequently, Krylenko proposed a solution in the form of a political amnesty and the reinstatement of voting rights for all persons sentenced before December 5, 1936, the date the new constitution was adopted, regardless of the crime for which they were sentenced. The Justice Commissar hoped that following an amnesty, the courts could begin keeping the necessary records from scratch and not worry about constructing old lists. Krylenko's proposed amnesty was an act of mercy intended not for the disenfranchised but for his own justice officials.[78] Nonetheless, TsIK rejected the Justice Commissar's suggestion. Shortly after Kiselev's tragic fate, Krylenko also fell victim to Stalinist repression in 1938.

The Soviet leader maintained that his 1936 Constitution would stand as proof of socialism's victory. In November 1936, Stalin argued that the class structure of Soviet society had been transformed and exploitation eliminated: "The boundaries between the working class and the peasantry, as well as between these classes and the intelligentsia are being effaced, and the old class exclusiveness vanishes."[79] This rhetoric was directed at a foreign as well as a domestic audience. Stalin's Constitution, according to Peter Solomon, was about appearances—the appearance of normalcy, fairness, and good performance. Both at home and abroad, the new constitution aimed at enhancing the legitimacy of the Soviet state by presenting an image of efficiency and democracy.[80] The domestic audience, particularly people without rights, took great interest in the new constitution and expected the fundamental law to introduce a new reality.

Raised Expectations

The new constitution did not provide a blanket amnesty for people who had earlier been deprived of rights, but many expected that the new law would fundamentally improve their status and expand their rights. Officials in Moscow reported in 1936 that some viewed article 135 as the legal basis for the return of confiscated property to those who were dekulakized.[81] Deported kulaks, in particular, expressed the highest expectations following publication of Stalin's Constitution. Persons deported to labor settlements were constantly writing Kalinin and other officials after the publication of the constitution asking whether they could have their rights back, acquire a passport, and move to another city. For example, in a typical petition signed by twenty-three workers on an NKVD construction project, the men confidently proclaimed their new identity. They made no requests but simply declared that rights were earned and now due: "We are workers, former deportees. According to Stalin's Constitution article 135 we consider ourselves reinstated into the rights of citizenship."[82]

Stalin's Constitution raised many questions concerning the status of former deportees (*trudpereselentsy, spetspereselentsy*). The paperworkers' trade union (*soiuz bumazhnikov*), which had a policy of excluding the disenfranchised, wondered how it should handle the many requests it now received from deportees who wished to join the trade union. Union officials wrote TsIK inquiring whether the new constitution automatically restored voting rights to deportees or whether they had to petition TsIK individually for the reinstatement of rights. In 1937, a party member and school director in a camp for deported kulaks in Uzbekistan wrote TsIK because deportees approached the director and the teachers daily asking whether the constitution applied to them. Officials of the Mordovia autonomous republic wrote the Commissariat of Justice asking what it should do with petitions from those who were deported to settlements outside the republic and now wished to return. Letters were sent to the Commissariat of Justice as well as the NKVD USSR labor-camp administration asking about the status of deportees following the adoption of the new constitution.[83] In October 1937, responding to this flurry of inquiries, TsIK issued a decree that only specified which deportees were to be placed on the list of voters.[84]

NKVD USSR officials who managed the settlements of deportees insisted that the constitution did not apply to their residents. In 1937, one man in Kazakhstan wrote the Supreme Soviet and complained that the NKVD USSR commander (*komandant*) "constantly says the law [the new constitution] doesn't apply to us because we are resettled workers [*trud-*

pereselentsy]." A group of deportees, coal miners from the Svedlovsk oblast, wrote Kalinin in December 1936, complaining that their NKVD commander "says that we are still deportees and disenfranchised."[85] Deportees very often described how the NKVD administration (*komendatura*) refused to review their status in light of the new constitution and continued to exact a 5 percent tax on their wages.[86] In a 1937 letter to the editor of the newspaper *Komsomol'skaia pravda,* the son of a deported kulak who had been living in Western Siberia since 1931 explained his situation: "When the Stalin Constitution was ratified, I tried to enter the trade union but they told me, 'You still don't have the right; you're not yet reinstated in the rights of citizenship. Once you get a passport, then you can become a member of the trade union.' Then I went to the NKVD administration, and they told me that they don't have the right yet to issue me a passport, [saying] 'You're not reinstated [in rights].' "[87]

In another 1937 letter, the children of deported kulaks complained about their living conditions, their poor treatment, and the unwillingness of the NKVD administration to give them citizenship status after the publication of Stalin's 1936 Constitution. The Sovnarkom All-Union Committee for Radio Broadcasts received their appeal through its letters division (*tsentral'naia gruppa pisem*). They wanted the radio station to serve as intermediary between them and TsIK, the body that would ultimately decide their status. Rather than write TsIK directly, they appealed initially to the radio station for sympathy, support, and advocacy: "We ask that you announce on the air and in writing when we will be granted the rights of citizenship. . . . We ask the radio center to pass along our letter to TsIK for an answer and inform us of their response. We will wait impatiently."[88] In 1936, one group of administrative exiles, deported on account of their parents' social origin, sent a joint telegram to Stalin, Molotov, and the security police chief, G. G. Iagoda, asking for their rights back and a chance to continue their schooling.[89] Not surprisingly, people who possessed minimal rights living in NKVD forced-labor settlements often placed the greatest hope in Stalin's Constitution. Their raised expectations were frustrated when it became clear that this document would not fundamentally improve their lives.

The Indelible Mark of Old Identities

People who were once disenfranchised or who could be classified as bourgeois aliens continued to generate suspicion and face harsh sanction. Neither priests nor their children could join a collective farm even after their civil rights were restored by the 1936 Constitution.[90] In her 1937 letter, one woman described being disillusioned by the promise of the constitution that "we would remain citizens, without deprivation of voting rights, thereby preserving everything societal and humane [*obshchestvennye i chelovecheskie*]."[91] Those who had been deprived of rights told many stories of discrimination. In a 1938 letter to the legislative commission of the Supreme Soviet, a man who had been a priest until 1934 explained his frustrating search for a job:

> Despite the assertions of the constitution, and although I stopped serving in a religious cult in 1934 and worked in soviet enterprises, I am refused work as a former priest. . . . Procurators and Soviet Control say, "Your right to work is unlimited, but we have no right to force an employer [to hire you]." They sometimes give me advice to complain to higher organs but these also refuse me work. Employers, it seems, are afraid to give me work as a priest and some suggest I get an official document [*spravka*] from the procurator attesting to my right to work. But the procurators refuse to give me a document saying that everyone knows the constitution.[92]

In April 1937, a man who identified himself as a "former person" composed the following diary entry about the specter of his damaging past. "For no matter what I say, it will all be twisted to mean something bad, everything will be interpreted as an attempt to discredit the party, an assault by a class enemy. They will never allow us to be equal, and they never will believe that we've forgotten and forgiven everything. We're damned, from now until the end of our lives."[93] Various Soviet institutions asked potential employees detailed questions about their past. According to one official, requests for documents on the social origin and social position of citizens came typically from the military concerning potential conscripts (*doprizyvniki*) or from agricultural enterprises under the Commissariat of Heavy Industry.[94] Yet military and heavy industries were not the only employers to investigate whether someone was formerly disenfranchised. In December 1937, the NKVD USSR issued a standard format for a questionnaire that was supposed to be completed by persons admitted to do "secret work." The VTsIK Secret Department (*sekretnyi otdel*) distributed the form for use by all institutions and enterprises under its jurisdiction. The extensive questionnaire inquired into practically every aspect of people's lives, including their estate (*soslovie*) in tsarist times and social origin, and whether they or their relatives had ever been disenfranchised and why.[95] The importance of social origin remained, and a person's past could still be used to justify discrimination or repression.

As Soviet institutions continued to ask people about their class identity, citizens and institutions alike flooded local administrative organs with requests for personal documents. In 1937, the city soviet of Grozni in the Chechen-Ingush autonomous oblast reported that it daily received dozens of visitors and written letters with such requests. The police required such documents before it would issue internal passports, and institutions made the same inquiry before hiring a prospective employee. One local official described how military industries in particular submitted numerous requests for detailed data on their employees and the standard questions included: Did the individual use hired labor and, if so, when? Did he or she ever engage in trade? Were they ever disenfranchised and, if so, when and for what reason? What used to be the job of the local soviet was now the responsibility of all employers. Since economic behavior remained a critical measure of identity, many local officials failed to understand the point of the new constitution. Would it be permissible, they asked, to issue a kind of personal document on an individual's social origin and previous disenfranchisement even in light of the new constitution? In January 1937, some officials asked whether documents concerning social origin and social position, when issued to formerly disenfranchised people, should include the fact that the person was deprived of rights and why. The VTsIK Presidium turned the question over to the Commissariat of Justice, and justice officials maintained that documents on social origin should not include the fact that someone was once disenfranchised because those grounds for disenfranchisement no longer existed, following the adoption of the new law.[96] VTsIK would later dispute the Commissariat of Justice's interpretation. Well after the adoption of Stalin's Constitution, the state continued to take great interest in the old identities and practices of Soviet citizens.

In discussions over the practical implications of the constitution, VTsIK took a more conservative position and insisted that social origin and past disenfranchisement remained relevant after 1936. The VTsIK Presidium's secretariat called the Commissariat of Justice's interpretation wrong and argued that people looking for work should indeed answer questions regarding whether they were once disenfranchised. Moreover, upon the request of institutions and organizations, local officials should include in documents on social position whether the individual had previously been disenfranchised or dekulakized.[97] In the spring of 1937, VTsIK sent the following standard reply to local officials who asked about whether the 1936 Constitution automatically changed the old practice of issuing documents on social origin: "The secretariat of the VTsIK Presidium states that the practice [*poriadok*] of completing a questionnaire before employment, of verifying the questionnaire responses [*anketnye dannye*], and of the soviets issuing official documents, upon request from institutions, enterprises and organizations, concerning the origin and past social position of citizens remains in place [*ostaetsia prezhnii*]."[98]

Class identity continued to be important even after the adoption of the 1936 Constitution, and when local officials assumed otherwise, they were sharply criticized. For example, the Kharkov regional soviet executive committee decided that issuing documents on the social origin of citizens contradicted article 135 of the USSR Constitution, so it instructed all the oblast soviets to stop issuing this kind of document. In a letter to the USSR General Procurator A. Ia. Vyshinskii dated December 1937, a member of the TsIK Presidium, S. Chutskaev, expressed alarm that some local officials were arriving at this interpretation of the constitution. Consistent with the views of his institution, Chutskaev firmly defended "the necessity of preserving the existing practice" in which institutions and enterprises, particularly military industries and transportation, can request and obtain documents on an employee or prospective employee's social origin.[99] He urged the Soviet General Procurator to distribute a list of institutions and enterprises to which local soviets must give such documents upon request, and Vyshinskii did so. After 1936, the formerly disenfranchised learned that their past still interested officials and employers and could continue to be damaging.

The threat of continued discrimination affected the former disenfranchised in different ways. Some chose to be quiet and discreet, knowing that if attention were drawn to them, their damaging past might be exposed. One man defended the wisdom of keeping a low profile and maintaining silence in 1937: "Open your soul to these revolutionary philistines, that is, tell them what you were, and they'll immediately come up with an axe to grind."[100] The formerly disenfranchised were often afraid of being subjected to another's scrutiny. For others, however, it appears that the threat of exposure did not represent a great burden. Some of those with stigmatized identities who had managed to accumulate years of service for Soviet power maintained a certain confidence that they would be protected from further repression. The son of a wealthy Ukrainian peasant before the revolution, Stepan Podlubny, was one of the few people who suffered only mildly when it was discovered in 1936 that he had concealed his kulak origins. Expelled from the komsomol, he nonetheless continued his studies at the Medical Institute. He even admitted that his past had become less significant for him: "I ask what the new year [1936] has in store for me, but it is a different question from the one I asked in years past. I used to ask how I would be punished for my past, and that was all, 100 percent. Now this is only 40 percent of my question, the other 60 percent is what will I achieve, will things go my way in 1936." On the other hand, his mother was arrested by the NKVD and sentenced to eight years "for concealing social origins," even though, he admitted, "the official powers knew about her social origin all the way back in 1934."[101] The persecution of those with a damaging past remained inconsistent, but the younger and more productive generation appears to have suffered less than their bourgeois parents.

Familiar Victims of the Great Terror

The beginning of Stalin's Great Terror is typically marked by the assassination of Sergei Kirov, the Leningrad party boss. This murder certainly signaled the start of a new wave of repression for class enemies. "Alien elements," such as former members of the nobility and bourgeoisie, were evicted from Leningrad and Moscow following Kirov's death in December 1934.[102] In the first few months of 1935, thousands of nonlaboring elements, including persons without passports, criminals, and "former people" were expelled from the city. A man who went to Leningrad after he was dekulakized in 1930 worked in a shoe-export factory and elsewhere, even surviving the passportization campaign, but he was discovered as an alien during this 1935 purge of the city.[103] Just as in the earlier years of discrimination, some welcomed the expulsions of aliens and other undesirables as a way of freeing scant housing space for those in need. One person held the opinion that "finally all the parasites will be expelled from Leningrad and the working class will have at least a little improvement in housing at their expense."[104] Once again, competition over insufficient resources generated support for repression.

A woman deported from Leningrad to Saratov, exiled with her husband on grounds that he was a former nobleman, sent an angry letter to Molotov in 1936. She charged officials with wrongly judging her husband, insulting her, separating her from her children, depriving her of the right to work, and advising her to petition for forgiveness. She found the mere suggestion outrageous and instead insisted that her suffering entitled her to rights. The letter was strikingly insolent and sharply disputed the party's assumption that noblemen possessed privileged status. Elise Kimberling Wirtschafter describes an Imperial Russian society in which "lesser nobles . . . blended imperceptibly into the general population," and hardly represented an elite in many cases.[105] This point is emphasized by the petitioner who noted her noble husband's humble upbringing and emphatically blamed Soviet power for the family's misery and humiliation.

In 1928 I married A.N. Kovalev, whose father was a nobleman. . . . At thirteen, Kovalev was orphaned and never managed even to finish middle school. At the time of the revolution he was 16 years old. From 1920 to 1923 he was in the Red Army. . . . I've known Kovalev for 8 years as an honest man, a toiler and a good family man. But this mattered little for granting a hardworking and peaceful life. . . . I haven't seen my children in a full year. Above all, I have lost my dignity as a human being, a woman, and a citizen. I am a socially dangerous element! . . .

Like a beggar, I have asked for work but can't even find a job as a cleaning lady with the kind of certificate the NKVD gave me. . . . I have submitted petitions asking that my husband's and my exile be changed, that the gun seized after our arrest be returned, that we be allowed to return to our children and parents—but within one month all of my petitions were rejected. Comrade Roginskii [in Moscow] told me to "send VTsIK a petition for mercy [*pomilovanie*]." In other words, I have to ask forgiveness for crimes I didn't commit. If I actually did commit a crime by marrying this kind of nobleman, then the hardship, deprivation, insult and separation from my children fully redeems me.[106]

The personal testimony of this woman from Leningrad vividly illustrates a theme that runs through many letters from outcasts. Emotional suffering, plus the experience of hardship and humiliation, entitled one to redemption before the state.

Like the woman deported to Saratov, many of the people being evicted from the major cities were deceived by officials who, in order to force compliance with deportation orders, denied that any harm would come to them. In 1935, a woman who was deported from Leningrad to Kazakhstan described in a letter to Kalinin that officials assured her she would not lose her voting rights. Yet only a week after arrival in Kazakhstan, her entire family was disenfranchised as "administrative exiles."[107] The former bourgeois classes became especially vulnerable to the waves of arrests that took place in Leningrad and other cities after the Kirov assassination. One woman described the arrest of an artist whose past was used to condemn him. "They sent Tverskoy into exile, the man had worked in the theater since the beginning of 1914, and had been awarded a title of merit, but he had been an officer in the war against Germany, and rumor had it he had been an adjutant to Kerensky, though I doubt it myself. He had worked in the Petrograd Department of Theater and Performance since the beginning of 1918. He had never been on the side of the Whites."[108]

The former bourgeois classes continued to be especially vulnerable to the purges that swept through institutions of party, state, and industry from 1936 to 1938. In autumn 1937, a wave of arrests targeted the disenfranchised groups, notably priests, before the first elections to the soviets since 1934. Some citizens believed that Stalin wanted to ensure that "alien elements" did not assert their power during the elections.[109] One woman described how clerics were largely the targets of the pre-election purge: "In Iaroslav Province, right where we used to live, everyone who had anything to do with the church was arrested, all the priests, church elders, pastors, et cetera, et cetera. In Detskoe, Irina came home from school and said, 'They told us there are mass arrests going on right now. We need to rid ourselves of undesirable elements before the election!'"[110] In the second half of 1937, Stalin instructed regional party organizations to arrest and either send to a Gulag or shoot, among others, clerics and former kulaks who had returned to their provinces after their term of exile (presumably, after the reinstatement of rights) since they were considered the "chief instigators" of anti-Soviet crimes.[111] The head of the Commissariat of Heavy Industry, Sergo Ordzhonikidze, tried to protect former White Army officers and family members of traders, industrialists, and noblemen employed in his institution, but the effort proved increasingly difficult during this intensified hunt for internal enemies.[112] A secret directive from the Moscow Party Committee in August 1936 instructed party cells in industrial factories to arrest "class alien elements," including peasants who had fled dekulakization.[113] Party purges also led to the arrest of people who hid damaging elements of their family history, such as a father who was a kulak or worked for a landowner, or brothers who had served in the White Army.[114]

As in the case of disenfranchisement, the campaign against internal "enemies of the people" targeted not only people from the former bourgeois classes but those who possessed their traits, particularly theft and deception. Former kulaks and clerics were grouped for arrest and execution together with "horse thieves, cattle-rustlers, robbers, thieves, et cetera."[115] During the Great Terror, the embezzler and the thief were likely to be accused not of stealing but of sabotage and counterrevolution. The enemy of the Soviet state continued to be characterized as a robber of public resources. Moreover, the Great Terror sought to ferret out masked enemies after the population's refashioning of self had effectively heightened suspicion of pretenders. As in the time of militant class war, during the purges of the late 1930s, Soviet authorities vilified tactics of evasion and idealized sincerity and transparency. In the witch hunts that propelled the Great Terror, deception remained a basic characteristic of the enemy, and its importance only increased. The Soviet Union in the 1930s represented a body politic with "a clear external boundary, and a confused internal state in which envy and favoritism flourish and continually confound the proper expectations of members," and in such an environment, as Mary Douglas has argued, people take seriously the witch who, like the body politic, appears normal but possesses hidden and extraordinary malevolent powers.[116]

Despite the similarities between the waves of intense political repression that swept the country in the periods 1928–1931 and 1936–1938, one critical difference remains. Stalin's Terror coincided with a campaign to promote the "stability of law": to significantly reduce appeals and contestations, to fix blame and identify the culpable without hesitation, and to force unambiguous confessions.[117] One observer in the camps noted that before 1938 the majority of sentences were commuted for good work, but after this fateful year commutations of sentences became rare.[118] The witch-hunting of the Great Terror pinned blame for misfortune squarely on the trouble-makers and deviants.[119] The official legal culture of high Stalinism unequivocally opposed the legal practices so common in the previous decade when disenfranchisement was coupled with a mechanism for the reinstatement of rights. The Prosecutor during the show trials of 1936–1938, Vyshinskii insisted that culpability was fixed and unambiguous and considered confession the supreme form of evidence. Stalin's Great Terror was characterized by the presence of incorrigible enemies, the necessity of confession, and the fixed location of blame. Laments, blameless victims, and redeemed laborers would represent things of the past.

Conclusion

In the 1930s, the numbers of people on the soviets' lists of the disenfranchised steadily declined, rates of rehabilitation increased, and the exclusion of nonlaboring elements occurred less frequently as elections to the soviets no longer took place annually. Signs of a significant change in policy were evident as early as 1932, but the dismantling of disenfranchisement would take place gradually. In 1936, Stalin promulgated his new constitution that declared the existence of a classless society and granted voting rights to all citizens regardless of social origin. This apparently benign picture veils the fact that class aliens continued to be viewed as a grave threat well after 1936. The drop in the numbers of people on the soviets' lists of the disenfranchised does not suggest an end to the repression of class aliens but simply a decline in the surveillance powers of the soviets. Instead, the task of identifying aliens for exclusion became the respon-

sibility of NKVD, police, and judicial organs who commanded greater coercive powers.

Stalin's decision to end the policy set forth in Lenin's 1918 Constitution
and extend voting rights to all people regardless of their former economic
activities or bourgeois identity appears at first as a dramatic shift in policy.
In fact, repression did not end but simply took different forms. The categories of people who at an earlier time faced disenfranchisement remained
especially vulnerable to new methods of discrimination and sanction.
Many social marginals, perceived nonlaboring and parasitic elements, and
members of the former bourgeois classes were denied passports and expelled from the cities in 1933, and thieves faced execution and other severe criminal sanction under Stalin's August 7, 1932, law. Class-alien elements were among the first groups of people expelled from Leningrad in
large numbers after the 1934 assassination of the city's party boss, Kirov,
and they also represented principal targets of the massive purges that followed in party, state, and industrial institutions during the Stalinist terror
of 1936–1938.

Moreover, even after the reinstatement of rights and the implementation of Stalin's Constitution, various forms of discrimination continued.
Deportees and resettled aliens were denied freedom to leave their settlements, and others still encountered distrust and suspicion when they
looked for work or attempted to join a trade union. Past disenfranchisement, former economic activities or parasitic, nonlaboring behavior remained relevant, and any attempt to "mask" a class-alien identity invited
severe sanction at the hands of the secret police. The country's most dangerous enemies were the pretenders, those who concealed their true interests behind a mask of loyalty, and these hidden enemies could not be reinstated or redeemed. An earlier policy of social engineering that involved
the dual practices of purging alien elements and evaluating worthy citizens
was replaced by a campaign of expulsion with almost no possibility of redemption.

Conclusion

As the Stalinist state expanded to absorb all social and material life in the late 1920s and early 1930s, persons excluded from participation appeared no different from noncitizen aliens. However, those who, like the disenfranchised, lost economic and civil rights were not technically stripped of their citizenship in the Soviet state. Legal differences existed between the status of persons disenfranchised and those deprived of Soviet citizenship, but the fact remains that by the mid-1930s, many had blurred the distinction. Soviet officials and *lishentsy* often spoke of disenfranchisement as the denial of citizenship and, correspondingly, understood the reinstatement of rights as conferring citizenship. When addressing the reinstatement of rights to deportees, the head of the Gulag, Matvei Berman, referred to the restoration of their citizenship (*grazhdanstvo*), and outcasts petitioning for rights frequently asked specifically for citizenship or the right to live as a Soviet citizen. Under Stalin, the loss of voting rights often meant complete marginalization. That outcasts as well as Soviet officials so often conflated the restoration of voting rights with the reinstatement of citizenship says less about Soviet law than social practice.

The practices of exclusion and inclusion expose the nature of the Soviet political community that emerged in the years of socialist construction. On the one hand, the boundary separating insiders from outsiders appears ambiguous. People became outcasts for a multitude of reasons, from selling kosher meats to insulting a local official or neighbor, to renting out space in a modest dwelling. Those without rights did not represent a uniform segment of society but included the elderly as well as able-bodied youth, male heads of households, and women who earned paltry sums in odd jobs, White Army officers with formal education and means, and

185

Buddhist lamas without, Russian peasants along with ethnic traders. Certainly, a degree of randomness and bad luck grouped these people together as outcasts, but misfortune alone did not separate them from the enfranchised Soviet citizenry.

If not united as a social group, Stalin's outcasts nonetheless share certain behaviors and cultural attributes. A close examination of exclusionary practices indicates that bourgeois aliens were often perceived by others as nonlaboring and exploitative elements. The traits and activities that people associated with the alien class fundamentally informed the boundary that separated insiders and outsiders in the Soviet state. Stalin's class-based society appears highly abstract unless the categories of bourgeois and proletarian are examined for the meanings they evoked. For example, behavior viewed as parasitic was considered part of a bourgeois identity, thus justifying exclusion, while the experience of hardship and exploitation could provide one marker of a proletarian self and legitimize belonging. To earn re-entry into Soviet society, aliens had to abandon their nonlaboring ways (namely, reject material dependency or private trade) and demonstrate loyalty to Soviet power through activism and socially useful labor. The terms of social membership were quite simple and straightforward, but the path to inclusion proved more complicated.

Not everyone in the diverse group of Stalin's outcasts could readily erase the stigma of the nonlaboring element. The elderly and disabled might gain "unearned income" from rent, but they could hardly be expected to labor on the shop floor of a Stalinist factory. Many state officials well understood this, and accepted various appeals for the reinstatement of rights. Social life and not party instruction often determined membership in Stalin's new society. People could re-enter Soviet life even without demonstrating the requisite personal transformation. Patterns of inclusion reveal that resourceful outcasts discovered various paths to civic incorporation. They offered emotional appeals or laments, sought the assistance of relatives and friends, re-wrote their personal histories, moved to new cities, and concealed their past. At the same time, others challenged the regime to follow its own laws and grant rights in exchange for productive labor. On the surface, it appears that little united the diverse group of people who successfully regained their rights. But here too, certain patterns emerge. Redeemed citizens managed to convince officials of their sincerity, suffering, and usefulness to the state.

In the forced labor camps of the Far North city of Kolyma, Varlam Shalamov wrote, "If you didn't fill your [production] quota, your bread ration got cut to three hundred grams. Soup once a day."[1] Stalin truly enforced the principle of Lenin's 1918 Constitution, that "he who does not work neither shall he eat." In the Soviet Union, the central duty of all Soviet subjects was work, and this determined one's material existence or "rights" in Stalinist society. The deprivation and reinstatement of rights fixed the state-society relationship as one based on the exchange of rights for socially useful labor. Many years after his father denounced Stalin, Sergei Khrushchev, the son of the former Soviet Premier Nikita Khrushchev, became an American citizen. When he was asked, "Do you think that your life will be any different now that you're an American citizen?" he replied without hesitation, "No. Each citizen has to work. . . . I am working now and I will work in the future."[2] The son of the man who initiated the process of de-Stalinization did not easily relinquish the notion of the citizen as laborer. The identity of the citizen as sufferer also apparently outlived the Stalin era. Nancy Ries describes how a language of litany dominated in the Gorbachev era, as people continuously spoke a fatalistic lament about Russia's exploited and poor population.[3] One wonders the degree to which fundamental notions such as the citizen as sufferer and useful laborer remained meaningful well beyond the Stalin era.

Stalinist repression took many forms and generated diverse outcomes. It is not unusual to discover contradictions in Stalin's rule, and one is struck by many in the policy and practice of disenfranchisement. A powerful instrument of exclusion is coupled with a system of reintegration, that is, the deprivation of rights is often followed by the reinstatement of rights. Stalin's victims do not make forced confessions or acknowledge their mistakes, but rather interact with state agents in often emotional and demanding ways. The lamenting supplicant regains rights with almost the same frequency as the redeemed laborer, the regime's proper constituency. The course of policy is shaped by the adaptive strategies of the disenfranchised and by the party leadership's paranoid perception of its rehabilitated citizens. And the Stalinist regime admits to being manipulated by the very people whom it has victimized. Nonetheless, these and other paradoxes in policy did not render this social engineering project meaningless. The deprivation and reinstatement of rights endeavored to make each individual a site for socialist construction, for discarding the old and installing the new. The policy's legacy consists primarily in the lives it fundamentally altered but also in the understandings and practices that the system effected. In the end, formative political practices, coherent alien and citizen identities, and distinct terms of membership in the new socialist society represent the project's significant legacy.

Notes

Introduction

1. On the disenfranchised, see A.I. Dobkin, "Lishentsy," *Zven'ia: Istoricheskii al'-manakh* (Moscow-St. Petersburg, 1992): 2:600–631; Sheila Fitzpatrick, "Cultural Revolution as Class War," in *Cultural Revolution in Russia, 1928–1931*, ed. Sheila Fitzpatrick (Bloomington, Ind., 1984); Sheila Fitzpatrick, "The Problem of Class Identity in NEP Society," in *Russia in the Era of NEP: Explorations in Soviet Society and Culture*, ed. Sheila Fitzpatrick, Alexander Rabinowitch, and Richard Stites (Bloomington, Ind., 1991), 12–33; Elise Kimberling, "Civil Rights and Social Policy in Soviet Russia, 1918–1936," *Russian Review* 41 (1982): 24–46; V.I. Tikhonov et al., *Lishenie izbiratel'nykh prav v Moskve v 1920–1930–e gody* (Moscow, 1998).

2. GARF f. 5248, op. 9, d. 8180, l. 24 (Karelia ASSR, 1929); GARF f. 5248, op. 13, d. 817, l. 18–22 (Gorkii krai, 1934). In over a third of all petitions examined in this study, the disenfranchised asked specifically for the rights of citizenship.

3. In theory, citizenship in the first socialist society was not determined by indicators common to other European states, such as place of birth or residence, blood descent, common language, culture, or even political doctrine. On how modern European states determined the rights and obligations of citizens, see Rogers Brubaker, *Citizenship and Nationhood in France and Germany* (Cambridge, Mass., 1992); Kathleen Paul, *Whitewashing Britain: Race and Citizenship in the Postwar Era* (Ithaca, N.Y., 1997); John Torpey, *The Invention of the Passport: Surveillance, Citizenship, and the State* (Cambridge, U.K., 2000).

4. S.S. Kishkin, *Sovetskoe grazhdanstvo* (Moscow, 1925), 19–20. See also V.S. Shevtsov, *Sovetskoe grazhdanstvo* (Moscow, 1965).

5. RSFSR Constitution of 1918, *Istoriia Sovietskoi komstitutsii 1917–1956* (Moscow, 1957), 79, 85. In the pre-war years, the Soviet Union had only general guidelines and no specific set of laws or practices that defined its policy concerning citizenship. According to the 1924 law on Soviet citizenship, persons could be deprived of the rights of citizenship by a decision of a court or on the basis of Soviet legislation, yet this later changed. The centralizing trend in state policy in the 1930s influenced the 1930 and 1931 laws on Soviet citizenship. They stipulate that only the republic TsIK has the right to deny people their citizenship. See *Sobranie zakonov i rasporiazhenii raboche-krest'ianskogo pravitel'stva SSSR* (hereafter SZ) 1924 no. 23, art. 202; SZ 1930 no. 34, art. 367; SZ 1931 no. 24, art. 196.

6. "Ocherednye zadachi Sovetskoi vlasti," in *V.I. Lenin i I.V. Stalin o sovetskoi konstitutsii* (Moscow, 1936), 22.

7. GARF f. 1235, op. 141, d. 1052 (1931).

8. Official data is quite uneven, and the state kept statistics on the disenfranchised not in absolute figures (which are difficult to come by) but as a percentage of the voting-age population. In the RSFSR or Soviet Russia, the data on people without voting rights in the years 1922–25 remained constant at about 1.4 percent of the voting age population. In the 1925–26 campaign, the disenfranchised in the RSFSR as a percentage of the voting-age population stood at 1.1 percent in the rural areas and 4.5 percent in the cities (where most *lishentsy* were traders, middlemen, and clerics). In the election of 1926–27, the percentage of outcasts jumped to 3.3 percent in rural areas and 7.7 percent in the cities. In the 1928–29 electoral campaign, nearly 72 percent of cities and settlements reported 7.2 percent disenfranchised, and nearly 86 percent of rural soviets reported 3.9 percent without voting rights. In other words, the soviets reported no significant increase in their outcast population from the previous election. In the 1930–31 campaign, the percentage of disenfranchised was reported to be 3.5 percent of the RSFSR population (roughly that recorded for 1926–27), and this figure declined to 2.6 percent in the 1934 electoral campaign. In 1937, after the adoption of Stalin's 1936 Constitution, the numbers of disenfranchised in the RSFSR fell dramatically to under 0.5 percent of the voting age population. See GARF f. 5248, op. 1, d. 68, l. 65–68, 229; GARF f. 393, op. 1, d. 156, l. 16–17; GARF f. 393, op. 1, d. 153, l. 20–23; GARF f. 5248, op. 1, d. 4, l. 78; GARF f. 7522, op. 1, d. 139, l. 37. The percentage of people deprived of voting rights in the RSFSR in 1930–31 does not appear to have changed considerably when one looks at the aggregate figures for the RSFSR overall. However, during that campaign many regions reported sharp declines in the number of people disenfranchised. For additional data, see Golfo Alexopoulos, *Marking Outcasts and Making Citizens* (Ph.D. diss., University of Chicago, 1996).

9. The Soviet secret police is identified as the Cheka of 1918–1921, the State Political Administration (GPU) of 1922–1923, and the Unified State Political Administration (OGPU) of 1923–1934. In July 1934, the Commissariat of Internal Affairs (NKVD) absorbed the OGPU when reorganized as an All-Union Commissariat. While the NKVD RSFSR continued to perform routine police functions—registered births, deaths, and marriages, and also managed prisons and forced labor camps—the NKVD SSSR assumed the responsibilities of the Soviet secret police. SZ 1934 no. 36, art. 283.

10. The mechanism for reinstating rights to the disenfranchised represents a rite of passage analogous to that which Van Gennep describes. Arnold Van Gennep, *The Rites of Passage* (Chicago, 1960). On rites of passage, see also Victor Turner, *Dramas, Fields, and Metaphors* (Ithaca, N.Y., 1974).

11. I use the definition in which ritual "is constituted of patterned and ordered sequences of words and acts . . . whose content and arrangement are characterized in varying degree by formality (conventionality), stereotype (rigidity), condensation (fusion), and redundancy (repetition)." Stanley J. Tambiah, "A Performative Approach to Ritual," *Proceedings of the British Academy* 65:113–169. Quoted in Michael Herzfeld, *The Social Production of Indifference: Exploring the Symbolic Roots of Western Bureaucracy* (Chicago, 1992), 18.

12. On deportees, many of whom were disenfranchised people, see *Spetspereselentsy v zapadnoi sibiri*, ed. V.P. Danilov and S.A. Krasil'nikov (Novosibirsk, 1992–1993); G.F. Dobronozhenko and L.S. Shabalova, *Spetsposelki v Komi oblasti* (Syktyvkar, 1997); N.A. Ivnitsky, *Repressivnaia politika sovetskoi vlasi v derevne (1928–1933)* (Moscow, 2000).

13. Peter Sahlins, *Boundaries: The Making of France and Spain in the Pyrenees* (Berkeley, Calif., 1989), 8.

14. J. Arch Getty and Roberta T. Manning, eds., *Stalinist Terror: New Perspectives* (Cambridge, U.K., 1993); Paul M. Hagenloh, "'Socially Harmful Elements' and The Great Terror," in *Stalinism: New Directions*, ed. Sheila Fitzpatrick (London, 2000); Peter Holquist, "Anti-Soviet 'Svodki' from the Civil War: Surveillance as a Shared Feature of Russian Political Culture," *Russian Review* 56 (1997): 445–450, and his "Information Is the Alpha and Omega of Our Work: Bolshevik Surveillance in Its Pan-European Context," *Journal of Modern History* 69 (1997): 415–451; Torpey, *Invention of the Passport*.

15. John L. Comaroff and Simon Roberts, *Rules and Processes: The Cultural Logic of Dispute in an African Context* (Chicago, 1981); Sally Falk Moore, "Inflicting Harm Righteously: Turning a Relative into a Stranger: An African Case," *Fremde der Gesellschaft* (Frankfurt, 1991); *Law as Process: An Anthropological Approach* (London, 1978).

16. Sheila Fitzpatrick, "Ascribing Class: The Construction of Social Identity in Soviet Russia," *Journal of Modern History* 65 (1993): 745–770; Sheila Fitzpatrick, "The Bolsheviks' Dilemma: Class, Culture, and Politics in the Early Soviet Years," *Slavic Review* 47 (1988): 599–613.

17. Providing false information on petitions to state institutions was considered a criminal offense according to article 187 of the Criminal Code and was punishable by a fine of up to 300 rubles or forced labor for up to three months. Examples of the questionnaire appear in AKhSF f. 5248, op. 4, d. 6464, l. 2; GARF f. 1235, op. 140, d. 416, l. 13–15.

18. Orlando Figes and Boris Kolonitskii, *Interpreting the Russian Revolution: The Languages and Symbols of 1917* (New Haven, 1999). Similar villainous attributes historically ascribed to the bourgeoisie are also broadly treated in Etienne Balibar and Immanuel Wallerstein, *Race, Nation, Class: Ambiguous Identities* (London, 1991). See also Donald J. Raleigh, "Languages of Power: How the Saratov Bolsheviks Imagined Their Enemies," *Slavic Review* 57 (1998): 320–350. On bourgeois identity and Russian chauvinism, see Matthew J. Payne, *Stalin's Railroad: Turksib and the Building of Socialism* (Pittsburgh, Pa., 2001), 149–152.

19. Lynne Viola, "The Second Coming: Class Enemies in the Soviet Countryside, 1927–1935," in *Stalinist Terror*.

20. GARF f. 1235, op. 141, d. 145, l. 25.

21. This logic is described with reference to how the Orthodox perceived pagans, Catholics, and others of the "alien faith." See Iurii M. Lotman and Boris A. Uspenskii, "Binary Models in the Dynamics of Russian Culture (to the End of the Eighteenth Century)" in *The Semiotics of Russian Cultural History*, ed. Alexander D. Nakhimovsky and Alice Stone Nakhimovsky (Ithaca, N.Y., 1985), 40.

22. Edward Hallett Carr and R. W. Davies, *Foundations of a Planned Economy, 1926–29* (London, 1969), 1:72; Edward Hallett Carr, *Foundations of a Planned Economy, 1926–1929* (London, 1971), 2:284. In particular, the works of Jochen Hellbeck and Stephen Kotkin explore this project of remaking individuals in a Stalinist context. See Jochen Hellbeck, "Fashioning the Stalinist Soul: The Diary of Stepan Podlubnyi, 1931–1939," in *Stalinism*, 77–117; Stephen Kotkin, *Magnetic Mountain: Stalinism as a Civilization* (Berkeley, Calif., 1995).

23. The French revolutionaries believed that politics could reshape human nature. See Lynn Hunt, *Politics, Culture, and Class in the French Revolution* (Berkeley, Calif., 1984), 47; Mussolini claimed that fascism could remake human life and individual character. See Simonetta Falasca-Zamponi, *Fascist Spectacle: The Aesthetics of Power in Mussolini's Italy* (Berkeley, Calif., 1997), 96. Aleksa Djilas describes how Communist Yugoslavia inherited the shared belief of Marxism and the Enlightenment that humanity could create new human beings and a fundamentally different society. Aleksa Djilas, *The Contested Country: Yugoslav Unity and Communist Revolution* (Cambridge, Mass., 1991), 183.

24. A number of works explore various aspects of the Soviet project of social engineering. See, for example, Oleg Kharkhordin, *The Collective and the Individual in Russia: A Study of Practices* (Berkeley, Calif., 1999); Stephen Kotkin, *Magnetic Mountain*; Terry Martin, *Affirmative Action Empire: Nations and Nationalism in the Soviet Union, 1923–1939* (Ithaca, N.Y., 2001); Elizabeth A. Wood, *The Baba and the Comrade: Gender and Politics in Revolutionary Russia* (Bloomington, Ind., 1997); Lewis H. Siegelbaum and Ron Suny, eds., *Making Workers Soviet: Power, Class, and Identity* (Ithaca, N.Y., 1994); Ronald Grigor Suny, *The Revenge of the Past: Nationalism, Revolution, and the Collapse of the Soviet Union* (Stanford, Calif., 1993).

25. Primo Levi, *Survival in Auschwitz* (New York, 1996), 90.

26. Fitzpatrick, "Problem of Class Identity," in *Russia in the Era of NEP*, 12–33; Sheila Fitzpatrick, *Everyday Stalinism: Ordinary Life in Extraordinary Times* (Oxford, U.K.,

1999); Sheila Fitzpatrick, *Stalin's Peasants: Resistance and Survival in the Russian Village after Collectivization* (Oxford, U.K., 1994).

27. See, for example, Nadezhda Mandelstam, *Hope Against Hope: A Memoir,* trans. Max Hayward (New York, 1970), 93; Varlam Shalamov, *Kolyma Tales* (New York, 1994), 457; Aleksandr Solzhenitsyn, *The Gulag Archipelago* (New York, 1973), 208–209. Solzhenitsyn asserted that "in each and every case your petition would have no effect whatever."

28. On party members' confessions particularly during Stalin's Great Purges, see J. Arch Getty, *Origins of the Great Purges: The Soviet Communist Party Reconsidered, 1933–1938* (Cambridge, U.K., 1985); Kharkhordin, *Collective and Individual;* Oleg V. Khlevniuk, *1937: Stalin, NKVD i sovetskoe obshchestvo* (Moscow, 1992); Vadim Z. Rogovin, *1937: Stalin's Year of Terror* (Oak Park, Mich., 1998); Robert Tucker and Stephen Cohen, eds., *The Great Purge Trial* (New York, 1965).

29. See, for example, Sarah R. Davies, *Popular Opinion in Stalin's Russia: Terror, Propaganda, and Dissent, 1934–1941* (Cambridge, U.K., 1997); Jeffrey J. Rossman, "The Teikovo Cotton Workers' Strike of April 1932: Class, Gender, and Identity Politics in Stalin's Russia," *Russian Review* 56 (1997): 44–69; Lynne Viola, *Peasant Rebels Under Stalin* (Oxford, U.K., 1996); Golfo Alexopoulos, "Portrait of a Con Artist as a Soviet Man," *Slavic Review* 57 (1998): 774–790; Fitzpatrick, *Everyday Stalinism;* Hellbeck, "Fashioning the Stalinist Soul"; Kotkin, *Magnetic Mountain.*

30. AKhSF f. 5248, op. 14, d. 4245, l. 9–10 (Western Siberia krai, 1934).

31. AKhSF f. 5248, op. 7, d. 13614, l. 6 (Arkhangelsk, n/a).

32. On soviet subjectivity, see Jochen Hellbeck, "Self-Realization in the Stalinist System: Two Soviet Diaries of the 1930s," in *Russian Modernity: Politics, Knowledge, Practices* (London, 2000), 221–242; Anna Krylova, "The Tenacious Liberal Subject in Soviet Studies," *Kritika* 1 (2000): 119–146.

33. Kotkin, *Magnetic Mountain.* The author was the first to apply this idea most notably from Michel Foucault, but also from Antonio Gramsci and Raymond Williams, to the study of Stalinism.

34. Guenter Lewy, *The Nazi Persecution of the Gypsies* (Oxford, U.K., 2000); Burleigh and Wipperman, *The Racial State,* 168–182; Detlev J.K. Peukert, *Inside Nazi Germany: Conformity, Opposition, and Racism in Everyday Life* (New Haven, Conn., 1987).

35. This issue is explored in depth in William H. Sewell, *Work and Revolution in France: The Language of Labor from the Old Regime to 1848* (Cambridge, U.K., 1980), 80. The author quotes from Sieyes, "What Is the Third Estate?"

36. Milovan Djilas, *The New Class: An Analysis of the Communist System* (New York, 1983); Alena Ledeneva, *Russia's Economy of Favours: Blat, Networking, and Informal Networks* (Cambridge, U.K., 1998); Elena Osokina, *Za fasadom "Stalinskogo izobiliia": raspredelenie i rynok v snabzhenii naseleniia v gody industrializatsii, 1927–41* (Moscow, 1999).

37. Brubaker, *Citizenship and Nationhood.*

38. Clifford Geertz, *The Interpretation of Cultures* (New York, 1973), 354–355.

39. Ann Laura Stoler argues that "physiological attributes only signal the nonvisual and more salient distinctions of exclusion on which racism rests." See her "Sexual Affronts and Racial Frontiers: European Identities and the Cultural Politics of Exclusion in Colonial Southeast Asia," in *Tensions of Empire: Colonial Cultures in a Bourgeois World,* ed. Frederick Cooper and Ann Laura Stoler (Berkeley, Calif., 1997), 203.

1. Marking Outcasts and Making Citizens

1. Maria Gough, "Switched On: Notes on Radio, Automata, and the Bright Red Star," in *Building the Collective: Soviet Graphic Design 1917–1937,* ed. Leah Dickerman (Princeton, N.J., 1996), 40.

2. Sarah Davies, " 'Us against Them': Social Identity in Soviet Russia, 1934–1941," *Russian Review* 56 (1997): 70–89; Jeffrey J. Rossman, "The Teikovo Cotton Workers' Strike of

April 1932: Class, Gender, and Identity Politics in Stalin's Russia," *Russian Review* 56 (1997): 44–69. Yanni Kotsonis explores this same rhetorical pattern in a prerevolutionary context. See his *Making Peasants Backward: Agricultural Cooperatives and the Agrarian Question, 1861–1914* (London, 1999).

3. "Iz programmy rossiiskoi kommunisticheskoi partii," in *V. I. Lenin i V. I. Stalin*, 191.

4. On masking in the Russian and French revolutionary traditions, see Hunt, *Politics, Culture, and Class*, 39–40, 66–67; Fitzpatrick, "Ascribing Class."

5. Fitzpatrick, "Bolshevik's Dilemma"; Moshe Lewin, *The Making of the Soviet System* (New York, 1985), 211–215; Carr, *Foundations*, 2:425.

6. S. M. Melgunov, *Krasnyi terror v Rossii: 1918–1923* (Simferopol, 1991); Diane P. Koenker, William G. Rosenberg, and Ronald Grigor Suny, eds., *Party, State, and Society in the Russian Civil War: Explorations in Social History* (Bloomington, Ind., 1989).

7. L. M. Spirin, *Klassy i partii v grazhdanskoi voine v Rossii* (Moscow, 1968), 386; Lewin, *Making*, 212; James W. Heinzen, "'Alien' Personnel in the Soviet State: The People's Commissariat of Agriculture under Proletarian Dictatorship, 1918–1929," *Slavic Review* 56 (1997): 87.

8. GARF f. 5404, op. 2, d. 4, l. 15.

9. AKhSF f. 5248, op. 1, d. 72, l. 72.

10. The class background of the accused would determine whether the offense qualified as political. Peter H. Solomon, *Soviet Criminal Justice Under Stalin* (Cambridge, U.K., 1996), 30, 92.

11. On the rear militia, see "Zakon ob obiazatel'noi voennoi sluzhbe," SZ 1925 no. 62, art. 463, and the new edition of this law in SZ 1930 no. 40, art. 424. See also S. M. Kliatskin, *Na zashchite oktiabria* (Moscow, 1965), 201–202. On the special tax for rear militiamen, see various Sovnarkom decrees, including SZ 1930 no. 7, art. 77.

12. On the RSFSR Constitutions of 1918 and 1925, see *Istoriia sovetskoi konstitutsii, 1917–1956* (Moscow, 1957); on the important electoral instructions of the late 1920s, see *Sobranie uzakonenii i rasporiazhenii rabochego i krest'ianskogo pravitel'stva RSFSR 1925* no. 30, art. 218; Potapov and Fedorovskii, *Kto lishaet'sia prava* (Perm, 1928).

13. This provision appeared as article twenty-three in the 1918 RSFSR Constitution, article fourteen in the 1925 RSFSR Constitution, and was incorporated into the 1930 Instructions on Elections to the Soviets as article seventeen. By the end of 1925, only the Central Executive Committee could disenfranchise according to this category. AKhSF f. 5248, op. 1, d. 2, l. 41.

14. *V. I. Lenin i I. V. Stalin o sovetskoi konstitutsii* (Moscow, 1936), 53.

15. According to Lynne Viola, "kulak status could be determined by political behavior" or any action perceived as "contrary to the politics of the party," to the point where "class stereotypes were subsumed by political stereotypes." See her *Peasant Rebels Under Stalin: Collectivization and the Culture of Peasant Resistance* (Oxford, U.K., 1996), 16, 23, 33. On how even striking workers could become class enemies, see Rossman, "Teikovo Cotton Workers," 53.

16. AKhSF f. 5248, op. 1, d. 129, l. 141–142.

17. Party purges also targeted individuals who exhibited deviant behavior. See Getty, *Origins*, 58–91; Wood, *Baba and Comrade*, 196–206.

18. Orlando Figes, *A People's Tragedy: A History of the Russian Revolution* (New York, 1997), 524.

19. Wood, *Baba and Comrade*, 176–177.

20. RGAE f. 396, op. 3, d. 36, l. 20.

21. Carr, *Foundations*, 2:250, 272–273.

22. From the resolutions and decrees of the XIII Party Congress in May 1924, *Kommunisticheskaia partiia sovetskogo soiuza v rezoliutsiiakh i resheniiakh s'ezdov, konferentsii i plenumov TsK* (Moscow, 1970), 3:99.

23. "Postanovlenie III s'ezda sovetov SSSR," in *Kommunisticheskaia partiia sovetskogo soiuza v rezoliutsiiakh i resheniiakh s'ezdov, konferentsii i plenumov TsK* (Moscow, 1960), 2:79. Graduate students from the Moscow Institute of Soviet Construc-

tion as well as workers from factories and Red Army soldiers were sent to various regions to assist with the electoral campaign. AKhSF f. 5248, op. 1, d. 1, l. 102; AKhSF f. 5248, op. 1, d. 57, l. 1.

24. Sally Falk Moore and Barbara G. Myerhoff, *Secular Ritual* (Amsterdam, 1977). On the importance of elections to the French revolutionary project, see Hunt, *Politics, Culture, and Class,* 125–126.

25. AKhSF f. 5248, op. 1, d. 26, l. 124.

26. AKhSF f. 5248, op. 1, d. 17, l. 150; AKhSF f. 5248, op. 1, d. 129, l. 86.

27. *Instruktsiia k sostavleniiu otchetnosti po perevyboram v sovety* (Moscow, 1930).

28. In the 1920s, the People's Commissariat of Internal Affairs in Russia (*NKVD RSFSR*) performed routine police and civic duties such as registering births, deaths, and marriages and was responsible for prisons and forced-labor camps. SZ 1930 no. 60, art. 640.

29. The NKVD RSFSR continued to receive reports on the campaigns and keep campaign statistics. AKhSF f. 5248, op. 1, d. 3, l. 17; GARF f. 1235, op. 140, d. 447, l. 1–2; AKhSF f. 5248, op. 1, d. 1, l. 1.

30. AKhSF f. 5248, op. 1, d. 1, l. 104.

31. Carr and Davies, *Foundations,* 1:282–283.

32. Carr, *Foundations,* 2:274–275, 296.

33. Alec Nove, *An Economic History of the USSR* (New York, 1984), 121, 132–144; Osokina, *Za fasadom,* 47–58.

34. *Kommunisticheskaia partiia,* 382.

35. *Stalin's Letters to Molotov,* ed. Lars T. Lih, Oleg V. Naumov, and Oleg V. Khlevniuk (New Haven, Conn., 1995), 128.

36. *Kommunisticheskaia partiia,* 335. On NEP, see Alan M. Ball, *Russia's Last Capitalists: The Nepmen, 1921–1929* (Berkeley, Calif., 1987); Alexander Erlich, *The Soviet Industrialization Debate, 1924–1928* (Cambridge, Mass., 1960); Sheila Fitzpatrick, Alexander Rabinowitch, and Richard Stites, *Russia in the Era of NEP* (Bloomington, Ind., 1991); Abbott Gleason, Peter Kenez, and Richard Stites, eds., *Bolshevik Culture* (Bloomington, Ind., 1985); William Chase, *Workers, Society, and the Soviet State: Labor and Life in Moscow, 1918–1929* (Urbana, Ill., 1987).

37. Lewin, *Making,* 127; Carr and Davies, *Foundations,* 1:129. Before 1934, the various editions of the Instructions on Elections to the Soviets did not explicitly call for the disenfranchisement of kulaks. Rather, the economic practices listed in the Instructions as grounds for disenfranchisement, such as the hiring of labor, were associated with the activities of this rural bourgeoisie. Thus despite the legal ambiguity, people disenfranchised could easily expect the terrible kulak designation. T.I. Slavko, ed. *Sotsial'nyi portret lishentsa (na materialakh Urala), sbornik dokumentov* (Ekaterinburg, 1996), 4.

38. GARF f. 393, op. 1, d. 156, l. 16–17.

39. Carr, *Foundations,* 2:278.

40. Officials issued target figures of 3–5 percent for the numbers of people who should be identified as kulaks. See Fitzpatrick, *Stalin's Peasants,* 29–30, 54, 82; I. Ia Trifonov, *Likvidatsiia ekspluatatorskikh klassov v SSSR* (Moscow, 1975), 253, 261; Lewin, *Making,* 127; Carr and Davies, *Foundations,* 1:131.

41. Carr and Davies, *Foundations,* 1:14, 388, 664, 668, 669, 674, 748, 749; I. Ia Trifonov, *Ocherki istorii klassovoi bor'by v SSSR, 1921–1937* (Moscow, 1960), 134; Alan Ball, "Private Trade and Traders during NEP," *Russia in the Era of NEP: Explorations in Soviet Society and Culture,* Sheila Fitzpatrick, Alexander Rabinowitch, and Richard Stites, eds. (Bloomington, Ind., 1991).

42. AKhSF f. 5248, op. 1, d. 4, l. 70.

43. Year-by-year figures on the number of the disenfranchised are fragmentary and often contradictory. The most consistent data concerns this sharp jump from 1 percent disenfranchised prior to 1926 to over 3 percent in 1927, and the decline in numbers from 1930 to 1934. However, archival sources provide different figures. For example, the number of disenfranchised in the RSFSR in 1927 is indicated at 1,286,670 in GARF f. 5248, op. 1, d. 4, l.

79, as 1,808,051 in GARF f. 5248, op. 1, d. 4, l. 78, and as 1,902,000 in GARF f. 1235, op. 105, d. 504, l. 68. Similarly, the figure for the disenfranchised as a percentage of the voting age population in 1930–1931 is given as 3.2 percent in GARF f. 5248, op. 1, d. 140, l. 116, and as 3.5 percent in GARF f. 5248, op. 1, d. 68, l. 65–68.

44. GARF f. 393, op. 1, d. 156, l. 16–17; GARF f. 1235, op. 105, d. 504, l. 68. In 1922 and 1923, the figure was 1.4 percent; in 1924–1925, 1.3 percent; and in 1925–1926, 1 percent. GARF f. 393, op. 1, d. 156, l. 16–17. In the 1925–1926 campaign in the RSFSR, only 0.8 percent of the rural population and nearly 3 percent of the urban population (persons of voting age) was disenfranchised, and most of them were traders, middlemen and clerics. GARF f. 393, op. 1, d. 153, l. 20. In 1924–1925, it was reported that 1.3 percent of the rural population of the RSFSR was disenfranchised. GARF f. 393, op. 1, d. 156, l. 16–17.

45. Carr and Davies, *Foundations,* 1:41, 132, 673.

46. AKhSF f. 5248, op. 1, d. 11, l. 3.

47. Priests were considered exploiters because their main source of income came from administering Christian rites (funerals, weddings, baptisms), for which peasants gave a large proportion of their income. Sheila Fitzpatrick, *Stalin's Peasants,* 35, 59. On the disenfranchisement of shamans, see Slezkine, *Arctic Mirrors,* 226–228, and Bruce Grant, *In the Soviet House of Culture: A Century of Perestroikas* (Princeton, N.J., 1995), 92–96.

48. Lewin, *Making,* 127.

49. GARF f. 1235, op. 141, d. 723, l. 3. 1925 RSFSR Constitution in *Istoriia sovetskoi konstitutsii,* 529–546; N. Zolotarevskii, *Sel'sovety, gorsovety, s'ezdy sovetov: novaia instruktsiia o vyborakh* (Leningrad, 1926), 17–18; psalmodists and cantors could be disenfranchised only if their primary source of income was derived from religious rites. SU 1925 no. 79, art. 603.

50. *Zakonodatel'stvo o lishenii i vosstanovlenii v izbiratel'nykh pravakh* (Leningrad, 1930), 24.

51. AKhSF f. 5248, op. 1, d. 15, l. 22. This move came at a time when "the Baptist 'Bapsomol' and Mennonite 'Mensomol' supposedly had more members together than the Soviet Komsomol." See Fitzpatrick, "Cultural Revolution as Class War," 20.

52. Slezkine, *Arctic Mirrors,* 289.

53. Letter to Molotov dated 10 August 1929, quoted in Lih, Naumov, and Khlevniuk, *Stalin's Letters,* 166.

54. Carr, *Foundations,* 2:297, 77–78. Bourgeois specialists also "lived off the labor of others" like other class enemies, while Nepmen live off the "economic exploitation of others" and accumulates wealth at the expense of others. Wood, *Baba and Comrade,* 177, 205.

55. Lev R. Sheinin, *Zapiski sledovatelia; Voennaia taina: Rasskazy, roman* (Kishinev, 1987), 161.

56. *Chastichnye perevybory sel'sovetov v 1933 g.* ed., N. Nurmanov (Moscow, 1933), 14.

57. On the Great Transformation that became synonymous with the First Five-Year Plan, see William G. Rosenberg and Lewis H. Siegelbaum, *Social Dimensions of Soviet Industrialization* (Bloomington, Ind., 1993); R. W. Davies, *The Industrialization of Soviet Russia,* vols. 1–3 (Cambridge, Mass., 1989), and his *The Socialist Offensive: The Collectivization of Soviet Agriculture* (Cambridge, Mass., 1980); Hiroaki Kuromiya, *Stalin's Industrial Revolution* (Cambridge, U.K., 1988); David R. Shearer, *Industry, State and Society in Stalin's Russia, 1926–1934* (Ithaca, N.Y., 1996).

58. Sheila Fitzpatrick, ed. *Cultural Revolution in Russia 1928–1931* (Bloomington, Ind., 1978); William G. Rosenberg, ed. *Bolshevik Visions: First Phase of the Cultural Revolution in Soviet Russia* (Ann Arbor, Mich., 1984).

59. Carr, *Foundations,* 2:304–305.

60. Fitzpatrick, *Stalin's Peasants,* 54–55.

61. Viola, *Peasant Rebels,* 27.

62. Carr and Davies, *Foundations,* 1:50–52; Carr, *Foundations,* 2:184; Lewin, *Making,*

97; Fitzpatrick, *Stalin's Peasants,* 38; Nove, *Economic History,* 151–152; Osokina, *Za fasadom,* 53–54.

63. FGATO f. 434, op. 5, d. 13, l. 13; Trifonov, *Likvidatsiia,* 270.

64. N.A. Ivnitskii, *Repressivnaia politika sovetskoi vlasti v derevne (1928–1933 gg)* (Moscow, 2000) and his *Klassovaia bor'ba v derevne i likvidatsiia kulachestva kak klassa (1929–1932)* (Moscow, 1972); Fitzpatrick, *Stalin's Peasants;* Viola, *Peasant Rebels.*

65. Regional party organizations purged between 6 and 18 percent of members; in one locality, over 42 percent of those expelled were identified as "alien elements." Carr, *Foundations,* 2:136–137, 147, 286, 331.

66. GARF f. 1235, op. 141, d. 145, l. 5.

67. GARF f. 1235, op. 106, d. 519, l. 254.

68. AKhSF f. 5248, op. 1, d. 129, l. 50.

69. On the legal status of women and children in Imperial Russia, see Gregory Freeze, "The Soslovie (Estate) Paradigm and Russian Social History," *American Historical Review* 91 (1986): 11–36; Elise Kimberling Wirtschafter, *Social Identity in Imperial Russia* (DeKalb, Ill., 1997); Michelle Marrese, *A Woman's Kingdom: Noblewomen and the Control of Property in Russia, 1700–1861* (Ithaca, N.Y., 2002).

70. Some examples include AKhSF f. 5248, op. 7, d. 10814, l. 1; AKhSF f. 5248, op. 8, d. 1146, l. 4; AKhSF f. 5248, op. 7, d. 6614, l. 1.

71. GARF f. 5248, op. 1, d. 4, l. 79.

72. GARF f. 5248, op. 1, d. 68, l. 229.

73. GARF f. 1235, op. 106, d. 526, l. 114.

74. GARF f. 393, op. 1, d. 154, l. 728; GARF f. 393, op. 1, d. 189, l. 9–10; GARF f. 393, op. 1, d. 154, l. 229–233; GARF f. 393, op. 1, d. 95, l. 205; GARF f. 393, op. 1, d. 95, l. 317; GARF f. 393, op. 1, d. 95, l. 72. Indeed, local data suggest that in the first half of the 1920s, the disenfranchised population was largely made up of clerics, bandits, and thieves. Local officials, so used to depriving rights to clerics and criminals, needed to be reminded to disenfranchise family dependents, consistent with the 1926 Instructions. Traders and family dependents appear prominently on these lists by the middle of the decade. Slavko, *Sotsial'nyi portret,* 17-19, 60; GATO f. 22, op. 3, d. 3, l. 80-82; GATO f. 22, op. 3, d. 2, l. 7.

75. GARF, f. 1235, op. 104, d. 1119, l. 1.

76. Central State Archive of the Moscow Oblast, Moscow. Hereafter TsGAMO, f. 2157, op. 1, d. 666, l. 11.

77. GARF f. 5248, op. 1, d. 68, l. 229.

78. Osokina, *Za fasadom,* 92–97; Burleigh and Wippermann, *Racial State;* Lewy, *Nazi Persecution of the Gypsies;* Peukert, *Inside Nazi Germany.*

79. Lagovier, *Perevybory sovetov,* 38.

80. GARF f. 1235, op. 141, d. 145, l. 28.

81. GARF f. 1235, op. 141, d. 145, l. 7.

82. GARF f. 1235, op. 141, d. 145, l. 20.

83. According to article 40 of the 1925 RSFSR Criminal Code, an individual sentenced by a court to deprivation of rights (*porazhenie prav, porazhenie v politicheskikh pravakh*) was denied precisely those rights denied the disenfranchised.

84. I. Kutuzov, *Organizatsiia ucheta, rassmotreniia zhalob i khodataistv lits, lishennykh izbiratel'nikh prav* (Moscow, 1935), 21–22. Military veterans and others receiving social security (*strakhovanie*) and social welfare (*obespechenie*) risked losing it if they were disenfranchised, unless they lost rights as mentally ill. SU 1926 no. 86, art. 627. The various rights denied the disenfranchised are enumerated in V.I. Tikhonov et al., *Lishenie izbitatel'nykh prav v Moskve v 1920–1930–e gody* (Moscow, 1998), 25.

85. AKhSF f. 5248, op. 1, d. 48, l. 74. Ration books were issued by consumers' cooperatives to the laboring population in their region and entitled people to receive a certain ration of food.

86. NKVD RSFSR circular in *Ezhenedel'nik sovetskoi iustitsii* 20 (1930): 30; "Informatsionnoe pis'mo . . ." in *Sovetskaia iustitsiia* 31 (1932): 25.

87. AKhSF f. 5248, op. 1, d. 25, l. 27; "O poriadke priobreteniia . . ." in SU 1932 no. 38, art. 174.

88. Carr and Davies, *Foundations,* 1:34, 660; "O nedopushchenii kulakov i lishentsev v kooperatsiiu," SZ 1930 no. 56, art. 591. The various cooperatives and artels to which the disenfranchised were denied membership are enumerated in AKhSF f. 5248, op. 1, d. 48, l. 74.

89. GARF f. 3316, op. 23, d. 51, l. 11. In March 1927, the Komsomol central committee banned the children of the disenfranchised from admission into the young communist league. Carr, *Foundations,* 2:162.

90. On how the disenfranchised were denied ration books in the city of Moscow, see "Kak v Moskve budut vydavat'sia zabornye knizhki," in *Pravda* 43 (February 21, 1929): 2; David Hoffmann, *Peasant Metropolis: Social Identities in Moscow, 1929–1941* (Ithaca, N.Y., 1994), 146–149; Osokina, *Za fasadom;* Fitzpatrick, *Everyday Stalinism.*

91. AKhSF f. 5248, op. 12, d. 4438, l. 11–12 (Moscow, 1933).

92. AKhSF f. 5248, op. 7, d. 13014, l. 5 (North Caucasus krai, 1931).

93. *Stalin's Letters,* 87. The goal of saving kopecks was clearly related to the purges of the period. One party activist called on female workers to get involved in "the fight against wreckers of the national economy—against embezzlers, thieves, drunkards, against all those who do not know how to save Soviet kopecks." Wood, *Baba and Comrade,* 211.

94. Carr and Davies, *Foundations,* 1:701; Motolov's view had some popular resonance among those concerned about the lifting of rations for the working class while the Soviet administrative elite enjoyed supply privileges ("They eat while we starve!"). See Rossman, "Teikovo Cotton Workers," 49.

95. AKhSF f. 5248, op. 2, d. 3, l. 8.

96. GARF f. 1235, op. 140, d. 723, l. 2.

97. AKhSF f. 5248, op. 13, d. 10513, l. 1–4.

98. AKhSF f. 5248, op. 14, d. 8265, l. 12–15.

99. AKhSF f. 5248, op. 13, d. 8897, l. 6.

100. Paul Josephson, "'Projects of the Century' in Soviet History: Large-Scale Technologies from Lenin to Gorbachev," in *Technology and Culture* 36, no. 3 (July 1995): 519–559; Kuromiya, *Stalin's Industrial Revolution;* Payne, *Stalin's Railroad;* Shearer, *Industry, State, and Society.*

101. GARF f. 5248, op. 2, d. 25, l. 51. They were barred from the on-site evening training schools until the ban on children of the disenfranchised in higher education was lifted. John Scott, *Behind the Urals: An American Worker in Russia's City of Steel* (Bloomington, Ind., 1973), 47.

102. AKhSF f. 5248, op. 14, d. 627.

103. Scott, *Behind the Urals,* 86; Slezkine, *Arctic Mirrors,* 229.

104. VTsIK published Instructions on Elections to the Soviets in December 1918, yet the law only dealt with rural soviets. The 1925 Instructions were the first republic instructions directed at both urban and rural areas, and that also addressed the reinstatement of rights. Tikhonov, *Lishenie,* 28–29.

105. Kutuzov, *Organizatsiia ucheta,* 21.

106. See, for example, AKhSF f. 5248, op. 1, d. 7, l. 71; TsGA g. Moskvy f. 3103, op. 1, d. 16, l. 83; AKhSF f. 5248, op. 1, d. 13, l. 6; AKhSF f. 5248, op. 1, d. 16, l. 19.

107. Wood, *Baba and Comrade,* 8. Similarly, in fascist Italy, active participation was the duty of all true believers. Falasca-Zamponi, *Fascist Spectacle,* 190.

108. Similarly, the Constitution gave the right of amnesty, remission, or rehabilitation for those sentenced by a court or administrative organ to the republic soviet executive committees. 1924 USSR Constitution in *Istoriia sovetskoi konstitutsii,* 226–237.

109. GARF f. 1235, op. 105, d. 173, l. 220.

110. GARF f. 1235, op. 105, d. 173, l. 203. This change then appeared as part of the 1930 TsIK Instructions. "Low-level technical workers" in the former police, gendarmerie, and prison establishment were distinguished from others of their classification and grouped to-

gether with the "class of exploiters" who could be rehabilitated by local officials if they had at least five years of productive, socially useful labor and demonstrated loyalty to Soviet power.

111. These individuals still had to petition through the soviets, as amnesty did not automatically enfranchise them. AKhSF f. 5248, op. 1, d. 9, l. 6.

112. GARF f. 1235, op. 105, d. 173, l. 220. The personal case files of this group can be found in GARF f. 5404.

113. Petitions for the reinstatement of rights and complaints regarding wrongful disenfranchisement were exempt from fees (*svobodno ot gerbovogo sbora*), as were other citizen complaints. GARF f. 1235, op. 105, d. 174, l. 183. See also *Kuda zhalovat'sia na neporiadki* (Moscow, 1926), 16.

114. AKhSF f. 5248, op. 1, d. 129, l. 13.

115. GARF f. 1235, op. 106, d. 519, l. 253.

116. This practice prompted VTsIK to issue a decree stating that new appeals after rejected petitions could not be made until at least a year after the rejection. See VTsIK decree of January 2, 1928.

117. AKhSF f. 5248, op. 17, d. 1205, l. 80–83. Other examples include AKhSF f. 5248, op. 13, d. 6877, l. 46–47, AKhSF f. 5248, op. 13, d. 5261, l. 28–29, and the case of a Tambov man who was disenfranchised in 1927, reinstated in rights that same year, and then dekulakized in 1930. AKhSF f. 5248, op. 17, d. 2805, l. 8.

118. AkhSF f. 5248, op. 1, d. 1, 1. 23.

119. AKhSF f. 5248, op. 2, d. 3, l. 11; AKhSF f. 5248, op. 1, d. 11, l. 10; AKhSF f. 5248, op. 2, d. 7, l. 33; GARF f. 1235, op. 76, d. 146, l. 34. In the 1930s, Solts and Kutuzov chaired other public commissions under the VTsIK Presidium. Solts was chairman of the Amnesty Commission and Kutuzov chairman of the commission that reviewed petitions concerning RSFSR citizenship. A. A. Solts served as chairman of the VTsIK Amnesty Commission until A. S. Kiselev was appointed in 1935. AKhSF f. 5248, op. 1, d. 33, l. 31. AKhSF f. 5248, op. 2, d. 1, l. 64.

120. AKhSF f. 5248, op. 1, d. 13, l. 22.

121. Lagovier, *Perevybory sovetov,* 15; TsGA g. Moskvy f. 3103, op. 1, d. 16, l. 83.

122. GARF f. 1235, op. 106, d. 519, l. 305; AKhSF f. 5248, op. 1, d. 23, l. 43.

123. GARF f. 1235, op. 105, d. 504, l. 68.

124. Tikhonov, *Lishenie,* 40.

125. Volodarskii and Terekhov, *Izbiratel'noe pravo,* 41.

126. GARF f. 1235, op. 106, d. 519, l. 233.

127. GARF f. 393, op. 1, d. 154, l. 592, 602. Officials also reported roughly 20–30 percent of the disenfranchised in the Urals oblast that year filed a petition for the reinstatement of rights.

128. AKhSF f. 5248, op. 2, d. 3, l. 14.

129. GARF f. 1235, op. 106, d. 519, l. 308.

130. AKhSF f. 5248, op. 1, d. 68, l. 229.

131. AKhSF f. 5248, op. 1, d. 13, l. 12; GARF f. 1235, op. 106, d. 519, l. 308.

132. The volume of inquiries led the paper to create a legal department (*iuridicheskii otdel*) that handled letters requesting legal information, clarification, and assistance. RGAE f. 396, op. 2.

133. In particular, the complaints bureaus (*biuro zhalob*) of the Worker-Peasant Inspectorate (*Rabkrin*) and the Soviet Control Commission under Sovnarkom received many complaints from the disenfranchised about the backlog and delays in getting replies from the Central Electoral Commission. AKhSF f. 5248, op. 2, d. 4, l. 46.

134. GARF f. 1235, op. 106, d. 519, l. 308. Kutuzov reported that the largest single group of petitions that was approved by the Central Electoral Commission that year was from former members of the White Army and police.

135. AKhSF f. 5248, op. 1, d. 86, l. 107, 132.

136. AKhSF f. 5248, op. 1, d. 69, l. 115.

137. The commission reinstated rights in 52 percent of the cases it reviewed from the

1927 campaign. GARF f. 1235, op. 105, d. 504, l. 68. After 1928, the rate of success on petitions for the reinstatement of rights that were reviewed by the Central Electoral Commission increased to almost 40 percent in 1929 and around 60 percent in 1930. The rehabilitation rate for outcasts whose cases were reviewed by the CEC remained roughly at this level for a few years, but declined in 1933–1935 to between 40 percent and 50 percent. The success of petitioners then jumped in the first six months of 1936 to around 70 percent of cases reviewed by the CEC. GARF f. 1235, op. 76, d. 126, l. 1-30.

138. GARF f. 1235, op. 106, d. 519, l. 136. Similarly, by the 1930s, while local procurators and judges responded to political pressure in a climate of class war by issuing harsh sentences, the RSFSR Supreme Court changed 90 percent of the sentences that it reviewed, including political cases. Solomon, *Soviet Criminal Justice,* 110.

139. GARF f. 1235, op. 106, d. 519, l. 155.

140. GARF f. 1235, op. 107, d. 368, l. 2; AKhSF f. 5248, op. 1, d. 23, l. 7.

141. GARF f. 3316, op. 23, d. 1189, l. 5–6.

142. GARF f. 1235, op. 106, d. 519, l. 37.

143. GARF f. 3316, op. 29, d. 286, l. 29, 88. The breakdown of republics was as follows: Ukraine and Armenia (32 percent), Azerbaizhan (38 percent), Georgia (36 percent), Tadzhikistan (37 percent). GARF f. 3316, op. 29, d. 286, l. 88.

144. AKhSF f. 5248, op. 1, d. 69, l. 2.

145. AKhSF f. 5248, op. 1, d. 87, l. 256; AKhSF f. 5248, op. 1, d. 7, l. 21; AKhSF f. 5248, op. 1, d. 69, l. 38; AKhSF f. 5248, op. 12, d. 1021, l. 21–22 (Ivanovo Industrial oblast, 1933).

146. AKhSF f. 5248, op. 2, d. 3, l. 55.

147. AKhSF f. 5248, op. 1, d. 69, l. 37.

148. AKhSF f. 5248, op. 1, d. 71, l. 197.

149. AKhSF f. 5248, op. 1, d. 84, l. 356.

150. Lynne Attwood and Catriona Kelly, "Programmes for Identity: The 'New Man' and the 'New Woman,'" in Catriona Kelly and David Shepherd, eds. *Constructing Russian Culture in the Age of Revolution: 1881–1940* (Oxford, U.K., 1998), 276–279.

151. AKhSF f. 5248, op. 1, d. 80, l. 23; AKhSF f. 5248, op. 1, d. 74, l. 69; AKhSF f. 5248, op. 1, d. 74, l. 199; AKhSF f. 5248, op. 1, d. 84, l. 229.

152. Katerina Clark, *The Soviet Novel: History as Ritual,* 3d ed. (Bloomington, Ind., 2000); Frederick C. Corney, *Writing October: History, Memory, Identity, and the Construction of the Bolshevik Revolution* (Ph.D. diss., Columbia University, 1997).

153. One man's petition was rejected because he returned from emigration illegally in 1924. See AKhSF f. 5248, op. 1, d. 74, l. 111.

154. AKhSF f. 5248, op. 1, d. 80, l. 285.

155. AKhSF f. 5248, op. 1, d. 85, l. 149; AKhSF f. 5248, op. 1, d. 83, l. 308.

156. AKhSF f. 5248, op. 1, d. 83, l. 291; AKhSF f. 5248, op. 1, d. 84, l. 356. In the late 1920s, Soviet officials believed that underground lawyers (*podpol'nye advokaty*) and mediators had taken shelter in the villages. One letter from an exasperated official alerted the public to the large presence of "generally illiterate" underground lawyers in the countryside: ". . . they write such nonsense [*chush'*] in their statements and complaints that they make a reader's head spin." *Krest'ianskii iurist* 11 (1929): 12–13. On the underground lawyer in Russia, see Eugene Huskey, *Russian Lawyers and the Soviet State* (Princeton, N.J., 1986); V.M. Kuritsyn, *Perekhod k NEPu i revoliutsionnaia zakonnost'* (Moscow, 1972); Wirtschafter, *Social Identity,* 94.

157. AKhSF f. 5248, op. 1, d. 85, l. 31; AKhSF f. 5248, op. 1, d. 86, l. 323.

158. AKhSF f. 5248, op. 1, d. 78, l. 15.

159. Lewin, *Making,* 281. See also Fitzpatrick, *Stalin's Peasants;* and Kharkhordin, *The Collective and the Individual.*

160. AKhSF f. 5248, op. 1, d. 70, l. 6; AKhSF f. 5248, op. 1, d. 79, l. 36; AKhSF f. 5248, op. 1, d. 87, l. 240.

161. TsGA g. Moskvy f. 3103, op. 1, d. 16, l. 6.

162. AKhSF f. 5248, op. 1, d. 7, l. 30.

163. Hunt, *Politics, Culture, and Class,* 44–45; Falasca-Zamponi, *Fascist Spectacle,* 101.

2. Faces of the Disenfranchised

1. RGAE f. 396, op. 3, d. 36, l. 20.

2. AKhSF f. 5248, op. 1, d. 11, l. 52.

3. GARF f. 1235, op. 74, d. 423, l. 201, 215; GARF f. 1235, op. 74, d. 427, l. 145; GARF f. 1235, op. 74, d. 427, l. 149; GARF f. 3316, op. 29, d. 967, l. 2; AKhSF f. 5248, op. 1, d. 48, l. 48; AKhSF f. 5248, op. 1, d. 26, l. 50; Lagovier, *Perevybory sovetov,* 45.

4. AKhSF f. 5248, op. 1, d. 26, l. 237; AKhSF f. 5248, op. 1, d. 16, l. 49. On self-evidence and classification, see Mary Douglas, *Implicit Meanings* (London, 1975).

5. GARF f. 1235, op. 141, d. 145, l. 17.

6. AKhSF f. 5248, op. 1, d. 51, l. 110.

7. GARF f. 1235, op. 140, d. 269, l. 505; Carr, *Foundations,* 2:283; GARF f. 1235, op. 141, d. 145, l. 25.

8. GARF f. 1235, op. 105, d. 174, l. 272; GARF f. 3316, op. 20, d. 962, l. 2.

9. GARF f. 1235, op. 74, d. 427, l. 109.

10. GARF f. 3316, op. 23, d. 1210, l. 19.

11. "Instruktsiia o vyborakh v sovety," in SZ 1926 no. 66, art. 501.

12. AKhSF f. 5248, op. 2, d. 3, l. 20.

13. AKhSF f. 5248, op. 1, d. 68, l. 22.

14. GARF f. 393, op. 1, d. 154, l. 602.

15. GARF f. 1235, op. 106, d. 526, l. 30–31.

16. GARF f. 1235, op. 141, d. 114, l. 142–144; GARF f. 1235, op. 106, d. 519, l. 80.

17. GARF f. 1235, op. 106, d. 519, l. 138, 143, 134–135. People were disenfranchised "without any documentation, solely on the basis of verbal complaints and slander." GARF f. 1235, op. 141, d. 126, l. 3. One inspector from Moscow went so far as to say, "I didn't find even one case in which disenfranchisement was grounded on documentary evidence." GARF f. 1235, op. 106, d. 519, l. 11–12.

18. GARF f. 1235, op. 106, d. 519, l. 146; GARF f. 1235, op. 106, d. 519, l. 227.

19. Tikhonov, *Lishenie,* 31, 45.

20. GARF f. 1235, op. 141, d. 1506, l. 31–32. GARF f. 3316, op. 23, d. 1204, l. 2. For example, a man was levied an excessive fixed-quota tax in 1930 and, after he failed to pay, he was disenfranchised. AKhSF f. 5248, op. 12, d. 1825, l. 17. Some villages witnessed the wholesale disenfranchisement of so-called "kratniki," peasants who were required to impose self-taxation. GARF f. 374, op. 27, d. 1966, l. 2–20.

21. AKhSF f. 5248, op. 14, d. 13491, l. 18, 24.

22. In a 1931 memo to VTsIK, the soviet executive committee of the Ivanovo Industrial province noted that the district and city soviets almost always get help from the police when they are reviewing voting rights cases and need supporting documents and data to verify a decision. GARF f. 1235, op. 141, d. 1141, l. 47. On how the housing management and police worked together in compiling the lists of disenfranchised persons in Moscow, see Tikhonov, *Lishenie,* 31, 45–46.

23. GARF f. 1235, op. 107, d. 368, l. 27.

24. GARF f. 374, op. 27, d. 1966, l. 2–20.

25. AKhSF f. 5248, op. 1, d. 50, l. 282–287.

26. GARF f. 374, op. 27, d. 1966, l. 2–20.

27. GARF f. 393, op. 1, d. 95, l. 10.

28. GARF f. 1235, op. 141, d. 1506, l. 31–32; AKhSF f. 5248, op. 17, d. 4805, l. 4–5; AKhSF f. 5248, op. 13, d. 4857, l. 7.

29. Kutuzov, *Organizatsiia ucheta,* 28.

30. GARF f. 1235, op. 104, d. 1148, l. 6. One man publicly called the chairman of the

·rural soviet a Red Army deserter for which he was later disenfranchised. AKhSF f. 5248, op. 13, d. 817, l. 18–22. People considered loud were deprived of rights "so that the campaign would progress with less criticism . . . peacefully, easily, and without any disturbances [*buzy*]." GARF f. 1235, op. 106, d. 519, l. 253.

31. AKhSF f. 5248, op. 1, d. 4, l. 13; GARF f. 1235, op. 106, d. 519, l. 134–135.

32. GARF f. 1235, op. 141, d. 114, l. 142–144.

33. Volodarskii and Terekhov, *Izbiratel'noe pravo,* 46. GARF f. 1235, op. 74, d. 423, l. 195.

34. Numerous examples include: AKhSF f. 5248, op. 13, d. 6271, l. 3; AKhSF f. 5248, op. 13, d. 3645, l. 5; AKhSF f. 5248, op. 12, d. 1825, l. 17; AKhSF f. 5248, op. 17, d. 3605, l. 10; AKhSF f. 5248, op. 14, d. 828, l. 8–9; AKhSF f. 5248, op. 1, d. 50, l. 282–287; AKhSF f. 5248, op. 17, d. 8405, l. 19.

35. AKhSF f. 5248, op. 10, d. 1191, l. 3. In 1933, the secretary of the CEC, I. Raab, stated that in most complaints of wrongful disenfranchisement petitioners claimed that they were deprived of rights because personal scores were being settled. GARF f. 1235, op. 141, d. 1506, l. 26–27.

36. GARF f. 1235, op. 141, d. 150, l. 16.

37. On backlash against those who write complaints, see Golfo Alexopoulos, "Exposing Illegality and Oneself: Complaint and Risk in Stalin's Russia," in *Reforming Justice in Russia, 1864–1994: Power, Culture, and the Limits of Legal Order,* ed. Peter Solomon (New York, 1997).

38. AKhSF f. 5248, op. 13, d. 3799, l. 36. People were deprived of rights for "unmasking the class enemy's criminal activity" within the rural soviet or kolkhoz management. GARF f. 1235, op. 141, d. 1506, l. 26–27.

39. GARF f. 1235, op. 141, d. 586, l. 5–8.

40. GARF f. 1235, op. 141, d. 1506, l. 26–27. In the Ulchinskii raion, a man was disenfranchised "because he had grain and did not share it with others who did not." GARF f. 1235, op. 141, d. 1506, l. 11.

41. AKhSF f. 5248, op. 17, d. 3605, l. 10.

42. AKhSF f. 5248, op. 1, d. 23, l. 34.

43. AKhSF f. 5248, op. 14, d. 13491, l. 46. A Moscow official reported in 1929 that a rumor had been circulating to the effect that all of the disenfranchised would be evicted from their apartments. This, he argued, caused a "mass of false denunciations." AKhSF f. 5248, op. 1, d. 129, l. 50.

44. AKhSF f. 5248, op. 12, d. 4438, l. 11–12.

45. According to Lenskii, the attacks against him began when his wife testified against the former chairman of the housing management, Tkachenko, who beat the doorman. This incited Tkachenko against him. RTsKhIDNI f. 613, op. 3, d. 109, l. 6–7.

46. RTsKhIDNI f. 613, op. 3, d. 109, l. 3.

47. Rabkrin wrote a letter to the OGPU asking for information on whether Lenskii had the name "Svinobaev" before the revolution, but the OGPU claimed that it had no information on Lenskii. RTsKhIDNI f. 613, op. 3, d. 109, l. 8–9, 11.

48. RTsKhIDNI f. 613, op. 3, d. 109, l. 14, 17–18, 19.

49. Richard Stites, *Revolutionary Dreams: Utopian Vision and Experimental Life in the Russian Revolution* (Oxford, U.K., 1989), 117. On the egotism and rudeness of the bourgeoisie and the demand for politeness in the new Soviet order, see also Figes and Kolonitskii, *Interpreting,* 115, 178.

50. RTsKhIDNI f. 613, op. 3, d. 109, l. 6–7.

51. RTsKhIDNI f. 613, op. 3, d. 109, l. 16.

52. GARF f. 1235, op. 106, d. 519, l. 131–132.

53. AKhSF f. 5248, op. 1, d. 55, l. 65.

54. RTsKhIDNI, f. 17, op. 85, d. 487, l. 228.

55. AKhSF f. 5248, op. 1, d. 129, l. 141–142. In fact, any contact with the courts was often used as justification to deny people their rights. AKhSF f. 5248, op. 1, d. 129, l. 141; GARF f. 1235, op. 106, d. 526, l. 30–31; GARF f. 1235, op. 106, d. 519, l. 146.

56. GARF f. 5248, op. 1, d. 129, l. 141.
57. TsGA g. Moskvy f. 3103, op. 1, d. 12, l. 28.
58. TsGA g. Moskvy f. 3103, op. 1, d. 16, l. 6; TsGA g. Moskvy f. 3103, op. 1, d. 14, l. 97; TsGA g. Moskvy f. 3103, op. 1, d. 13, l. 19.
59. GARF f. 393, op. 1, d. 95, l. 136; GARF f. 1235, op. 104, d. 265, l. 133–135.
60. AKhSF f. 5248, op. 7, d. 4414, l. 15–16.
61. Davies, *Popular Opinion,* 136.
62. AKhSF f. 5248, op. 7, d. 12814, l. 8, 15, 29–31, 56.
63. Carr, *Foundations,* 2:139–143.
64. AKhSF f. 5248, op. 7, d. 12814, l. 29–31.
65. Terry Martin, "The Origins of Soviet Ethnic Cleansing," *Journal of Modern History* 70 (1998): 813–861.
66. Carr, *Foundations,* 2:287, 395–397.
67. Carr, *Foundations,* 2:287.
68. GARF f. 393, op. 1, d. 94, l. 130.
69. GARF f. 1235, op. 104, d. 1119, l. 49. In 1926–1927 private trade as a percentage of total rural trade was officially determined to be highest in Central Asia and Transcaucasia. Carr and Davies, *Foundations,* 1:665.
70. GARF f. 1235, op. 104, d. 1146, l. 36.
71. GARF f. 1235, op. 104, d. 1119, l. 7.
72. GARF f. 1235, op. 104, d. 263.
73. GARF f. 5248, op. 1, d. 68, l. 229; GARF f. 1235, op. 141, d. 155, l. 3; GARF f. 5248, op. 1, d. 4, l. 74–78; GARF f. 3316, op. 23, d. 1189, l. 17; GARF f. 393, op. 1, d. 156, l. 16–17; GARF f. 393, op. 1, d. 153, l. 20–23; GARF f. 393, op. 1, d. 94, l. 129–130.
74. Isaac Babel, *1920 Diary* (New Haven, Conn., 1995), 33, 85.
75. GARF f. 1235, op. 141, d. 126, l. 3. See also Martin, *Affirmative Action Empire,* 43.
76. GARF f. 1235, op. 141, d. 126, l. 3.
77. GARF f. 1235, op. 141, d. 126, l. 3. Also considered "aliens," Jews in Imperial Russia were similarly restricted in place of residence and freedom of movement, excluded from the legal professions and participation in local government and limited in their right to vote, serve in the military and acquire an education. See Benjamin Pinkus, *The Jews of the Soviet Union: The History of a National Minority* (Cambridge, U.K., 1988), 23–27; Ben Nathans, *Beyond the Pale: The Jewish Encounter with Late Imperial Russia* (Berkeley, Calif., 2002).
78. AKhSF f. 5248, op. 11, d. 620, l. 27 (Western oblast, 1932).
79. GARF f. 393, op. 1, d. 95, l. 467.
80. GARF f. 1235, op. 112, d. 28, l. 6.
81. GARF f. 1235, op. 104, d. 1148, l. 4.
82. GARF f. 1235, op. 104, d. 1148, l. 7.
83. AKhSF f. 5248, op. 1, d. 14, l. 6.
84. AKhSF f. 5248, op. 1, d. 4, l. 49.
85. Slezkine, *Arctic Mirrors,* 152, 226–228; Grant, *Soviet House of Culture,* 92–96.
86. AKhSF f. 5248, op. 1, d. 54, l. 219.
87. In prerevolutionary Russia, the ratio of total clergy (deacons, and so on) to laymen was roughly 1:3 and for priests only it was as low as 1:1,000. Gregory L. Freeze, *The Parish Clergy in Nineteenth-Century Russia* (Princeton, N.J., 1983), 64.
88. GARF f. 1235, op. 141, d. 150, l. 19.
89. AKhSF f. 5248, op. 2, d. 13, l. 19.
90. TsGA g. Moskvy f. 3103, op. 1, d. 14, l. 37.
91. AKhSF f. 5248, op. 1, d. 52, l. 19.
92. GARF f. 1235, op. 141, d. 150, l. 19; AKhSF f. 5248, op. 1, d. 129, l. 141. A peasant was deprived of voting rights because a bloodhound barked at him, and he was consequently perceived as a suspicious element. Lagovier, *Perevybory sovetov,* 34.
93. AKhSF f. 5248, op. 1, d. 140, l. 23.
94. AKhSF f. 5248, op. 1, d. 129, l. 141.

95. AKhSF f. 5248, op. 1, d. 4, l. 84.
96. GARF f. 393, op. 1, d. 95, l. 10.
97. Lagovier, *Perevybory sovetov*, 35.
98. GARF f. 1235, op. 141, d. 118, l. 35.
99. AKhSF f. 5248, op. 1, d. 129, l. 141; GARF f. 1235, op. 141, d. 114, l. 5.
100. GARF f. 1235, op. 141, d. 150, l. 19.
101. AKhSF f. 5248, op. 1, d. 129, l. 141; In the Don okrug, people were deprived of rights "for drunkenness and playing cards." GARF f. 1235, op. 141, d. 155, l. 2.
102. GARF f. 1235, op. 106, d. 519, l. 131–132.
103. AKhSF f. 5248, op. 1, d. 17, l. 6.
104. GARF f. 1235, op. 106, d. 519, l. 253; Tikhonov, *Lishenie,* 28.
105. AKhSF f. 5248, op. 1, d. 4, l. 13; In the Omsk okrug, someone was deprived of rights for having a "restless disposition." AKhSF f. 5248, op. 1, d. 129, l. 141.
106. AKhSF f. 5248, op. 1, d. 4, l. 84.
107. AKhSF f. 5248, op. 1, d. 51, l. 363; Tikhonov, *Lishenie,* 28; AKhSF f. 5248, op. 1, d. 129, l. 50, 142.
108. AKhSF f. 5248, op. 1, d. 129, l. 141; AKhSF f. 5248, op. 1, d. 39, l. 2.
109. On prostitution, see Wood, *Baba and Comrade,* 111–114; N. B. Lebina, *Povsednevnaia zhizn' sovetskogo goroda 1920–1930 gody: normy i anomalii* (St. Petersburg, 1999), 79–98.
110. AKhSF f. 5248, op. 1, d. 129, l. 50.
111. AKhSF f. 5248, op. 1, d. 129, l. 141.
112. GARF f. 1235, op. 106, d. 526, l. 30–31. This incident was also mentioned in AKhSF f. 5248, op. 2, d. 3, l. 21; and at a meeting of the CEC Plenum in April, 1929, in GARF f. 1235, op. 106, d. 519, l. 66.
113. AKhSF f. 5248, op. 1, d. 129, l. 141. In contrast, women who married young were rewarded with rights. Some regions in the 1926–1927 campaign included married women seventeen years old and under the legal voting age on the list of voters. AKhSF f. 5248, op. 1, d. 140, l. 23.
114. "Rank two" constituted trade by an individual or family members conducted with booths, tables, carts, and so on at markets and bazaars or trade by no more than two people from small permanent facilities, such as a kiosk. Ball, "Private Trade," 92–93.
115. GARF f. 1235, op. 74, d. 423, l. 182 (n/a, 1930).
116. GARF f. 1235, op. 106, d. 519, l. 251; GARF f. 1235, op. 106, d. 519, l. 131–132.
117. Viola, "The Second Coming."
118. AKhSF f. 5248, op. 1, d. 129, l. 142.
119. GARF f. 1235, op. 106, d. 519, l. 140; GARF f. 1235, op. 104, d. 263, l. 138–140. According to a TsIK and Sovnarkom decree of March 21, 1924, invalids from labor or war have the right to conduct trade on a free license up to rank two. Trade was intended as social security (*sotsial'noe obespechenie*) for invalids and could not be grounds for disenfranchisement. SU 1924 no. 45, art. 426. In 1926, Kalinin issued a circular from VTsIK that described the free license to trade for invalids (those injured from work and war) "as an equivalent of social security for invalids." Therefore, they should maintain their voting rights although they engaged in trade. AKhSF f. 5248, op. 1, d. 1, l. 50.
120. GARF f. 1235, op. 106, d. 519, l. 138.
121. GARF f. 1235, op. 106, d. 519, l. 141.
122. GARF f. 1235, op. 104, d. 262, l. 2. Other examples include AKhSF f. 5248, op. 12, d. 3634, l. 3–4 (Samara, 1930); AKhSF f. 5248, op. 10, d. 5943, l. 4–5 (Udmurtsk AO, 1932).
123. AKhSF f. 5248, op. 14, d. 3240, l. 21–22 (Leningrad oblast, 1935).
124. Wood, *Baba and Comrade,* 173–175.
125. For example, a former trader insisted that he borrowed money from local traders to enable him to trade; he did not have his own capital but was poor. AKhSF f. 5248, op. 9, d. 7782, l. 21 (Western oblast, 1930). A man from Dagestan, deprived of rights for hiring a shepherd, claimed that the employment agreement was in fact made by someone else. AKhSF f. 5248, op. 9, d. 3603, l. 18 (Dagestan ASSR, 1931).

126. AKhSF f. 5248, op. 9, d. 10966, l. 12 (Western oblast, 1931).

127. AKhSF f. 5248, op. 9, d. 5991, l. 8 (Central Black Earth oblast, 1930).

128. This image is examined further in Golfo Alexopoulos, "Victim Talk: Defense Testimony and Denunciation Under Stalin," *Law and Social Inquiry* 24 (1999): 501–518.

129. GARF f. 1235, op. 105, d. 173, l. 84; GARF f. 1235, op. 106, d. 519, l. 176.

130. GARF f. 1235, op. 141, d. 114, l. 39.

131. GARF f. 1235, op. 106, d. 519, l. 141.

132. Lagovier, *Perevybory sovetov*, 32. GARF f. 1235, op. 106, d. 519, l. 194; AKhSF 5248, op. 1, d. 129, l. 141–142; GARF f. 1235, op. 105, d. 174, l. 251.

133. Kimberling, "Civil Rights and Social Policy," 39.

134. Lagovier, *Perevybory sovetov*, 33.

135. GARF f. 1235, op. 106, d. 519, l. 134–135.

136. Christine Worobec, "Witchcraft Beliefs and Practices in Prerevolutionary Russian and Ukrainian Villages," *Russian Review* 54 (1995): 165–187.

137. A study in 1928 that counted the "bourgeoisie" in Russia included among them peddlers, people renting out a room in an apartment, and small merchants, as well as entrepreneurs for an inflated total of 855,000 people (2,705,000 including their families). Lewin, *Making*, 214.

138. GARF f. 374, op. 27, d. 1966, l. 2–20.

139. AKhSF f. 5248, op. 1, d. 129, l. 142; GARF f. 1235, op. 106, d. 519, l. 100–101; GARF f. 374, op. 27, d. 1966, l. 2–20; GARF f. 1235, op. 106, d. 519, l. 306.

140. AKhSF f. 5248, op. 2, d. 2, l. 13. In the Far North, grooms working for their brides, widows living with relatives, and poorer kinsmen provided with temporary reindeer herds became 'hired labor', so those who hired them were subject to disenfranchisement. Slezkine, *Arctic Mirrors*, 198.

141. GARF f. 1235, op. 105, d. 173, l. 167–168.

142. Lewin, *Making*, 86, 133, 214–215; Carr and Davies, *Foundations*, 1:135–136.

143. Slezkine, *Arctic Mirrors*, 199.

144. Volodarskii and Terekhov, *Izbiratel'noe pravo*, 32, 43; GARF f. 1235, op. 141, d. 151, l. 143.

145. Lagovier, *Perevybory sovetov*, 35; GARF f. 1235, op. 106, d. 519, l. 176; RGAE f. 396, op. 3, d. 416, l. 6.

146. GARF f. 5248, op. 1, d. 129, l. 141; AKhSF f. 5248, op. 1, d. 129, l. 141.

147. GARF f. 1235, op. 141, d. 586, l. 9–13.

148. GARF f. 1235, op. 106, d. 519, l. 202.

149. Lagovier, *Perevybory sovetov*, 35; TsGA g. Moskvy, f. 3103, op. 1, d. 15, l. 3, 6.

150. Lagovier, *Perevybory sovetov*, 35.

151. Potapov and Fedorovskii, *Kto lishaetsia*, 15.

152. AKhSF f. 5248, op. 1, d. 129, l. 142.

153. GARF f. 1235, op. 104, d. 1148, l. 6. Deaf mutes were disenfranchised in many other regions as well. See GARF f. 1235, op. 106, d. 519, l. 194; AKhSF f. 5248, op. 1, d. 129, l. 141; AKhSF f. 5248, op. 2, d. 3, l. 18; GARF f. 393, op. 1, d. 154, l. 632; FGATO f. 434, op. 4, d. 26, l. 12.

154. GARF f. 393, op. 1, d. 154, l. 612.

155. Lagovier, *Perevybory sovetov*, 34.

156. AKhSF f. 5248, op. 1, d. 129, l. 141.

157. Wirtschafter, *Social Identity*, 106–107; Steven Hoch, *Serfdom and Social Control in Russia: Petrovskoe, a Village in Tambov* (Chicago, 1986), 154–159; Kotsonis, *Making Peasants Backward*, 145–147; Viola, *Peasant Rebels*, 230. Even in contemporary Russia, former Soviet citizens applying for Russian citizenship face a similar obstacle, as local authorities are reluctant to register immigrants because they do not want "to have to supply them with social services" and this is "particularly difficult for non-Russians." NPR Morning Edition, February 21, 2001, Hour 1, Burrelle's Transcript, 8.

158. Carr and Davies, *Foundations*, 1:605–609.

159. TsGA g. Moskvy f. 3118, op. 1, d. 285, l. 22.
160. Carr, *Foundations,* 2:279, 287.
161. AKhSF f. 5248, op. 1, d. 5, l. 36.
162. GARF f. 1235, op. 106, d. 519, l. 227; AKhSF f. 5248, op. 1, d. 140, l. 23; AKhSF f. 5248, op. 1, d. 129, l. 141; AKhSF f. 5248, op. 2, d. 3, l. 19; GARF f. 1235, op. 106, d. 526, l. 30–31. In 1923, a man from the Khabarovsk gubernia wrote a letter to *Krest'ianskaia gazeta* asking whether his rural soviet acted properly by disenfranchising all peasants age 50 and over. RGAE f. 396, op. 3, d. 715, l. 20.
163. AKhSF f. 5248, op. 17, d. 10805, l. 3–4.
164. GARF f. 1235, op. 141, d. 150, l. 19.
165. GARF f. 1235, op. 141, d. 114, l. 18. It was not unusual for women who lived alone to be the target of rural repression. Not only was property vandalized and seized from nobles, officers, priests, Jews, and foreigners shortly after the Revolution but from widows and single women as well. See Andrea Graziosi, *The Great Soviet Peasant War: Bolsheviks and Peasants, 1917–1933* (Cambridge, Mass., 1996), 12.
166. AKhSF f. 5248, op. 1, d. 11, l. 33.
167. GARF f. 1235, op. 141, d. 145, l. 28–29.
168. GARF f. 1235, op. 106, d. 519, l. 133.
169. GARF f. 1235, op. 106, d. 519, l. 77; AKhSF f. 5248, op. 1, d. 68, l. 24.
170. GARF f. 1235, op. 106, d. 519, l. 147; Lagovier, *Perevybory sovetov,* 24–25; GARF f. 1235, op. 141, d. 150, l. 19; GARF f. 393, op. 1, d. 154, l. 612.
171. GARF f. 1235, op. 106, d. 519, l. 134–135.
172. Slezkine, *Arctic Mirrors,* 200; Lagovier, *Perevybory sovetov,* 24–25; GARF f. 1235, op. 106, d. 519, l. 146; Viola, *Peasant Rebels,* 88. Viola describes the peasant claim that "we have no kulaks here" as "an implicit form of resistance, an implicit act of defense on behalf of the whole village."
173. AKhSF f. 5248, op. 1, d. 5, l. 36.
174. Lagovier, *Perevybory sovetov,* 24–25.
175. AKhSF f. 5248, op. 1, d. 129, l. 142.
176. AKhSF f. 5248, op. 1, d. 68, l. 11.
177. AKhSF f. 5248, op. 1, d. 68, l. 11.
178. AKhSF f. 5248, op. 1, d. 129, l. 142; AKhSF f. 5248, op. 1, d. 66, l. 30; AKhSF f. 5248, op. 1, d. 63, l. 100; AKhSF f. 5248, op. 2, d. 3, l. 19; GARF f. 1235, op. 106, d. 519, l. 129; GARF f. 1235, op. 112, d. 28, l. 2.
179. GARF f. 1235, op. 105, d. 173, l. 167–168.
180. GARF f. 1235, op. 104, d. 265, l. 133.
181. AKhSF f. 5248, op. 14, d. 6657, l. 12–13. In another case, a Siberian man claimed that he was deprived of rights while he was away from his village and working in industry. AKhSF f. 5248, op. 9, d. 8578, l. 5.
182. AKhSF f. 5248, op. 10, d. 3765, l. 7; AKhSF f. 5248, op. 16, d. 213, l. 21.
183. AKhSF f. 5248, op. 9, d. 3802, l. 24; AKhSF f. 5248, op. 14, d. 6054, l. 12–15; AKhSF f. 5248, op. 17, d. 8405, l. 19.
184. AKhSF f. 5248, op. 9, d. 10170, l. 13–14.
185. TsGA g. Moskva f. 3118, op. 1, d. 324, l. 5.

3. Dangers, Disappearances, and False Appearances

1. GARF f. 1235, op. 106, d. 526, l. 114.
2. AKhSF f. 5248, op. 1, d. 51, l. 110.
3. GARF f. 1235, op. 141, d. 145, l. 20.
4. GARF f. 1235, op. 141, d. 145, l. 19.
5. AKhSF f. 5248, op. 7, d. 5814, l. 5 (Moscow, 1930); AKhSF f. 5248, op. 9, d. 3603, l. 36 (Dagestan ASSR, 1930).

6. AKhSF f. 5248, op. 9, d. 8976, l. 7 (Crimea ASSR, 1931).

7. AKhSF f. 5248, op. 7, d. 9014, l. 13 (Nizhnyi Novgorod krai, 1930).

8. GARF f. 1235, op. 141, d. 145, l. 16.

9. Ledeneva, *Russia's Economy of Favours,* 19, 21.

10. AKhSF f. 5248, op. 1, d. 129, l. 92.

11. AKhSF f. 5248, op. 1, d. 11, l. 54.

12. AKhSF f. 5248, op. 1, d. 51, l. 120.

13. AKhSF f. 5248, op. 1, d. 44, l. 37.

14. GARF f. 1235, op. 106, d. 526, l. 66.

15. AKhSF f. 5248, op. 1, d. 51, l. 350.

16. GARF f. 1235, op. 106, d. 526, l. 66–67.

17. Tikhonov, *Lishenie,* 39.

18. AKhSF f. 5248, op. 1, d. 129, l. 10.

19. GARF f. 1235, op. 106, d. 519, l. 100–101, 134–135.

20. GARF f. 1235, op. 141, d. 145, l. 19, 21.

21. GARF f. 1235, op. 141, d. 195, l. 1.

22. AKhSF f. 5248, op. 1, d. 9, l. 21; GARF f. 1235, op. 106, d. 339, l. 66; GARF f. 1235, op. 104, d. 262, l. 218; AKhSF f. 5248, op. 1, d. 15, l. 29.

23. *V. I. Lenin i I. V. Stalin,* 61.

24. GARF f. 1235, op. 141, d. 145, l. 25. Solts made statements against what he perceived to be the excessively harsh and unfair punishment of ordinary "toilers," in such policies as dekulakization and the August 7, 1932, law on socialist property. See Solomon, *Soviet Criminal Justice,* 105.

25. GARF f. 1235, op. 141, d. 145, l. 20.

26. GARF f. 1235, op. 141, d. 145, l. 24.

27. GARF f. 1235, op. 141, d. 145, l. 28–29.

28. Quoted in Daniel Field, *Rebels in the Name of the Tsar* (Boston, Mass., 1989), 2.

29. AKhSF f. 5248, op. 13, d. 9099, l. 37 (Leningrad oblast, 1933).

30. AKhSF f. 5248, op. 14, d. 12687, l. 13 (Gorkii, 1935).

31. AKhSF f. 5248, op. 7, d. 9014, l. 7 (Nizhnyi Novgorod krai, 1930).

32. AKhSF f. 5248, op. 17, d. 2205, l. 43–44 (Krasnoiarsk krai, 1936).

33. AKhSF f. 5248, op. 10, d. 2577, l. 33–34 (Western oblast, 1929).

34. Michel Foucault, *The History of Sexuality: An Introduction* (New York, 1978), 95.

35. GARF f. 1235. op. 141, d. 1052 (1931).

36. AKhSF f. 5248, op. 7, d. 11614, l. 5 (Central Black Earth oblast, 1930).

37. AKhSF f. 5248, op. 9, d. 11762, l. 30–31 (Rostov on Don, n/a).

38. AKhSF f. 5248, op. 9, d. 3603, l. 3 (Dagestan ASSR, 1931).

39. RGAE f. 396 op. 3, d. 36, l. 26 (1925).

40. GARF f. 1235, op. 141, d. 145, l. 18.

41. *Ezhenedel'nik sovetskoi iustitsii* 18 (1929), 424.

42. *Ezhenedel'nik sovetskoi iustitsii* 19 (1929): 445. Originally published in *Trud* 63 (1929).

43. *Ezhenedel'nik sovetskoi iustitsii* 20 (1929): 471. The issue is also discussed in *Sudebnaia praktika* 16 (1930): 7; *Sudebnaia praktika* 14/15 (1930): 10.

44. Fitzpatrick, *Stalin's Peasants,* 62–63.

45. *Izvestiia* 81 (March 23, 1930).

46. *Zakonodatel'stvo o lishenii i vostanovlenii v izbiratel'nykh pravakh* (Leningrad, 1930), 6–10.

47. GARF f. 374, op. 27, d. 1966, l. 15.

48. *Ezhenedel'nik sovetskoi iustitsii* 20 (1930): 30.

49. AKhSF f. 5248, op. 1, d. 48, l. 75. Those who engaged in socially useful labor were supposed to receive ration books, see *Sovetskaia iustitsiia* 30 (1930): 23.

50. Kutuzov, *Organizatsiia ucheta,* 21–22, 30; *Izvestiia* 60 (March 14, 1929). On the 1930 law, see Lagovier, *Perevybory sovetov,* 48; *Zakonodatel'stvo o lishenii,* 9.

51. AKhSF f. 5248, op. 1, d. 32, l. 9–10.

52. GARF f. 1235, op. 104, d. 263, l. 142–143; Volodarskii and Terekhov, *Izbiratel'noe pravo*, 26.

53. AKhSF f. 5248, op. 1, d. 15, l. 14.

54. AKhSF f. 5248, op. 1, d. 13, l. 6.

55. AKhSF f. 5248, op. 1, d. 42, l. 40.

56. AKhSF f. 5248, op. 1, d. 16, l. 15.

57. AKhSF f. 5248, op. 1, d. 22, l. 33; GARF f. 1235, op. 106, d. 519, l. 387.

58. GARF f. 3316, op. 20, d. 958, l. 3; GARF f. 3316, op. 21, d. 133, l. 1.

59. GARF f. 1235, op. 141, d. 145, l. 28–29.

60. GARF f. 3316, op. 21, d. 132, l. 3; AKhSF f. 5248, op. 1, d. 40, l. 33; GARF f. 3316, op. 20, d. 947, l. 12.

61. GARF f. 1235, op. 141, d. 500, l. 1, 5.

62. Ibid.

63. AKhSF f. 5248, op. 1, d. 42, l. 8, 29.

64. From a meeting of the Supreme Court Plenum on July 16, 1930, in *Sudebnaia praktika* 11 (1930): 2.

65. *Sovetskaia iustitsiia* 29 (1934): 6.

66. AKhSF f. 5248, op. 1, d. 51, l. 120.

67. AKhSF f. 5248, op. 1, d. 48, l. 13. The decree appeared in *Izvestiia*, November 12, 1931. See also *Sovetskaia iustitsiia* 10 (April 10, 1932): 26.

68. AKhSF f. 5248, op. 1, d. 48, l. 13, 74–75.

69. Il'ia Il'f and Evgenii Petrov, *Sobranie sochenenii*,(Moscow, 1961) 2:53.

70. Tikhonov, *Lishenie*, 35.

71. GARF f. 1235, op. 106, d. 337, l. 13.

72. GARF f. 1235, op. 141, d. 1141, l. 63.

73. AKhSF f. 5248, op. 1, d. 48, l. 52–53; AKhSF f. 5248, op. 1, d. 40, l. 15; AKhSF f. 5248, op. 1, d. 40, l. 10.

74. AKhSF f. 5248, op. 1, d. 18, l. 6.

75. AKhSF f. 5248, op. 1, d. 6, l. 15.

76. GARF f. 1235, op. 141, d. 145, l. 19.

77. GARF f. 1235, op. 106, d. 526, l. 114.

78. GARF f. 1235, op. 141, d. 145, l. 9.

79. Tikhonov, *Lishenie*, 44.

80. AKhSF f. 5248, op. 1, d. 51, l. 7.

81. Administrative exiles and others sentenced to deprivation of rights by a court were included on the list of the disenfranchised in the place where they served their term of exile and not in their former place of residence. AKhSF f. 5248, op. 1, d. 50, l. 268.

82. GARF f. 1235, op. 106, d. 519, l. 11–12.

83. AKhSF f. 5248, op. 1, d. 51, l. 181.

84. Fitzpatrick, "The Problem of Class Identity," and "Ascribing Class."

85. Tikhonov, *Lishenie*, 35.

86. AKhSF f. 5248, op. 1, d. 51, l. 110.

87. GARF f. 5248, op. 1, d. 140, l. 116.

88. Carr and Davies, *Foundations,* 1:62, 256, 393–394, 397.

89. Fitzpatrick, *Stalin's Peasants,* 77.

90. AKhSF f. 5248, op. 1, d. 129, l. 92.

91. GARF f. 1235, op. 106, d. 526, l. 66, 95; AKhSF f. 5248, op. 1, d. 61, l. 31.

92. AKhSF f. 5248, op. 1, d. 51, l. 120.

93. AKhSF f. 5248, op. 1, d. 51, l. 1.

94. AKhSF f. 5248, op. 1, d. 50, l. 4.

95. GARF f. 1235, op. 106, d. 526, l. 95.

96. AKhSF f. 5248, op. 1, d. 51, l. 120.

97. Kutuzov, *Organizatsiia ucheta*, 27.

98. GARF f. 1235, op. 141, d. 145, l. 8.

99. GARF f. 1235, op. 141, d. 151, l. 188.

100. GARF f. 3316, op. 29, d. 965, l. 20; FGATO f. 434 op. 4, d. 3, l. 33.

101. However, in the case of former White Army officers, leaders of counterrevolutionary bands, and others of their category, rehabilitation rates hovered around 20 percent. GARF f. 1235, op. 76, d. 20, l. 9. In 1929, Kutuzov reported that the largest single group of petitions approved by the Central Electoral Commission came from former members of the White Army and Imperial police. GARF f. 1235, op. 106, d. 519, l. 308; AKhSF f. 5248, op. 1, d. 51, l. 364.

102. GARF f. 1235, op. 106, d. 519, l. 314. Many were reinstated in rights only to be disenfranchised again. The government made a mild attempt to eliminate the cycle of disenfranchisement, rehabilitation, and disenfranchisement again. VTsIK issued a decree in March 1929 stating that those who had already been reinstated in voting rights by VTsIK could not be disenfranchised again except on new grounds. GARF f. 1235, op. 107, d. 369, l. 1.

103. AKhSF f. 5248, op. 1, d. 52, l. 16.

104. AKhSF f. 5248, op. 1, d. 51, l. 364.

105. AKhSF f. 5248, op. 1, d. 38, l. 393.

106. The Industrial Party show trial in November–December 1930 concerned eight defendants, high-level Soviet engineers and technicians, who were accused of committing various acts of treason, wrecking, and sabotage. See Loren R. Graham, *The Ghost of the Executed Engineer: Technology and the Fall of the Soviet Union* (Cambridge, Mass., 1993).

107. AKhSF f. 5248, op. 1, d. 51, l. 120.

108. GARF f. 1235, op. 141, d. 1401, l. 3–4.

109. GARF f. 1235, op. 141, d. 114, l. 134.

110. AKhSF f. 5248, op. 1, d. 23, l. 43.

111. GARF f. 1235, op. 106, d. 519, l. 305.

112. Volodarskii and Terekhov, *Izbiratel'noe pravo*, 70–71.

113. Ibid. Such party rhetoric was nothing new. In an earlier period, the bourgeois enemy was also a fake and saboteur with a "cushy job" in the Soviet bureaucracy. See Raleigh, "Languages of Power," 345–347.

114. AKhSF f. 5248, op. 7, d. 5214, l. 7 (Leningrad, 1930).

4. Hardship and Citizenship

1. Tikhonov, *Lishenie,* 51; A. I. Dobkin, "Lishentsy: 1918–1936," *Zven'ia: Istoricheskii al'manakh* (Moscow-St. Petersburg, 1992), 600.

2. Nadezhda Mandelstam, *Hope Against Hope: A Memoir,* trans. Max Hayward (New York, 1970), 93.

3. Carr, *Foundations,* 2:420; Fitzpatrick, *Stalin's Peasants,* 19.

4. Fitzpatrick, *Stalin's Peasants,* 226.

5. AKhSF f. 5248, op. 9, d. 11165, l. 14–15 (Saratov, 1930).

6. Svetlana Boym, *Common Places: Mythologies of Everyday Life in Russia* (Cambridge, Mass., 1994), 99–101.

7. Court report from a Moscow oblast newspaper, "Vrag proletarskoi distsipliny," *Podol'skii rabochii* (April 2, 1934).

8. AKhSF f. 5248, op. 9, d. 10966, l. 12 (Western oblast, 1931).

9. See Golfo Alexopoulos, "Voices Beyond the Urals: The Discovery of a Central State Archive," *Cahiers du Monde russe* 40 (1999): 1–17.

10. Viola, *Peasant Rebels,* 91–99.

11. James C. Scott, *Domination and the Arts of Resistance* (New Haven, Conn., 1990).

12. TsGA g. Moskvy f. 3118, op. 1, d. 33, l. 2 (Moscow, 1934).

13. AKhSF f. 5248, op. 7, d. 14614, l. 3–4 (Moscow, 1930).

14. AKhSF f. 5248, op. 13, d. 6877, l. 46–47 (Chuvash ASSR, 1934).

15. AKhSF f. 5248, op. 14, d. 6255, l. 11 (Kursk oblast, 1935).

16. On the confessions of party members, see Getty, *Origins of the Great Purges;* Kharkhordin, *The Collective and the Individual;* Klevniuk, *1937.* Unlike the letters of the disenfranchised, a confession of wrongdoing appears frequently in other letters to the party leadership. See RTsKhIDNI f. 78, op. 1 (letters to Kalinin on amnesty); RTsKhIDNI f. 613, op. 3 (letters to the Party Control Commission).

17. Examples of these petitions include AKhSF f. 5248, op. 5, d. 110, l. 2: "I await from you, comrade Kalinin, mercy [*milost'*]" (Smolensk gubernia, 1929); AKhSF f. 5248, op. 7, d. 13814, l. 8: "I have atoned for my sin" (Ivanovo Industrial oblast, 1930); AKhSF f. 5248, op. 9, d. 7185, l. 11: "I ask of you, [grant] me great mercy."; AKhSF f. 5248, op. 9, d. 9175, l. 29–30: "I acknowledge my guilt" (Leningrad oblast, 1931); "I have atoned for my mistake, for which I repent [*iskuplili moiu oshibku v kotoroi raskaivaius'*]" AKhSF f. 5248, op. 7, d. 2414, l. 8 (Leningrad, 1929).

18. AKhSF f. 5248, op. 17, d. 405, l. 13–14 (Rostov na Donu, 1935).

19. Fitzpatrick, *Stalin's Peasants,* 295, 312. See also Davies, *Popular Opinion;* Viola, *Peasant Rebels.*

20. The discursive strategies employed by violators of labor discipline are similar to those used by the disenfranchised. See Lewis H. Siegelbaum, "Defining and Ignoring Labor Discipline in the Early Soviet Period: The Comrades-Disciplinary Courts, 1918–1922," in *Slavic Review* 51 (1992): 705–731.

21. This particular style of argument is examined in Alexopoulos, "Victim Talk."

22. Making what he called "a plea for excuses," the British philosopher J. L. Austin urged scholars to investigate excuses, pleas, defenses, and justifications. J. L. Austin, *Philosophical Papers* (Oxford, U.K., 1961). On habits of explanation in another context, see Natalie Zemon Davis, *Fiction in the Archives: Pardon Tales and Their Tellers in Sixteenth Century France* (Stanford, Calif., 1987).

23. AKhSF f. 5248, op. 7, d. 3414, l. 14–15 (Leningrad oblast, 1930).

24. AKhSF f. 5248, op. 7, d. 9414, l. 4 (Leningrad, 1930).

25. AKhSF f. 5248, op. 9, d. 7782, l. 21 (Western oblast, 1930).

26. AKhSF f. 5248, op. 3, d. 1223, l. 12 (Briansk gubernia, 1927).

27. GARF f. 1235, op. 140, d. 1220, l. 8 (Siberia krai, 1929).

28. AKhSF f. 5248, op. 11, d. 2, l. 3 (Dagestan ASSR, 1931).

29. AKhSF f. 5248, op. 7, d. 1414, l. 12 (Moscow, 1929).

30. AKhSF f. 5248, op. 7, d. 9614, l. 7 (Moscow, 1930).

31. TsGAMO f. 807, op. 1, d. 2426, l. 186 (Moscow, 1930–1932); AKhSF f. 5248, op. 7, d. 14814, l. 8–9 (Votkinsk oblast, n/a).

32. AKhSF f. 5248, op. 9, d. 10566 (Nizhnyi Novgorod krai, 1928).

33. AKhSF f. 5248, op. 10, d. 1389, l. 26–27 (Mari AO, 1932).

34. AKhSF f. 5248, op. 13, d. 11119, l. 7 (Novosibirsk, 1934).

35. AKhSF f. 5248, op. 13, d. 5665, l. 37.

36. AKhSF f. 5248, op. 9, d. 8379, l. 17 (Vladimir, 1930).

37. AKhSF f. 5248, op. 17, d. 9405, l. 14 (Iaroslavl oblast, 1932).

38. TsGA g. Moskvy f. 3118, op. 1, d. 385, l. 17 (Moscow, 1936).

39. AKhSF f. 5248, op. 9, d. 6389, l. 4 (Central Black Earth oblast, 1931).

40. AKhSF f. 5248, op. 9, d. 8180, l. 24 (Karelia ASSR, 1929).

41. George Steiner, *Real Presences* (Chicago, 1989), 206.

42. AKhSF f. 5248, op. 9, d. 3802, l. 24 (North Caucasus krai, 1929).

43. AKhSF f. 5248, op. 7, d. 3014, l. 8–10 (Nizhnyi Novgorod krai, n/a).

44. AKhSF f. 5248, op. 14, d. 10878, l. 4 (Western oblast, 1935).

45. AKhSF f. 5248, op. 17, d. 5205, l. 5–6 (Omsk oblast, 1936).

46. GARF f. 1235, op. 141, d. 1133, l. 1–2 (Abkhazia, 1931).

47. RTsKhIDNI f. 78, op. 1, d. 314, l. 104 (Vologda gubernia, 1928).

48. AKhSF f. 5248, op. 9, d. 15145, l. 12–15 (Western Siberia krai, 1931).

49. GARF f. 5404, op. 2, d. 5, l. 17 (Voronezh, 1925).

50. AKhSF f. 5248, op. 10, d. 9705, l. 16–17 (Moscow oblast, n/a).

51. AKhSF f. 5248, op. 7, d. 1414, l. 12 (Moscow, 1929).

52. GARF f. 5404, op. 2, d. 5 (Voronezh, 1924).

53. AKhSF f. 5248, op. 9, d. 11762, l. 25 (Rostov on Don, 1930).

54. In its effort to license and tax private traders, the state established five ranks corresponding to the size of a business, with rank one assigned to traders selling goods that they carried while rank five designated large stores of more than twenty workers. Ball, "Private Trade," 92–93.

55. GARF f. 1235, op. 140, d. 416, l. 2–3; AKhSF f. 5248, op. 1, d. 22, l. 13.

56. TsGA g. Moskvy f. 3118, op. 1, d. 385, l. 17 (Moscow, 1936).

57. GARF f. 5404, op. 2, d. 103, l. 6 (Stalingrad gubernia, 1926).

58. AKhSF f. 5248, op. 9, d. 2608, l. 3–4 (Leningrad, 1931).

59. The *politseiskie strazhniki* or police watchmen represented a section of the rural police force in tsarist Russia. See "Ob uchrezhdenii v 46–ti guberniiakh Evropeiskoi Rossii politseiskoi strazhi," in *Polnoe sobranie zakonov rossiiskoi imperii* 1903, no. 23, art. 22906.

60. RGAE f. 396, op. 6, d. 85, l. 106 (Sharinsk volost, 1928).

61. AKhSF f. 5248, op. 4, d. 1212, l. 11 (Saratov, 1927).

62. AKhSF f. 5248, op. 5, d. 111, l. 17 (Viatka gubernia, 1928).

63. AKhSF f. 5248, op. 7, d. 10814, l. 13 (Volga German Republic, 1930).

64. AKhSF f. 5248, op. 9, d. 11165, l. 14–15 (Saratov, 1930).

65. AKhSF f. 5248, op. 7, d. 6214, l. 22 (Moscow oblast, 1930).

66. AKhSF f. 5248, op. 10, d. 5943, l. 4–5 (Udmurt AO, 1932).

67. AKhSF f. 5248, op. 4, d. 414, l. 9 (Crimea ASSR, 1927–1928).

68. AKhSF f. 5248, op. 7, d. 2014, l. 6 (Rostov on Don, 1929).

69. AKhSF f. 5248, op. 10, d. 2973, l. 11 (Kursk, 1931).

70. AKhSF f. 5248, op. 7, d. 12414, l. 4 (Voronezh, 1930).

71. GARF f. 5404, op. 2, d. 114, l. 6 (Ivanovo-Vozn. gubernia, 1926). One man wrote, "I enlisted in the former police like many others, as the saying goes, 'not for Jesus but for a crumb of bread,'" that is, hunger and not ideology motivated his actions.

72. Slezkine, *Arctic Mirrors,* 24–26.

73. AKhSF f. 5248, op. 7, d. 2614, l. 5 (Moscow, 1929).

74. AKhSF f. 5248, op. 9, d. 12359, l. 19 (Penza, 1931). "I traded . . . because of circumstances that at the time were independent of me." AKhSF f. 5248, op. 9, d. 5195, l. 8–9 (Novgorod, 1930).

75. AKhSF f. 5248, op. 9, d. 11762, l. 25 (Rostov on Don, 1930).

76. AKhSF f. 5248, op. 7, d. 11614, l. 5 (Central Black Earth oblast, 1930).

77. AKhSF f. 5248, op. 9, d. 7782, l. 21 (Western oblast). Another attributed his trading to the desperate situation he found himself in after all his property was lost in a fire: "Nothing remained except the shirt on my back." AKhSF f. 5248, op. 9, d. 220, l. 32 (Mari AO, n/a). One person claimed "There was nothing to exist on." AKhSF f. 5248, op. 9, d. 12359, l. 19 (Penza, 1927).

78. TsGA g. Moskvy f. 3103, op. 1, d. 18, l. 2 (Moscow, 1933).

79. AKhSF f. 5248, op. 14, d. 7662, l. 24–25 (Azov-Black Sea krai, 1935).

80. AKhSF f. 5248, op. 3, d. 204, l. 17 (Kursk gubernia, 1926).

81. AKhSF f. 5248, op. 9, d. 8777, l. 7–8 (Perm, 1930).

82. AKhSF f. 5248, op. 7, d. 4614, l. 23–25 (Nizhnyi Novgorod krai, 1929).

83. AKhSF f. 5248, op. 10, d. 4953, l. 12 (Chuvash ASSR, n/a).

84. AKhSF f. 5248, op. 9, d. 9573, l. 21 (Ufa, 1930). The argument that one was motivated by necessity and not the desire for profit appears in AKhSF f. 5248, op. 9, d. 3404, l. 17 (Moscow, 1930); AKhSF f. 5248, op. 9, d. 16538 (Central Volga krai, 1931).

85. AKhSF f. 5248, op. 9, d. 9175, l. 29–30 (Leningrad oblast, 1931).

86. AKhSF f. 5248, op. 7, d. 3014, l. 8–10 (Nizhnyi Novgorod krai, n/a).

87. AKhSF f. 5248, op. 7, d. 7014, l. 14 (Siberian krai, 1928).

88. AKhSF f. 5248, op. 7, d. 1214, l. 5 (Moscow, 1929).

89. GARF f. 5404, op. 2, d. 2522, l. 8 (Krasnyi Kut, 1925).

90. AKhSF f. 5248, op. 10, d. 9309, l. 12 (Leningrad, 1931).

91. AKhSF f. 5248, op. 7, d. 10014, l. 6 (Western oblast, 1930).

92. AKhSF f. 5248, op. 9, d. 14548, l. 7 (Moscow oblast, 1931). Another who suffered from migraines also implicated the doctor in his story. The doctor told his patient to stop working given his ailment, an instruction that led the man to trade as a source of income. AKhSF f. 5248, op. 9, d. 9772, l. 21 (Western oblast, n/a).

93. AKhSF f. 5248, op. 9, d. 5792, l. 21 (Omsk, n/a). A couple from Ufa argued that they were not physically able to do any other job. AKhSF f. 5248, op. 7, d. 11214, l. 7 (Ufa, n/a).

94. AKhSF f. 5248, op. 7, d. 5414, l. 10 (Moscow, 1929).

95. TsGA g. Moskvy f. 3103, op. 1, d. 24, l. 4 (Moscow, 1935).

96. AKhSF f. 5248, op. 7, d. 13414, l. 4 (Leningrad oblast, 1930); AKhSF f. 5248, op. 9, d. 11165, l. 14–15 (Saratov, 1930).

97. For example, see AKhSF f. 5248, op. 7, d. 12214, l. 11 (Kaluga, 1930): "I began to trade because of unemployment."; AKhSF f. 5248, op. 7, d. 13224, l. 17 (Rostov on Don, 1930): "Under the influence of need and unemployment, I was drawn into an Artel."; AKhSF f. 5248, op. 10, d. 5943, l. 4–5 (Udmurtsk AO, 1932): "I was unemployed for a long time; I couldn't find work anywhere; I had no means of existence at all and so as not to die of starvation in 1924 I was forced to take a license rank one for the right to trade pastries."; AKhSF f. 5248, op. 12, d. 6448, l. 5 (Tambov, n/a): "I traded after I was left without work."

98. Hoffmann, *Peasant Metropolis,* 7; Wood, *Baba and Comrade,* 147–169.

99. AKhSF f. 5248, op. 7, d. 4614, l. 23–25 (Nizhnyi Novgorod krai, 1929).

100. AKhSF f. 5248, op. 7, d. 2214, l. 8 (Moscow, 1929). In another case, a former tsarist policeman insisted that he could not find work when he returned from military service in 1908. Since he was poor, semiliterate, and had a large family to support, he found work as a policeman for several months. AKhSF f. 5248, op. 10, d. 6141, l. 3–4 (Western oblast, 1932).

101. AKhSF f. 5248, op. 3, d. 611, l. 4 (Tambov gubernia, 1927).

102. AKhSF f. 5248, op. 9, d. 2608, l. 3–4 (Leningrad, 1931).

103. AKhSF f. 5248, op. 7, d. 2414, l. 8 (Leningrad, 1929).

104. AKhSF f. 5248, op. 9, d. 1613, l. 9 (Leningrad, 1929).

105. AKhSF f. 5248, op. 7, d. 6814, l. 7 (Central Black Earth oblast, 1929).

106. AKhSF f. 5248, op. 12, d. 2629, l. 45 (North Caucasus krai, n/a).

107. AKhSF f. 5248, op. 9, d. 8379, l. 17–18 (Vladimir, 1930). A former trader testified, "Being completely unable to engage in physical labor, and lacking material assistance, I really was forced to trade." AKhSF f. 5248, op. 10, d. 4755, l. 16 (Western oblast, 1932).

108. AKhSF f. 5248, op. 10, d. 1587, l. 29 (Moscow, n/a).

109. AKhSF f. 5248, op. 7, d. 5414, l. 10 (Moscow, 1929).

110. On the image of peasants in the Bolshevik imagination, see Viola, *Peasant Rebels;* Fitzpatrick, *Stalin's Peasants;* Moshe Lewin, *Making.*

111. AKhSF f. 5248, op. 9, d. 4598 (Western oblast, 1931).

112. AKhSF f. 5248, op. 7, d. 5814, l. 5 (Moscow, 1930).

113. AKhSF f. 5248, op. 8, d. 1356, l. 6–9 (Ivanovo Industrial oblast, 1930).

114. AKhSF f. 5248, op. 2, d. 10, l. 35 (Moscow, 1937).

115. AKhSF f. 5248, op. 3, d. 1412, l. 18 (Tambov gubernia, 1927).

116. AKhSF f. 5248, op. 9, d. 16737, l. 4 (Leningrad, 1931).

117. AKhSF f. 5248, op. 10, d. 7923, l. 32 (Nizhnyi Novgorod krai, 1930).

118. AKhSF f. 5248, op. 12, d. 619, l. 64–65 (Leningrad oblast, 1931).

119. GARF f. 5404, op. 2, d. 4, l. 16 (Urals oblast, 1925).

120. AKhSF f. 5248, op. 9, d. 8379, l. 17–18 (Vladimir, 1930).

121. RGAE f. 396, op. 3, d. 36, l. 13 (n/a, 1925).

122. "Diary of Lyubov Vasilievna Shaporina," in *Intimacy and Terror: Soviet Diaries of the 1930s,* ed. Veronique Garros, Natalia Korenevskaya, and Thomas Lahusen (New York, 1995), 335.

123. AKhSF f. 5248, op. 10, d. 6339, l. 15–16 (Moscow oblast, 1932).

124. AKhSF f. 5248, op. 7, d. 3014, l. 8–10 (Nizhnyi Novgorod krai, n/a).

125. GARF f. 1235, op. 141, d. 582, l. 96 (n/a, 1930).

126. AKhSF f. 5248, op. 7, d. 13614, l. 6 (Arkhangelsk, n/a). Similarly, Sarah Davies found that in letters to Soviet authorities in the 1930s, people represented themselves as laborers who suffer and are hence morally good as compared with the powerful who do not work and are thus reprehensible. *Popular Opinion*, 134.

127. Grant, *Soviet House of Culture*; Slezkine, *Arctic Mirrors*; Gregory J. Massell, *The Surrogate Proletariat: Moslem Women and Revolutionary Strategies in Soviet Central Asia, 1919–1929* (Princeton, N.J., 1974).

128. AKhSF f. 5248, op. 9, d. 12757, l. 28 (North Caucasus krai, 1928).

129. AKhSF f. 5248, op. 9, d. 9772, l. 17–18 (Western oblast, 1931).

130. AKhSF f. 5248, op. 7, d. 12414, l. 4 (Voronezh, 1930).

131. AKhSF f. 5248, op. 9, d. 6389, l. 4 (Central Black Earth oblast, 1931).

132. GARF f. 5404, op. 1, d. 452, l. 30 (Tambov, 1927).

133. AKhSF f. 5248, op. 7, d. 14414, l. 10 (Sevastopol, 1930).

134. AKhSF f. 5248, op. 10, d. 399, l. 39–40 (Kuzbass, 1931).

135. AKhSF f. 5248, op. 10, d. 4161, l. 7–9 (Sverdlovsk, 1932).

136. AKhSF f. 5248, op. 9, d. 12757, l. 28 (North Caucasus krai, 1928).

137. AKhSF f. 5248, op. 3, d. 1412, l. 8 (Tambov gubernia, 1927).

138. AKhSF f. 5248, op. 9, d. 2608, l. 2–3 (Leningrad, 1931).

139. AKhSF f. 5248, op. 7, d. 5214, l. 7 (Leningrad, 1930).

140. AKhSF f. 5248, op. 9, d. 16538, l. 7 (Central Volga krai, 1931).

141. AKhSF f. 5248, op. 7, d. 414, l. 8 (Nizhnyi Novgorod krai, 1929).

142. AKhSF f. 5248, op. 13, d. 8493, l. 23–26 (Central Black Earth oblast, 1932).

143. On the Russian lament, see B.E. Chustova and K.V. Chustov, *Prichitaniia* (Leningrad, 1960); Yuri M. Sokolov, *Russian Folklore*, trans. Catherine Ruth Smith (Hatboro, Penn., 1966); Natalie Kononenko, *Ukrainian Minstrels: And the Blind Shall Sing* (Armonk, N.Y., 1998). Other literature on the lament narrative examines the Greek ritual laments. See Nadia Seremetakis, *The Last Word: Women, Death, and Divination in Inner Mani* (Chicago, 1991), and Margaret Alexiou, *The Ritual Lament in Greek Tradition* (Cambridge, U.K., 1974).

144. On emotion and communication, see Catherine Lutz and Geoffrey M. White, "The Anthropology of Emotions," *Annual Review of Anthropology* 15 (1986): 405–436; Catherine A. Lutz and Lila Abu-Lughod, eds., *Language and the Politics of Emotion* (Cambridge, U.K., 1990).

145. Sokolov, *Russian Folklore*, 679.

146. Olga Meerson, "Old Testament Lamentation in the Underground Man's Monologue: A Refutation of the Existentialist Reading of 'Notes from Underground,'" *Slavic and East European Journal* 36 (1992): 317–322. I thank Carol Flath for calling this to my attention. On the language of litany and lament in the Gorbachev era, see Nancy Ries, *Russian Talk: Culture and Conversation during Perestroika* (Ithaca, N.Y., 1997).

147. Natalie Kononenko, "Women as Performers of Oral Literature: A Re-examination of Epic and Lament," *Women Writers in Russian Literature*, ed. Toby W. Clyman and Diana Greene (Westport, Conn., 1994), 22.

148. Sokolov, *Russian Folklore*, 230, 237.

149. AKhSF f. 5248, op. 13, d. 1221, l. 8–9 (Leningrad oblast, 1935).

150. AKhSF f. 5248, op. 7, d. 4614, l. 23–25 (Nizhnyi Novgorod krai, 1929).

151. AKhSF f. 5248, op. 9, d. 1215, l. 6 (Leninsk-Omsk, 1930).

152. AKhSF f. 5248, op. 12, d. 2629, l. 45 (North Caucasus krai, n/a).

153. AKhSF f. 5248, op. 9, d. 14349, l. 8–9 (Samara, 1931).

154. AKhSF f. 5248, op. 9, d. 7583, l. 32 (Nizhnyi Novgorod krai, 1930).

155. AKhSF f. 5248, op. 9, d. 12160, l. 20 (Central Black Earth oblast, 1931).

156. AKhSF f. 5248, op. 7, d. 3014, l. 8–10 (Nizhnyi Novgorod krai, n/a).

157. AKhSF f. 5248, op. 9, d. 6190, l. 11 (Moscow oblast, 1931).

158. AKhSF f. 5248, op. 9, d. 13155, l. 18–19 (Leningrad, 1931).

159. Sokolov, *Russian Folklore,* 233.

160. On women's use of lament as social commentary, to air grievances particular to women, see Anna Caraveli-Chaves, "Bridge Between Worlds: The Greek Women's Lament as Communicative Event," *Journal of American Folklore* 93 (1980): 129–158; Anna Caraveli, "The Bitter Wounding: The Lament as Social Protest in Rural Greece," in *Gender and Power in Rural Greece,* ed. Jill Dubisch (Princeton, N.J., 1986), 169–194; Richard P. Werbner, "Atonement Ritual and Guardian-Spirit Possession Among Kalanga," *Africa* 34 (1964): 221–222.

161. AKhSF f. 5248, op. 8, d. 1146, l. 4 (Penza, 1930).

162. AKhSF f. 5248, op. 7, d. 11814, l. 27 (Ialta, n/a).

163. AKhSF f. 5248, op. 13, d. 8493, l. 23–26 (Central Black Earth oblast, 1932).

164. AKhSF f. 5248, op. 9, d. 10369, l. 6 (Samara, 1931).

165. AKhSF f. 5248, op. 9, d. 11165, l. 14–15 (Saratov, 1930).

166. AKhSF f. 5248, op. 17, d. 5, l. 5–6 (Ivanovo Industrial oblast, 1936).

167. AKhSF f. 5248, op. 10, d. 5745, l. 9 (Nizhnyi Novgorod krai, n/a); AKhSF f. 5248, op. 10, d. 5745, l. 12 (Nizhnyi Novgorod krai, 1930).

168. AKhSF f. 5248, op. 14, d. 13290, l. 17 (Leningrad oblast, 1935).

169. Lynne Viola, "Bab'i Bunty and Peasant Women's Protest During Collectivization," *Russian Review* 45 (1986); Viola, *Peasant Rebels;* Wood, *Baba and Comrade.*

170. AKhSF f. 5248, op. 14, d. 2034, l. 13 (Western oblast, 1935).

171. AKhSF f. 5248, op. 13, d. 413, l. 31–32, 42–43 (Crimea ASSR, 1934).

172. TsGA g. Moskvy f. 3108, op. 1, d. 121, l. 14.

173. AKhSF f. 5248, op. 7, d. 13614, l. 6 (Arkhangelsk, n/a).

174. Irina Andreevna Fedosova, published in E. V. Barsov, *Lamentations,* 1:272–273, cited in Sokolov, *Russian Folklore,* 230.

175. AKhSF f. 5248, op. 9, d. 14150, l. 18 (Western Siberia krai, 1930).

176. Davis, *Fiction in the Archives,* 52–58.

177. William E. Connolly, "Suffering, Justice, and the Politics of Becoming," *Culture, Medicine, and Psychiatry* 20 (1996): 253–255.

178. AKhSF f. 5248, op. 12, d. 4438, l. 11–12 (Moscow, 1933).

179. AKhSF f. 5248, op. 9, d. 11961, l. 54 (Western Siberia krai, 1930).

180. AKhSF f. 5248, op. 8, d. 938, l. 1 (Nizhnyi Novgorod krai, 1930).

181. AKhSF f. 5248, op. 14, d. 6054, l. 12–15 (Leningrad oblast, 1934).

182. AKhSF f. 5248, op. 7, d. 4614, l. 19 (Nizhnyi Novgorod krai, 1929).

183. AKhSF f. 5248, op. 7, d. 1614, l. 7–8 (Moscow, 1929).

184. AKhSF f. 5248, op. 7, d. 3614, l. 5–6 (Moscow, 1930).

185. In a discussion with his brother, Alyosha (which many Russians knew well), Ivan argues: "I meant to speak of the suffering of mankind generally, but we had better speak of the sufferings of the children. . . . If they, too, suffer horribly on earth, they must suffer for their father's sins, they must be punished for their fathers. . . . The innocent must not suffer for another's sins, and especially such innocents!" Fyodor Dostoyevsky, *The Brothers Karamazov,* trans. Constance Garnett (New York, 1950), 282.

186. AKhSF f. 5248, op. 9, d. 4001, l. 13 (Moscow oblast, 1930).

187. AKhSF f. 5248, op. 14, d. 7260, l. 9 (Moscow, 1935).

188. AKhSF f. 5248, op. 9, d. 10566, l. 10–11 (Nizhnyi Novgorod krai, 1928).

189. GARF f. 5404, op. 1, d. 452, l. 62 (Tambov, 1923).

190. GARF-TsGA RSFSR f. 406, op. 12, d. 2210.

191. GARF f. 1235, op. 64, d. 193, l. 262 (n/a, 1928).

192. TsGA g. Moskvy f. 3103, op. 1, d. 18 (Moscow, 1933).

193. TsGA g. Moskvy f. 3109, op. 2, d. 2179, l. 5 (Moscow, 1933).

194. GARF f. 1235, op. 141, d. 582, l. 96 (1930)

195. AKhSF f. 5248, op. 7, d. 11814, l. 27 (Ialta, n/a); On prostitution and female unemployment, see Lebina, *Povsednevnaia zhizn',* and Wood, *Baba and Comrade.*

196. Quoted in Nathan Leites, *A Study of Bolshevism* (Glencoe, Ill., 1953), 208; One man was excluded from the party after he "gave in to the tears" of his petty-bourgeois fiancée for a church wedding, causing his comrades to wonder what else he might concede if "there are more tears." Wood, *Baba and Comrade,* 206.

197. See Jeffrey Brooks, *Thank You, Comrade Stalin! Soviet Public Culture from Revolution to Cold War* (Princeton, N.J., 2000); Karen Petrone, *Life Has Become More Joyous Comrades: Celebrations in the Time of Stalin* (Bloomington, Ind., 2000); James Von Geldern and Richard Stites, *Mass Culture in Soviet Russia: Tales, Poems, Movies, Plays, and Folklore, 1917–1953* (Bloomington, Ind. 1995).

198. Grant, *Soviet House of Culture,* 83.

199. "Chronicle of the Year 1937 as Recorded by the Newspaper *Izvestiya* and Collective Farmer Ignat Danilovich Frolov," in *Intimacy and Terror,* 52.

200. Lewin, *Making,* 76.

201. Davies, *Popular Opinion;* Hoffmann, *Peasant Metropolis.*

202. Geldern and Stites, *Mass Culture,* 70–71, 234–35.

5. The Talents and Traits of Soviet Citizens

1. AKhSF f. 5248, op. 7, d. 2014, l. 17 (Rostov on Don, 1929).
2. AKhSF f. 5248, op. 13, d. 7685, l. 7.
3. AKhSF f. 5248, op. 13, d. 8493.
4. AKhSF f. 5248, op. 13, d. 7887, l. 16.
5. AKhSF f. 5248, op. 13, d. 7281, l. 17.
6. AKhSF f. 5248, op. 13, d. 10917, l. 1–2; AKhSF f. 5248, op. 13, d. 10109, l. 24–25; FGATO f. 434, op. 4, d. 21, l. 4.
7. AKhSF f. 5248, op. 13, d. 9503, l. 10, 12.
8. AKhSF f. 5248, op. 1, d. 69, l. 130–132.
9. AKhSF f. 5248, op. 9, d. 16538, l. 7 (Central Volga krai, 1931).
10. People concealing their identity would be tried under statute 91 of the Criminal Code "by analogy." GARF f. 1235, op. 106, d. 337, l. 5.
11. GARF f. 7511, op. 1, d. 143, l. 105.
12. GARF f. 7511, op. 1, d. 143, l. 104.
13. Carr and Davies, *Foundations,* 1:659; TsGA g. Moskva f. 3103, op. 1, d. 15, l. 23, 32.
14. The 1926 RSFSR Criminal Code punished those who passed forged documents to state and social organizations with as much as three years incarceration. *Ugolovnyi kodeks RSFSR, redaktsii 1926 goda* (Moscow, 1927), art. 72. For example, a rural soviet chairman was sentenced for giving out false documents. AKhSF f. 5248, op. 1, d. 69, l. 29. In 1929, the CEC reaffirmed that those who deceive Soviet organs by presenting false information in petitions for the reinstatement of rights should be severely prosecuted. AKhSF f. 5248, op. 1, d. 24, l. 13.
15. "Diary of Stepan Filippovich Podlubny," in *Intimacy and Terror,* 291. The definitive analysis of this case is Jochen Hellbeck, "Fashioning the Stalinist Soul: The Diary of Stepan Podlubnyi, 1931–1939," in *Stalinism: New Directions,* ed. Sheila Fitzpatrick (London, 2000), 77–117.
16. Rogovin, *1937,* 147; Vasily Grossman, *Forever Flowing* (Evanston, Ill., 1997), 70–71.
17. Timothy Garton Ash, *The File: A Personal History* (New York, 1998), 115, 137.
18. Moshe Lewin, "Society, State, and Ideology During the First Five-Year Plan," in *Cultural Revolution in Russia, 1928–1931,* 56. Rural-urban migration was estimated at 945,000 in 1926, 1,062,000 in 1928, and 1,392,000 in 1929; see Carr and Davies, *Foundations,* 1:454. In 1930, more than two and a half million peasants moved to the cities, and in 1931 approximately four million peasants did so, totaling about twelve million in the years 1928–1932; see Fitzpatrick, *Stalin's Peasants,* 80.
19. Hoffmann, *Peasant Metropolis,* 53; Viola, *Peasant Rebels,* 84.

20. In the aftermath of the civil war, Siberia, the Far East, the south and southeastern regions of Russia accommodated an influx of refugees from the central regions who, according to one author, were largely "representatives of the former ruling classes" such as landowners and White Army officers. See Spirin, *Klassy i partii,* 381–382.
21. AKhSF f. 5248, op. 1, d. 69, l. 68.
22. Viola, *Peasant Rebels,* 26.
23. AKhSF f. 5248, op. 2, d. 3, l. 75.
24. AKhSF f. 5248, op. 1, d. 51, l. 110; GARF f. 1235, op. 141, d. 151, l. 188; GARF f. 1235, op. 106, d. 519, l. 155.
25. GARF f. 1235, op. 141, d. 155, l. 1.
26. AKhSF f. 5248, op. 1, d. 51, l. 7.
27. AKhSF f. 5248, op. 1, d. 76, l. 75.
28. AKhSF f. 5248, op. 1, d. 79, l. 98.
29. AKhSF f. 5248, op. 1, d. 69, l. 79.
30. AKhSF f. 5248, op. 9, d. 10966, l. 12 (Western oblast, 1931).
31. AKhSF f. 5248, op. 10, d. 399, l. 39–40 (Western Siberia krai, 1931).
32. GARF f. 1235, op. 140, d. 416, l. 2–3; 11–12.
33. TsGA g. Moskvy f. 3108, op. 1, d. 67.
34. AKhSF f. 5248, op. 2, d. 38, l. 31.
35. AKhSF f. 5248, op. 13, d. 10311, l. 6; AKhSF f. 5248, op. 4, d. 6060, l. 13; AKhSF f. 5248, op. 13, d. 10311, l. 6; AKhSF f. 5248, op. 1, d. 129, l. 142; GARF f. 1235, op. 106, d. 519, l. 253.
36. Herzfeld, *The Social Production of Indifference.*
37. AKhSF f. 5248, op. 1, d. 74, l. 199.
38. AKhSF f. 5248, op. 1, d. 85, l. 495. For someone deprived of voting rights because of mental illness, a petition for rehabilitation might include a note from the local psychiatrist attesting to the individual's mental health. TsGA g. Moskvy f. 3103, op. 1, d. 12, l. 125.
39. RTsKhIDNI f. 78, op. 1, d. 314, l. 109; AKhSF f. 5248, op. 1, d. 7, l. 1.
40. TsGA g. Moskvy f. 3108, op. 1, d. 67.
41. On the Stakhanovites or "outstanding labor heroes" who overfulfilled their production norms and for this received bonuses, see Lewis H. Siegelbaum, *Stakhanovism and the Politics of Productivity in the USSR, 1935–1941* (Cambridge, U.K., 1988). On Stalinist heroes, see also John McCannon, *Red Arctic: Polar Exploration and the Myth of the North in the Soviet Union, 1932–1939* (Oxford, U.K., 1988).
42. TsGA g. Moskvy f. 3108, op. 1, d. 296, l. 4.
43. TsGAMO f. 7335, op. 1, d. 457, l. 66–75.
44. AKhSF f. 5248, op. 1, d. 70, l. 46.
45. AKhSF f. 5248, op. 1, d. 87, l. 504.
46. AKhSF f. 5248, op. 1, d. 86, l. 450.
47. AKhSF f. 5248, op. 1, d. 78, l. 79.
48. AKhSF f. 5248, op. 1, d. 69, l. 90.
49. GARF f. 1235, op. 141, d. 2214, l. 37.
50. AKhSF f. 5248, op. 1, d. 78, l. 182. Paltry evidence of the Central Electoral Commission acting against secret police recommendations appears in cases prior to 1930. AKhSF f. 5248, op. 1, d. 71, l. 80; AKhSF f. 5248, op. 1, d. 7, l. 43.
51. AKhSF f. 5248, op. 1, d. 71, l. 59.
52. GARF f. 5248, op. 2, d. 6, l. 66.
53. GARF f. 1235, op. 141, d. 2214, l. 50–69.
54. AKhSF f. 5248, op. 1, d. 71, l. 56; AKhSF f. 5248, op. 1, d. 78, l. 39; AKhSF f. 5248, op. 1, d. 78, l. 37; AKhSF f. 5248, op. 1, d. 83, l. 32.
55. AKhSF f. 5248, op. 1, d. 71, l. 56.
56. AKhSF f. 5248, op. 1, d. 69, l. 29.
57. GARF f. 1235, op. 106, d. 519, l. 138.
58. GARF f. 1235, op. 141, d. 1506, l. 26–27.

59. Kotkin, *Magnetic Mountain;* Falasca Zamponi, *Fascist Spectacle.*
60. AKhSF f. 5248, op. 13, d. 4453, l. 4 (Leningrad oblast, 1934).
61. AKhSF f. 5248, op. 9, d. 3802, l. 24 (North Caucasus krai, 1929).
62. AKhSF f. 5248, op. 9, d. 12558, l. 10–11 (Urals oblast, 1931).
63. AKhSF f. 5248, op. 7, d. 814, l. 7 (Tver, 1929).
64. AKhSF f. 5248, op. 17, d. 6805, l. 47 (Western Siberia krai, 1936).
65. AKhSF f. 5248, op. 9, d. 16140, l. 11 (Moscow oblast, 1930).
66. AKhSF f. 5248, op. 14, d. 426, l. 9–11 (Moscow, 1936).
67. AKhSF f. 5248, op. 7, d. 2614, l. 5 (Moscow, 1929).
68. AKhSF f. 5248, op. 10, d. 1983, l. 49–50 (Mordovia AO, 1933). Other examples include: "My only son has been a commander for nine years already in the Red Army." AKhSF f. 5248, op. 7, d. 614, l. 14 (Moscow oblast, 1929). "My oldest son served in the Red Army . . . and I received a 75% cut in my taxes." AKhSF f. 5248, op. 9, d. 15543, l. 19–20 (Western oblast, no date).
69. AKhSF f. 5248, op. 14, d. 13491, l. 23–24 (Moscow, 1935).
70. AKhSF f. 5248, op. 7, d. 4014, l. 5–6 (Bashkir ASSR, 1929).
71. AKhSF f. 5248, op. 14, d. 4044, l. 4–5 (Leningrad oblast, 1935).
72. AKhSF f. 5248, op. 7, d. 14814, l. 8–9 (Votkinsk oblast, no date).
73. David Hoffmann, "Mothers in the Motherland: Stalinist Pronatalism and Its Pan-European Context" (Washington, D.C., 2000); Wood, *Baba and Comrade,* 192, 208.
74. GARF f. 3316, op. 37, d. 51, l. 4 (Moscow, 1935).
75. AKhSF f. 5248, op. 12, d. 4438, l. 11–12 (Moscow, 1933).
76. The Union of Struggle for the Liberation of the Working Class was an illegal Marxist organization in St. Petersburg which organized strikes among workers in the 1890s.
77. AKhSF f. 5248, op. 1, d. 84, l. 54.
78. AKhSF f. 5248, op. 7, d. 2814, l. 4 (Tobolsk, 1930).
79. AKhSF f. 5248, op. 7, d. 11414, l. 33–35 (Central Black Earth oblast, 1929).
80. Clark, *The Soviet Novel.*
81. AKhSF f. 5248, op. 9, d. 3205, l. 5 (Western oblast, 1931).
82. AKhSF f. 5248, op. 7, d. 10614, l. 13 (Moscow, 1930).
83. On the symbol of blood and national belonging, see Amir Weiner, *Making Sense of War: The Second World War and the Fate of the Bolshevik Revolution* (Princeton, N.J., 2001); Michael Ignatieff, *Blood and Belonging: Journeys into the New Nationalism* (New York, 1993); Herzfeld, *Social Production of Indifference;* Seth Koven, "Remembering and Dismemberment: Crippled Children, Wounded Soldiers, and the Great War in Great Britain," *American Historical Review* 99 (1994): 1167–1202.
84. Other examples include AKhSF f. 5248, op. 7, d. 15014, l. 5 (Central Black Earth oblast, 1930); AKhSF f. 5248, op. 7, d. 14214, l. 5–6 (Kuban okrug, 1930); AKhSF f. 5248, op. 9, d. 3603, l. 36 (Dagestan ASSR, 1930).
85. AKhSF f. 5248, op. 9, d. 12956, l. 18–19 (Leningrad oblast, 1931).
86. AKhSF f. 5248, op. 5, d. 66, l. 1 (Lower Volga krai, 1929).
87. AKhSF f. 5248, op. 9, d. 10966, l. 12 (Western oblast, 1931). On the necessity to "show activism," see Kotkin, *Magnetic Mountain,* 222.
88. GARF f. 1235, op. 106, d. 519, l. 78.
89. Official statements on the subject of child homelessness and adoption encouraged such action. See TsIK and Sovnarkom decrees of August 13, 1926, "O meropriiatiiakh po borbe s detskoi besprizornost'iu," SZ 1926 no. 5, art. 407; and April 2, 1926, "Ob osvobozhdenii ot edinogo sel'sko-khoziastvennogo naloga v techenie trekh let nadelov zemli, otvodimykh krest'ianam, prinimaiushchim vospitannikov detskikh domov," SZ 1926 no. 27, art. 164.
90. AKhSF f. 5248, op. 17, d. 5605, l. 6 (Iaroslavl, 1935).
91. AKhSF f. 5248, op. 7, d. 7214, l. 16.
92. AKhSF f. 5248, op. 7, d. 7214, l. 13 (Leningrad, 1929).
93. AKhSF f. 5248, op. 7, d. 7214, l. 18 (Leningrad, 1930).
94. AKhSF f. 5248, op. 7, d. 7214, l. 8, 11.

95. N. A. Ivnitskii, *Kollektivizatsiia i raskulachivanie (nachalo 30-x godov)* (Moscow, 1996); Galina Mikhailovna Ivanova, *Labor Camp Socialism: The Gulag in the Soviet Totalitarian System* (New York, 2000); Lynne Viola, "The Other Archipelago: Kulak Deportations to the North in 1930," *Slavic Review* (2001): 730–756.

96. V. N. Zemskov, "Spetsposelentsy," *Sotsiologicheskie issledovaniia* 11 (1990): 6.

97. N. A. Ivnitskii and V. G. Makurov, *Iz istorii raskulachivaniia v Karelii, 1930–1931* (Petrozavodsk, 1991), 228–229.

98. SZ 1931 no. 44, art. 298. The July decree did not specify which organ would be responsible for granting rehabilitation to kulaks, but three years later, in 1934, I. Raab issued a statement on procedure, noting that the local administrative organs (district soviet executive committee, city soviet, and district soviet) of the person's current place of residence should reinstate the rights of kulaks consistent with article 38 of the VTsIK Instructions. GARF f. 1235, op. 141, d. 2205, l. 12–13.

99. GARF f. 3316, op. 24, d. 313, l. 2.

100. GARF f. 3316, op. 25, d. 1027, l. 1.

101. SZ 1932 no. 57, art. 343.

102. "Obzor opublikovannykh zakonov," *Vlast' sovetov* 22 (1933): 40. Ivnitskii, *Kollektivizatsiia*, 275.

103. GARF f. 3316, op. 26, d. 153, l. 7. On the reinstatement of rights for children of deported kulaks, see TsIK decree of March 17, 1933, in SZ 1933 no. 21, art. 117; "Obzor opublikovannykh zakonov," *Vlast' sovetov* 22 (1933): 40; 1934 Instructions on Elections to the Soviets.

104. GARF f. 1235, op. 141, d. 2205, l. 34.

105. GARF f. 3316, op. 25, d. 657, l. 94–121.

106. The language here specifically refers to an unregulated (*neustavnyi*) agricultural artel, that is, a collective farm (*kolkhoz*) which did not possess the rights guaranteed by the 1935 Kolkhoz Charter.

107. GARF f. 1235, op. 141, d. 2205, l. 34. In the case of deportees, when a head of household was reinstated in rights, rehabilitation applied to the entire family.

108. GARF f. 3316, op. 25, d. 195, l. 3.

109. GARF f. 3316, op. 29, d. 965, l. 9–11.

110. The head of the political section (*politotdel*) of the Red Army's Rear Militia reported in 1936 that local executive committees and soviets were reinstating the rights of rear militiamen even though such authority was reserved only for TsIK, according to a decree of 1933. GARF f. 3316, op. 29, d. 965, l. 4, 17.

111. GARF f. 3316, op. 29, d. 965, l. 9–11.

112. GARF f. 3316, op. 29, d. 965, l. 1, 30–31.

113. See SZ 1936 no. 44, art. 424 for the law on military service; also article 23 of the 1934 TsIK Instructions, SZ 1934 no. 55, art. 395.

114. GARF f. 3316, op. 29, d. 965, l. 4.

115. "Ssylnye muzhiki. Pravda o spetsposelkakh," *Neizvestnaia Rossiia XX vek* (Moscow, 1992) 1:195–211.

116. AKhSF f. 5248, op. 2, d. 8, l. 31 (1937).

117. GARF f. 3316, op. 30, d. 656, l. 11.

118. AKhSF f. 5248, op. 12, d. 3031, l. 7 (Ivanovo Industrial oblast, 1932).

119. TsGA g. Moskvy f. 3118, op. 1, d. 385, l. 15 (Moscow, 1935).

120. GARF f. 3316, op. 39, d. 108, l. 3 (Kazak ASSR, 1936).

121. TsGA g. Moskvy f. 3118, op. 1, d. 385, l. 17.

122. AKhSF f. 5248, op. 17, d. 3205, l. 4–5 (Gorkii krai, 1931).

123. AKhSF f. 5248, op. 14, d. 4245, l. 9–10 (Western Siberia krai, 1934).

124. AKhSF f. 5248, op. 17, d. 5005, l. 26–27 (Ivanovo Industrial oblast, 1935); Kotkin, *Magnetic Mountain*, 513n.

125. AKhSF f. 5248, op. 14, d. 627, l. 25.

126. AKhSF f. 5248, op. 14, d. 627, l. 3 (Voronezh, 1935).

127. AKhSF f. 5248, op. 12, d. 3634, l. 13 (Samara, 1933).

128. John Scott, *Behind the Urals* (Bloomington, Ind., 1973), 18–19, 30. See also Ivanova, *Labor Camp Socialism*, 77.

129. AKhSF f. 5248, op. 16, d. 1479, l. 2–3 (Kalinin oblast, 1936). Similarly, one petitioner wrote, "I cannot let myself believe that Soviet power could so harshly and unjustly punish its worker," and another observed that "Soviet power not only justly punishes, but it also justly forgives (*miluet*)." AKhSF f. 5248, op. 5, d. 22, l. 2 (Saratov, 1930); AKhSF f. 5248, op. 12, d. 1624, l. 9 (Ivanovo Industrial oblast, 1933).

130. AKhSF f. 5248, op. 7, d. 7414, l. 6 (Crimea ASSR, 1930).

131. AKhSF f. 5248, op. 14, d. 3843, l. 3–4 (Leningrad oblast, 1935).

132. AKhSF f. 5248, op. 17, d. 2405, l. 10–11 (Cherkesskii AO, no date).

133. AKhSF f. 5248, op. 5, d. 111, l. 17 (Viatsk gubernia, 1928).

134. AKhSF f. 5248, op. 12, d. 3433, l. 17–20 (Moscow, 1932).

135. RTsKhIDNI f. 78, op. 1, d. 314, l. 104 (Vologoda gubernia, 1928).

136. AKhSF f. 5248, op. 10, d. 4161, l. 7–9 (Sverdlovsk, 1932).

137. AKhSF f. 5248, op. 9, d. 7981, l. 3 (Leningrad, 1931).

138. AKhSF f. 5248, op. 10, d. 993, l. 13 (Kursk, 1932).

139. AKhSF f. 5248, op. 10, d. 8319, l. 13 (Central Volga krai, 1932).

140. GARF f. 3316, op. 30, d. 656, l. 11.

141. Geoffrey Hosking, *Russia: People and Empire* (Cambridge, Mass., 1997), 315; See also Wirtschafter, *Social Identity*, 121; On women activists, see Wood, *Baba and Comrade*, 104.

6. Endings and Enduring Legacies

1. Solomon, *Soviet Criminal Justice*, 25.

2. RSFSR Procuracy circular of November 24, 1931, "Ob otvetstvennosti za dachu lozhnykh svedenii ob izbiratel'nykh pravakh," in *Sovetskaia iustitsiia* 33 (1931): 33.

3. On the Law of August 7, 1932, see Solomon, *Soviet Criminal Justice*.

4. "Ob ustanovlenii edinoi pasportnoi sistemy . . ." in SZ 1932 no. 84, arts. 516–517.

5. Paul M. Hagenloh, " 'Socially Harmful Elements' and The Great Terror," in *Stalinism: New Directions*, 297; In 1932, the RSFSR Supreme Court also urged the eviction of people who earned unearned income of over 3,000 rubles per year. *Sovetskaia iustitsiia* 31 (1932): 25.

6. Fitzpatrick, *Stalin's Peasants*, 93–94.

7. Davies, *Popular Opinion*, 25.

8. Khlevniuk, *1937*, 12.

9. Fitzpatrick, *Stalin's Peasants*, 94.

10. Ibid, 94–95.

11. Hoffmann, *Peasant Metropolis*, 52–53.

12. Solomon, *Soviet Criminal Justice*, 160–161.

13. AKhSF f. 5248, op. 1, d. 40, l. 2.

14. "Nikakogo sniskozhdeniia," in *Podol'skii rabochii* (March 28, 1934); "Khuligany osuzhdeny" in *Kolomenskii rabochii* (June 25, 1934).

15. Khlevniuk, *1937*, 23–27.

16. Fitzpatrick, *Stalin's Peasants*, 76–77.

17. Getty, *Origins of the Great Purges;* Merle Fainsod, *How Russia is Ruled* (Cambridge, Mass., 1963).

18. RTsKhIDNI f. 78, op. 1, d. 590, l. 47.

19. Here again, good job references were important for reinstatement. GARF f. 7511, op. 1, d. 97, l. 100, 89.

20. AKhSF f. 5248, op. 1, d. 68, l. 8.

21. AKhSF f. 5248, op. 1, d. 63, l. 100.

22. GARF f. 7511, op. 1, d. 53, l. 29–30.

23. GARF f. 1235, op. 112, d. 28, l. 2; GARF f. 1235, op. 112, d. 28, l. 2; AKhSF f. 5248, op. 1, d. 63, l. 100.

24. AKhSF f. 5248, op. 1, d. 66, l. 30.

25. GARF f. 1235, op. 112, d. 19, l. 37.

26. AKhSF f. 5248, op. 1, d. 38, l. 273.

27. GARF f. 1235, op. 106, d. 519, l. 305; AKhSF f. 5248, op. 1, d. 23, l. 43; GARF f. 1235, op. 76, d. 126; GARF f. 7511, op. 1, d. 143, l. 79–80, 92; AKhSF f. 5248, op. 2, d. 4, l. 1–2; GARF f. 1235, op. 76, d. 126.

28. GARF f. 3316, op. 30, d. 731, l. 26.

29. GARF f. 1235, op. 141, d. 1506, l. 27–27; GARF f. 7511, op. 1, d. 143, l. 80.

30. TsGA g. Moskvy f. 3103, op. 1, d. 16, l. 86.

31. GARF f. 1235, op. 111, d. 10, l. 4, 29; GARF f. 1235, op. 111, d. 10, l. 1, 43.

32. GARF f. 7511, op. 1, d. 143, l. 109.

33. "V priemnoi M. I. Kalinina," *Vlast' Sovetov* 6 (1934): 31.

34. GARF f. 1235, op. 141, d. 1506, l. 26–27. Kutuzov, *Organizatsiia ucheta,* 33. "Iz Sibirskoi provintsii," *Vlast' sovetov* 24 (1935): 36.

35. GARF f. 7511, op. 1, d. 143, l. 66.

36. AKhSF f. 5248, op. 2, d. 3, l. 207.

37. AKhSF f. 5248, op. 11, d. 414, l. 12–14 (Moscow oblast, 1931); AKhSF f. 5248, op. 13, d. 9301, l. 6 (Ivanovo Industrial oblast, 1935); AKhSF f. 5248, op. 9, d. 16538, l. 7 (Central Volga krai, 1931).

38. Tikhonov, *Lishenie,* 48–49.

39. TsGA g. Moskva f. 3103, op. 1, d. 15, l. 23. Another was deprived of rights in 1933 as a "kulak-exploiter" because he failed to fulfill his grain quota; shortly thereafter, he was sentenced to one-and-a-half years of imprisonment and four years of exile. AKhSF f. 5248, op. 16, d. 1268, l. 2–5.

40. Such persons, whether they fled or were deported, were listed as "zagrafnye." See Tikhonov, *Lishenie,* 47.

41. Kutuzov, *Organizatsiia ucheta,* 28–29.

42. Julie Hessler, "Cultured Trade: The Stalinist Turn Towards Consumerism," in *Stalinism: New Directions,* 182-210; Julie Hessler, "A Postwar Perestroika? Toward a History of Private Enterprise in the USSR," *Slavic Review* 57 (1998): 516–542.

43. Raab indicated that these individuals should be reinstated in rights after their release from OGPU camps according to articles 38 and 41 of the 1930 VTsIK Instructions. GARF f. 1235, op. 141, d. 2205, l. 12. See also Kotkin, *Magnetic Mountain,* 234–35.

44. GARF f. 1235, op. 141, d. 2205, l. 9.

45. GARF f. 3316, op. 29, d. 965, l. 4. The reinstatement of rights for rear militiamen was proposed in a draft version of a 1931 TsIK decree. GARF f. 3316, op. 26, d. 154, l. 2.

46. GARF f. 3316, op. 25, d. 657, l. 146. See TsIK decrees of April 27, 1932; May 3, 1932; and May 17, 1932, on reinstating the rights of deportees.

47. GARF f. 1235, op. 141, d. 2205, l. 2–6.

48. GARF f. 1235, op. 141, d. 2205, l. 34.

49. GARF f. 1235, op. 141, d. 2205, l. 3.

50. GARF f. 1235, op. 141, d. 2205, l. 4.

51. GARF f. 3316, op. 27, d. 182, l. 3; AKhSF f. 5248, op. 2, d. 2, l. 46. The decree was published in *Izvestiia* (January 26, 1935), see also SZ 1935 no. 7, art. 57. This supplemented the TsIK decrees of July 3, 1931, and May 27, 1934: "On the Procedure for Reinstating the Civil Rights of Deported Kulaks." See SZ 1931 no. 44, art. 298; SZ 1934 no. 33, art. 257. Three months later TsIK made explicit that this law applied to all who lived in special settlements, including people who had already been reinstated in rights prior to publication of the 1935 supplemental provision. GARF f. 3316, op. 27, d. 182, l. 9. The prohibition on mobility applied also to kulak children.

52. Fitzpatrick, *Stalin's Peasants,* 83, 239; Ivnitskii, *Kollektivizatsiia,* 276.

53. Fitzpatrick, "Ascribing Class," 758; SZ 1936 no. 1, art. 2; Fitzpatrick, *Stalin's Peasants*, 244.

54. See "Rech' tov. A. G. Tilby" *Pravda* 331 (December 2, 1935): 3; see also in Fitzpatrick, "Ascribing Class," 758–759.

55. AKhSF f. 5248, op. 14, d. 9069, l. 8–9 (Moscow, 1934); see also AKhSF f. 5248, op. 13, d. 1019, l. 3 (Ivanovo, 1933).

56. AKhSF f. 5248, op. 16, d. 2, l. 28–31 (Azov-Black Sea krai, 1936).

57. P. Zaitsev, *Kto i pochemu sovetskaia vlast' lishaet izbiratel'nykh prav* (Moscow, 1931), 9.

58. *Molotov on the New Soviet Constitution* (New York, 1937), 3–7. Molotov attacked the bourgeois critics who "claimed that the disenfranchisement of two or three percent of the population, i.e., the former exploiters . . . was a great violation of democratic rights in the USSR," 10–11.

59. GARF f. 3316, op. 64, d. 1610, l. 25–26, 57, 64–65, 83.

60. GARF f. 3316, op. 29, d. 965, l. 1.

61. GARF f. 3316, op. 64, d. 1610, l. 160. It appears that the decision to eliminate the categories of the disenfranchised in the 1936 Constitution came just weeks before this March draft. For in February 1936, the USSR Procurator, Vyshinskii, sent a memo to TsIK regarding voting rights policy, which made no suggestion of any decision to so radically revise disenfranchisement policy.

62. AKhSF f. 5248, op. 2, d. 4, l. 2.

63. AKhSF f. 5248, op. 2, d. 6, l. 1.

64. *Postanovleniia o rassmotrenii zhalob trudiashchikhsia* (Kursk, 1936), 1–5. See also TsIK decree of December 14, 1935, "On handling workers' complaints" published in SZ 1936 no. 31, art. 274.

65. *Izvestiia* 136 (June 12, 1936): 1–2.

66. From the 1936 USSR Constitution, in *Istoriia Sovetskoi konstitutsii*, 358.

67. J. Arch Getty, "State and Society under Stalin," *Slavic Review* 50 (1991): 26.

68. GARF f. 1235, op. 114, d. 47, l. 24–30; see also Davies, *Popular Opinion*, 103–105.

69. Getty, "State and Society," 26. In 1937, people continued to express concern that alien elements and enemies would easily be elected in an uncontrolled system. Getty, *Origins of the Great Purges*. 180.

70. Davies, *Popular Opinion*, 70, 139.

71. GARF f. 1235, op. 76, d. 146, l. 22; SZ 1937 no. 20, art. 75.

72. AKhSF f. 5248, op. 2, d. 4, l. 1.

73. SZ 1937 no. 49, art. 205.

74. *Sovetskaia iustitsiia* 16 (1937): 42.

75. "O tsentralizovannom uchete lishennykh izbiratel'nykh prav po sudu," *Sovetskaia iustitsiia* 6 (1937): 55. Every time a court, be it military, transport or civil, sentenced someone to deprivation of voting rights, a special form had to be completed and sent to the USSR Commissariat of Justice documenting the disenfranchisement decision. Every five years, the Commissariat was to compile a comprehensive account (*spravochnaia kniga*) of those disenfranchised according to a decision of a court.

76. GARF f. 3316, op. 30, d. 731, l. 4.

77. GARF f. 3316, op. 30, d. 156, l. 23.

78. GARF f. 3316, op. 64, d. 1839, l. 1–4.

79. Carr, *Foundations*, 2:435n.

80. Solomon, *Soviet Criminal Justice*, 191–193.

81. GARF f. 1235, op. 114, d. 47, l. 1–11.

82. AKhSF f. 5248, op. 2, d. 8, l. 18 (1937).

83. GARF f. 3316, op. 30, d. 656, l. 2, 15, 20, 16.

84. SZ 1937 no. 69, art. 315.

85. GARF f. 3316, op. 30, d. 656, l. 11, 4.

86. GARF f. 5248, op. 2, d. 25, l. 6.

87. GARF f. 3316, op. 30, d. 656, l. 34.

88. GARF f. 3316, op. 30, d. 656, l. 22.

89. GARF f. 8131, op. 13, d. 11, l. 44.

90. Fitzpatrick, *Stalin's Peasants*, 211. Children apparently were allowed membership at the end of the 1930s, and many collective farms ignored the ban and treated priests as members anyway.

91. GARF f. 3316, op. 30, d. 731, l. 10.

92. GARF f. 7523, op. 9, d. 59, l. 71.

93. "Diary of Andrei Stepanovich Arzhilovsky," in *Intimacy and Terror*, 114.

94. GARF f. 1235, op. 76, d. 146, l. 105.

95. GARF f. 1235, op. 141, d. 2060, l. 45–47.

96. GARF f. 1235, op. 76, d. 146, l. 35, 37, 39, 91, 93, 109, 114.

97. GARF f. 1235, op. 76, d. 146, l. 109. This dispute must have ended in favor of the Commissariat of Justice's ruling because the VTsIK Presidium issued a decree on April 4, 1937, informing the local soviets that when they issue personal documents they should not mention whether the individual in the past had been disenfranchised. GARF f. 1235, op. 76, d. 146, l. 105.

98. GARF f. 1235, op. 76, d. 146, l. 91, 95.

99. GARF f. 3316, op. 30, d. 215, l. 25.

100. "Diary of Andrei Stepanovich Arzhilovsky," in *Intimacy and Terror*, 158.

101. "Diary of Stepan Filippovich Podlubny," in *Intimacy and Terror*, 291, 330; Hellbeck, "Fashioning the Stalinist Soul."

102. Khlevniuk, *1937*, 50; Getty, *Origins of the Great Purges*, 209.

103. GARF f. 7511, op. 1, d. 143, l. 105.

104. Davies, *Popular Opinion*, 143.

105. Wirtschafter, *Social Identity*, 60–61. The author quotes one high-ranking tsarist official who claimed that the Russian nobility was "so boundless that at one end it touches the foot of the throne and at the other is almost lost in the peasantry," 67.

106. GARF f. 8131, op. 13, d. 11, l. 54.

107. GARF f. 3316, op. 30, d. 731, l. 10.

108. "Diary of Lyubov Vasilievna Shaporina," in *Intimacy and Terror*, 338.

109. Davies, *Popular Opinion*, 80, 122.

110. "Diary of Lyubov Vasilievna Shaporina," in *Intimacy and Terror*, 353.

111. Fitzpatrick, *Stalin's Peasants*, 202. John Scott described how in 1938 several thousand children of the disenfranchised who had been working in Magnitogorsk were moved to Cheliabinsk on twenty-four hours' notice, "herded off in a freight train." Scott, *Behind the Urals*, 131.

112. Khlevniuk, *1937*, 116.

113. Hoffmann, *Peasant Metropolis*, 103.

114. Khlevniuk, *1937*, 60–62.

115. Fitzpatrick, *Stalin's Peasants*, 202.

116. Mary Douglas, *Natural Symbols: Explorations in Cosmology* (London, 1996), 112.

117. Solomon, *Soviet Criminal Justice*.

118. Scott, *Behind the Urals*, 193–194.

119. Douglas, *Natural Symbols*, 113.

Conclusion

1. Varlam Shalamov, *Kolyma Tales* (New York: Penguin Books, 1994), p. 44.

2. From Sergei Khrushchev's interview with Terry Gross on *Fresh Air*, National Public Radio, June 23, 1999.

3. Ries, *Russian Talk*.

Selected Bibliography

Archives in Russia

AKhSF	*Arkhiv po khraneniiu strakhovykh fondov,* also known as the *Tsentr khraneniia strakhovogo fonda.* Archive for the Preservation of Reserve Records. Ialutorovsk.
FGATO	*Filial gosudarstvennyi arkhiv Tiumenskoi oblasti g. Tobol'sk.* Affiliate of the State Archive of the Tiumen Oblast in the city of Tobolsk.
GARF	*Gosudarstvennyi arkhiv Rossiiskoi Federatsii.* State Archive of the Russian Federation. Moscow.
GARF-TsGA RSFSR	*Gosudarstvennyi arkhiv Rossiiskoi Federatsii.* State Archive of the Russian Federation. Moscow. Formerly TsGA RSFSR.
GATO	*Gosudarstvennyi arkhiv Tiumenskoi oblasti.* State Archive of the Tiumen Oblast. Tuimen.
RGAE	*Rossiiskii gosudarstvennyi arkhiv ekonomiki.* Russian State Archive of the Economy. Moscow.
RTsKhIDNI	*Rossiiskii tsentr khraneniia i izucheniia dokumentov noveishei istorii.* Russian Center for the Preservation and Study of Documents of Modern History. Moscow.
TsGA g. Moskvy	*Tsentral'nyi gosudarstvennyi arkhiv g. Moskvy.* Central State Archive for the City of Moscow.
TsGAMO	*Tsentral'nyi gosudarstvennyi arkhiv Moskovskoi oblasti.* Central State Archive for the Moscow Oblast.

Published Primary and Secondary Sources

Alexiou, Margaret. *The Ritual Lament in Greek Tradition.* Cambridge, U.K., 1974.

Alexopoulos, Golfo. "Exposing Illegality and Oneself: Complaint and Risk in Stalin's Russia." In *Reforming Justice in Russia, 1864–1994: Power, Culture, and the Limits of Legal Order.* Ed. Peter Solomon. Armonk, N.Y., 1997.

——. *Marking Outcasts and Making Citizens.* Ph.D. diss., University of Chicago, 1996.

——. "Portrait of a Con Artist as a Soviet Man." *Slavic Review* 57 (1998): 774–790.

——. "Victim Talk: Defense Testimony and Denunciation Under Stalin." *Law and Social Inquiry* 24 (1999): 501–518.

——. "Voices beyond the Urals: The Discovery of a Central State Archive." *Cahiers du Monde russe* 40 (1999): 1–17.

Allport, Gordon W. *The Nature of Prejudice.* New York, 1958.

Arendt, Hannah. *Eichmann in Jerusalem: A Report on the Banality of Evil.* London, 1963.

——. *The Origins of Totalitarianism.* New York, 1979.

Ash, Timothy Garton. *The File: A Personal History.* New York, 1998.

Austin, J.L. "A Plea for Excuses." *Philosophical Papers.* Oxford, U.K., 1961.

Babel, Isaac. *1920 Diary.* New Haven, Conn., 1995.

Balibar, Etienne, and Immanuel Wallerstein. *Race, Nation, Class: Ambiguous Identities.* London, 1991.

Ball, Alan. "Private Trade and Traders During NEP." In *Russia in the Era of NEP.* Ed. Sheila Fitzpatrick, Alexander Rabinowitch, and Richard Stites. Bloomington, Ind., 1991.

——. *Russia's Last Capitalists: The Nepmen, 1921–1929.* Berkeley, Calif., 1987.

Bhabha, Homi K., ed. *Nation and Narration.* London, 1990.

Bourdieu, Pierre. *The Logic of Practice.* Trans. Richard Nice. Stanford, Calif., 1980.

——. *Outline of a Theory of Practice.* Trans. Richard Nice. Cambridge, U.K., 1977.

Boym, Svetlana. *Common Places: Mythologies of Everyday Life in Russia.* Cambridge, Mass., 1994.

Brodovich, S.M. *Sovetskoe izbiratel'noe pravo.* Leningrad, 1925.

Brooks, Jeffrey. *Thank You, Comrade Stalin! Soviet Public Culture from Revolution to Cold War.* Princeton, N.J., 2000.

Broom, Leonard, Helen P. Beem, and Virginia Harris. "Characteristics of 1,107 Petitioners for Change of Name." *American Sociological Review* 20 (1955): 33–39.

Brubaker, Rogers. *Citizenship and Nationhood in France and Germany.* Cambridge, Mass., 1992.

Burleigh, Michael, and Wolfgang Wippermann. *The Racial State: Germany 1933–1945.* Cambridge, U.K., 1991.

Caraveli-Chaves, Anna. "The Bitter Wounding: The Lament as Social Protest in Rural Greece." In *Gender and Power in Rural Greece,* ed. Jill Dubisch, 169–194. Princeton, N.J., 1986.

——. "Bridge Between Worlds: The Greek Women's Lament as Communicative Event." *Journal of American Folklore* 93 (1980): 129–158.

Carr, Edward Hallett. *Foundations of a Planned Economy, 1926–1929.* Vol. 2. London, 1971.

——. *Socialism in One Country, 1924–1926.* Vol. 1. New York, 1958.

——. *Socialism in One Country, 1924–1926.* Vol. 2. New York, 1960.

Carr, Edward Hallett, and R.W. Davies. *Foundations of a Planned Economy, 1926–29.* Vol. 1 (London, 1969).

Chan, Anita, Richard Madsen, and Jonathan Unger. *Chen Village: The Recent History of a Peasant Community in Mao's China.* Berkeley, Calif., 1984.

Chase, William. *Workers, Society, and the Soviet State: Labor and Life in Moscow, 1918–1929.* Urbana, Ill., 1987.

Chustova, B.E., and K.V. Chustov. *Prichitaniia.* Leningrad, 1960.

Clark, Katerina. *The Soviet Novel: History as Ritual.* 3rd ed. Bloomington, Ind., 2000.

Connolly, William E. "Suffering, Justice, and the Politics of Becoming." *Culture, Medicine, and Psychiatry.* 20 (1996): 251–277.

Corney, Frederick C. "Writing October: History, Memory, Identity, and the Construction of the Bolshevik Revolution." Ph.D. diss., Columbia University, 1997.

Danilov, V.P., and S.A. Krasil'nikov, ed. *Spetspereselentsy v zapadnoi sibiri.* Novosibirsk, 1992–1993.

Davies, R.W. *The Industrialization of Soviet Russia.* Vols. 1–3. Cambridge, Mass., 1989.

——. *The Socialist Offensive: The Collectivization of Soviet Agriculture.* Cambridge, Mass., 1980.

Davies, Sarah. *Popular Opinion in Stalin's Russia: Terror, Propaganda, and Dissent, 1934–1941.* Cambridge, Mass., 1997.

——. "'Us against Them': Social Identity in Soviet Russia, 1934–1941." *Russian Review* 56 (1997): 70–89.

Davis, Natalie Zemon. *Fiction in the Archives: Pardon Tales and Their Tellers in Sixteenth-Century France.* Stanford, Calif., 1987.

de Certeau, Michel. *The Practice of Everyday Life.* Trans. Steven Rendall. Berkeley, Calif., 1984.

Dentith, Simon, and Philip Dodd. "The Uses of Autobiography." *Literature and History* 14 (1988): 4–47.

Dewey, Horace W., and Ann Marie Kleimola. "The Petition (chelobitnaja) as an Old Russian Literary Genre." *The Slavic and East European Journal* 14 (1970): 284–301.

Djilas, Aleksa. *The Contested Country: Yugoslav Unity and Communist Revolution.* Cambridge, Mass., 1991.

Dobkin, A.I., "Lishentsy." In *Zven'ia: Istoricheskii al'manakh.* Vol. 2. Moscow-St. Petersburg, 1992..

Dostoevsky, Fyodor. *The Brothers Karamazov.* Trans. Constance Garnett. New York, 1950.

Douglas, Mary. *Implicit Meanings.* London, 1975.

——. *Natural Symbols: Explorations in Cosmology.* London, 1996.

——. *Purity and Danger: An Analysis of Concepts of Pollution and Taboo.* New York, 1966.

——. *Risk and Blame: Essays in Cultural Theory.* London, 1992.

——. "Witchcraft and Leprosy: Two Strategies of Exclusion." *Man* 26 (1991): 723–736.

Douglas, Mary, and David Hull, eds. *How Classification Works: Nelson Goodman among the Social Sciences.* Edinburgh, U.K., 1992.

Dubisch, Jill, ed. *Gender and Power in Rural Greece.* Princeton, N.J., 1986.

Engelstein, Laura, and Stephanie Sandler. *Self and Story in Russian History.* Ithaca, N.Y., 2000.

Erlich, Alexander. *The Soviet Industrialization Debate, 1924–1928.* Cambridge, Mass., 1960.

Evans, Richard, ed. *The German Underworld: Deviants and Outcasts in German History.* New York, 1988.

Fainsod, Merle. *How Russia is Ruled.* Cambridge, Mass., 1963.

Falasca-Zamponi, Simonetta. *Fascist Spectacle: The Aesthetics of Power in Mussolini's Italy.* Berkeley, Calif., 1997.

Field, Daniel. *Rebels in the Name of the Tsar.* Boston, 1989.

Figes, Orlando. *A People's Tragedy: A History of the Russian Revolution.* New York, 1997.

———. "The Russian Revolution and Language in the Village." *Russian Review* 56 (1997): 331.

Figes, Orlando, and Boris Kolonitskii. *Interpreting the Russian Revolution: The Languages and Symbols of 1917.* New Haven, Conn., 1999.

Fitzpatrick, David. *Oceans of Consolation: Personal Accounts of Irish Migration to Australia* (Ithaca, N.Y., 1994).

Fitzpatrick, Sheila. "After NEP: The Fate of NEP Entrepreneurs, Small Traders, and Artisans in the 'Socialist Russia' of the 1930s," *Russian History/Histoire Russe* 12 (1986): 187–234.

———. "Ascribing Class: The Construction of Social Identity in Soviet Russia," *Journal of Modern History* 65 (1993): 745–770.

———. "The Bolsheviks' Dilemma: Class, Culture, and Politics in the Early Soviet Years." *Slavic Review* 47 (1988): 599–613.

———. "Cultural Revolution as Class War." *Cultural Revolution in Russia, 1928–1931.* Bloomington, Ind., 1978.

———. *Everyday Stalinism: Ordinary Life in Extraordinary Times: Soviet Russia in the 1930s.* Oxford, U.K., 1999.

———. "The Problem of Class Identity in NEP Society." *Russia in the Era of NEP.* Ed. Sheila Fitzpatrick, Alexander Rabinowich, and Richard Stites. Bloomington, Ind., 1991.

———, ed. *Stalinism: New Directions.* New York, 2000.

———. *Stalin's Peasants: Resistance and Survival in the Russian Village after Collectivization.* Oxford, U.K., 1994.

———. "Supplicants and Citizens: Public Letter-Writing in Soviet Russia in the 1930s." *Slavic Review* 55 (1996): 78–106.

Foucault, Michel. *The History of Sexuality: An Introduction.* New York, 1978.

Freeze, Gregory. *From Supplication to Revolution: A Documentary Social History of Imperial Russia.* Oxford, U.K., 1981.

———. *The Parish Clergy in Nineteenth-Century Russia.* Princeton, N.J., 1983.

———. "The Soslovie (Estate) Paradigm and Russian Social History." *American Historical Review* 91 (1986): 11–36.

Garros, Veronique, Natalia Korenevskaya, and Thomas Lahusen, eds. *Intimacy and Terror: Soviet Diaries of the 1930s.* New York, 1995.

Geertz, Clifford. *The Interpretation of Cultures.* New York, 1973.

Gellately, Robert. *The Gestapo and German Society.* Oxford, U.K., 1990.

Getty, J. Arch. *Origins of the Great Purges: The Soviet Communist Party Reconsidered, 1933–1938.* Cambridge, U.K., 1985.

———. "State and Society under Stalin." *Slavic Review* 50 (1991): 18–35.

Getty, J. Arch, and Roberta T. Manning, eds. *Stalinist Terror: New Perspectives.* Cambridge, U.K., 1993.

Gleason, Abbott, Peter Kenez, and Richard Stites, ed. *Bolshevik Culture. Experiment, and Order in the Russian Revolution.* Bloomington, Ind., 1985.

Goffman, Erving. *Stigma.* New Jersey, 1963.

Gough, Maria. "Switched On: Notes on Radio, Automata, and the Bright Red Star." In *Building the Collective: Soviet Graphic Design 1917–1937.* Ed. Leah Dickerman, 39–55. Princeton, N.J., 1996.

Graham, Loren R. *The Ghost of the Executed Engineer: Technology and the Fall of the Soviet Union.* Cambridge, Mass., 1993.

Grant, Bruce. *In the Soviet House of Culture: A Century of Perestroikas.* Princeton, N.J., 1995.

Graziosi, Andrea. *The Great Soviet Peasant War: Bolsheviks and Peasants, 1917–1933.* Cambridge, Mass., 1996.

Greenblatt, Stephen. *Renaissance Self-Fashioning.* Chicago, 1980.

Grodzins, Morton. *The Loyal and the Disloyal: Social Boundaries of Patriotism and Treason.* Chicago, 1956.

———. "Making Un-Americans." *American Journal of Sociology* 60 (1955): 570–583.

Gross, Jan T. *Revolution from Abroad.* Princeton, N.J., 1988.

Grossman, Vasily. *Forever Flowing.* Evanston, Ill., 1997.

Hackett, Nan. "A Different Form of 'Self': Narrative Style in British Nineteenth-Century Working-Class Autobiography." *Biography* 12 (1989): 208–226.

Hagenloh, Paul M. "'Socially Harmful Elements' and The Great Terror." In *Stalinism: New Directions.* Ed. Sheila Fitzpatrick. London, 2000.

Haimson, Leopold H. "The Problem of Social Identities in Early Twentieth-Century Russia." *Slavic Review* 47 (1988): 1–20.

Heinzen, James W. "'Alien' Personnel in the Soviet State: The People's Commissariat of Agriculture under Proletarian Dictatorship, 1918–1929." *Slavic Review* 56 (1997): 73–100.

Hellbeck, Jochen. "Fashioning the Stalinist Soul: The Diary of Stepan Podlubnyi, 1931–1939." In *Stalinism: New Directions,* ed. Sheila Fitzpatrick, 77–117. London, 2000.

———, "Self-Realization in the Stalinist System: Two Soviet Diaries of the 1930s." In *Russian Modernity: Politics, Knowledge, Practices,* 221–242. London, 2000.

Hepworth, M. and B. Turner, "Confession, Guilt and Responsibility." *British Journal of Law and Society* 6 (1979): 219–234.

Herzfeld, Michael. "Exploring a Metaphor of Exposure." *Journal of American Folklore* 92 (1992): 285–301.

———. "Social Borderers: Themes of Conflict and Ambiguity in Greek Folk-Song." *Byzantine and Modern Greek Studies* 6 (1980): 61–80.

———. *The Social Production of Indifference: Exploring the Symbolic Roots of Western Bureaucracy.* Chicago, 1992.

Hessler, Julie. "Cultured Trade: The Stalinist Turn Towards Consumerism." In *Stalinism: New Directions,* 182–210.

———. "A Postwar Perestroika? Toward a History of Private Enterprise in the USSR." *Slavic Review* 57 (1998): 516–542.

Hobsbawm, Eric. "Inventing Traditions." In *The Invention of Tradition.* Cambridge, U.K., 1983.

Hoch, Steven. *Serfdom and Social Control in Russia: Petrovskoe, a Village in Tambov.* Chicago, 1986.

Hoffmann, David. "Mothers in the Motherland: Stalinist Pronatalism and Its Pan-European Context." Washington, D.C., 2000.

———. *Peasant Metropolis: Social Identities in Moscow, 1929–1941.* Ithaca, N.Y., 1994.

———, and Yanni Kotsonis. *Russian Modernity: Politics, Knowledge, Practices.* New York, 2000.

Holquist, Peter. "Anti-Soviet *Svodki* from the Civil War: Surveillance as a Shared Feature of Russian Political Culture." *Russian Review* 56 (1997): 445–450.

———. "Information is the Alpha and Omega of Our Work: Bolshevik Surveillance in its Pan-European Context." *Journal of Modern History* 69 (1997): 415–451.

Hosking, Geoffrey. *Russia: People and Empire.* Cambridge: Harvard University Press, 1997.

Hunt, Lynn. *Politics, Culture, and Class in the French Revolution.* Berkeley, Calif., 1984.

Huskey, Eugene. *Russian Lawyers and the Soviet State.* Princeton, N.J., 1986.

Ignatieff, Michael. *Blood and Belonging: Journeys into the New Nationalism.* New York, 1993.

Il'f, Il'ia, and Evgenii Petrov. *Sobranie sochenenii,* vol. 2. Moscow, 1961.

Instruktsiia k sostavleniiu otchetnosti po perevyboram v sovety. Moscow, 1930.

Istoriia sovetskoi konstitutsii, 1917–1956 (Moscow, 1957).

Ivanova, Galina Mikhailovna. *Labor Camp Socialism: The Gulag in the Soviet Totalitarian System.* New York, 2000.

Ivnitskii, N. A., *Klassovaia bor'ba v derevne i likvidatsiia kulachestva kak klassa (1929–1932).* Moscow, 1972.

———. *Kollektivizatsiia i raskulachivanie (nachalo 30-x godov).* Moscow, 1996.

———. *Repressivnaia politika sovetskoi vlasti v derevne (1928–1933 gg).* Moscow, 2000.

Ivnitskii, N. A., and V. G. Makurov. *Iz istorii raskulachivaniia v Karelii, 1930–1931.* Petrozavodsk, 1991.

Josephson, Paul. "'Projects of the Century' in Soviet History: Large-Scale Technologies from Lenin to Gorbachev." In *Technology and Culture* 36 (1995): 519–559.

Kelly, Catriona, and David Shepherd, eds. *Constructing Russian Culture in the Age of Revolution: 1881–1940.* Oxford, U.K., 1998.

Kharkhordin, Oleg. *The Collective and the Individual in Russia: A Study of Practices.* Berkeley, Calif., 1999.

Khlevniuk, Oleg V. *In Stalin's Shadow: The Career of "Sergo" Ordzhonikidze.* Armonk, N.Y., 1995.

——. *1937: Stalin, NKVD i Sovetskoe obshchestvo.* Moscow, 1992.

Khrushchev, Sergei. "Interview with Terry Gross on 'Fresh Air.' " National Public Radio. June 23, 1999.

Kimberling, Elise. "Civil Rights and Social Policy in Soviet Russia, 1918–1936." *Russian Review* 41 (1982): 24–46.

Kimberling Wirtschafter, Elise. *Social Identity in Imperial Russia.* DeKalb, Ill., 1997.

Kleimola, Ann M. "The Duty to Denounce in Muscovite Russia." *Slavic Review* 31 (1972): 759–779.

Kliatskin, S.M. *Na zashchite oktiabria.* Moscow, 1965.

Kligman, Gail. *The Wedding of the Dead: Ritual, Poetics, and Popular Culture in Transylvania.* Berkeley, Calif., 1988.

Koenker, Diane P., William G. Rosenberg, and Ronald Grigor Suny, eds. *Party, State, and Society in the Russian Civil War: Explorations in Social History.* Bloomington, Ind., 1989.

Kokurin, A.I., and N.V. Petrov, eds. *Gulag 1918–60* Moscow, 2000.

Kommunisticheskaia partiia sovetskogo soiuza v rezoliutsiiakh i resheniiakh s'ezdov, konferentsii i plenumov TsK. Vol. 2. Moscow, 1960.

Kommunisticheskaia partiia sovetskogo soiuza v rezoliutsiiakh i resheniiakh s'ezdov, konferentsii i plenumov TsK. Vol. 3. Moscow, 1970.

Kononenko, Natalie. *Ukrainian Minstrels: And the Blind Shall Sing.* Armonk, N.Y., 1998.

——. "Women as Performers of Oral Literature: A Re-examination of Epic and Lament." *Women Writers in Russian Literature.* Ed. Toby W. Clyman and Diana Greene. Westport, Conn., 1994.

Kotkin, Stephen. *Magnetic Mountain: Stalinism as a Civilization.* Berkeley, Calif., 1995.

Kotsonis, Yanni. *Making Peasants Backward: Agricultural Cooperatives and the Agrarian Question, 1861–1914.* New York, 1999.

Koven, Seth. "Remembering and Dismemberment: Crippled Children, Wounded Soldiers, and the Great War in Britain." *American Historical Review* 99 (1994): 1167–1202.

Krylova, Anna. "The Tenacious Liberal Subject in Soviet Studies." *Kritika* 1 (2000): 119–146.

Kuda zhalovat'sia na neporiadki. Moscow, 1926.

Kuritsyn, V.M. *Perekhod k NEPu i revoliutsionnaia zakonnost'.* Moscow, 1972.

Kuromiya, Hiroaki. *Stalin's Industrial Revolution.* Cambridge, U.K., 1988.

Kutuzov, I. *Organizatsiia ucheta, rassmotreniia zhalob i khodataistv lits, lishennykh izbiratel'nykh prav.* Moscow, 1935.

Kvashonkin, A.V., A.V. Livshin, and O.V. Khlevniuk, eds. *Stalinskoe politbiuro v 30–e gody.* Moscow, 1995.

Lagovier, N. *Perevybory sovetov i revoliutsionnaia zakonnost'.* Moscow, 1930.

Lebina, N. B. *Povsednevnaia zhizn' sovetskogo naroda: normy i anomalii, 1920–1930 gody*. St. Petersburg, 1999.

Ledeneva, Alena V. *Russia's Economy of Favours: Blat, Networking and Informal Exchange*. Cambridge, U.K., 1998.

Levi, Primo. *Survival in Auschwitz*. New York, 1996.

Lewin, Moshe. *The Making of the Soviet System*. New York, 1985.

Lewy, Guenter. *The Nazi Persecution of the Gypsies*. New York, 2000.

Lih, Lars T., Oleg V. Naumov, and Oleg V. Khlevniuk, eds. *Stalin's Letters to Molotov*. New Haven, Conn., 1995.

Lucas, Colin. "The Crowd and Politics." In *The French Revolution and the Creation of Modern Political Culture*. Ed. Colin Lucas, 259–285. Oxford, U.K., 1988.

——. "Revolutionary Violence, the People and Terror." In *The French Revolution and the Creation of Modern Political Culture*. Ed. Keith Michael Baker, 57–81. Oxford, U.K., 1994.

Lutz, Catherine, and Geoffrey M. White, "The Anthropology of Emotions." *Annual Review of Anthropology* 15 (1986): 405–436.

Lutz, Catherine A., and Lila Abu-Lughod, eds., *Language and the Politics of Emotion*. Cambridge, U.K., 1990.

Mandelstam, Nadezhda. *Hope Against Hope: A Memoir*. Trans. Max Hayward. New York, 1970.

Marrese, Michelle. *A Woman's Kingdom: Noblewomen and the Control of Property in Russia, 1700–1861*. Ithaca, N.Y., 2002.

Martin, Terry. *Affirmative Action Empire: Nations and Nationalism in the Soviet Union, 1923–1939*. Ithaca, N.Y., 2001.

——. "The Origins of Soviet Ethnic Cleansing." *Journal of Modern History* 70 (1998): 813–861.

Massell, Gregory J. *Surrogate Proletariat: Muslim Women and Revolutionary Strategies in Soviet Central Asia, 1919–1929*. Princeton, N.J., 1974.

McCannon, John. *Red Arctic: Polar Exploration and the Myth of the North in the Soviet Union, 1932–1939*. Oxford, U.K., 1998.

Meerson, Olga. "Old Testament Lamentation in the Underground Man's Monologue: A Refutation of the Existentialist Reading of 'Notes from Underground.'" *Slavic and East European Journal* 36 (1992): 317–322.

Melgunov, S. M. *Krasnyi terror v Rossii: 1918–1923*. Simferopol, 1991.

Mikhailov, G. *Sovetskoe predstavitelstvo i izbiratel'noe pravo*. Moscow, 1922.

Molotov on the New Soviet Constitution (New York, 1937).

Moore, Sally Falk. "Inflicting Harm Righteously: Turning a Relative into a Stranger: An African Case." *Fremde der Gesellschaft*. Frankfurt, 1991.

——. *Law as Process: An Anthropological Approach*. London, 1978.

——. *Social Facts and Fabrications*. Cambridge, U.K., 1986.

Moore, Sally Falk, and Barbara G. Myerhoff. *Secular Ritual*. Amsterdam, 1977.

Naiman, Eric. *Sex in Public: The Incarnation of Early Soviet Ideology*. Princeton, N.J., 1997.

Nakhimovsky, Alexander D., and Alice Stone Nakhimovsky, eds.*The Semiotics of Russian Cultural History*. Ithaca, N.Y., 1985.

Nathans, Ben. *Beyond the Pale: The Jewish Encounter with Late Imperial Russia.* Berkeley, Calif., 2002.

Neizvestnaia Rossiia XX vek. Vol. 1. Moscow, 1992.

Nove, Alec. *An Economic History of the USSR.* New York, 1984.

Nurmanov, N. *Chastichnye perevybory sel'sovetov v 1933 g.* Moscow, 1933.

Osokina, Elena. *Za fasadom "Stalinskogo izobiliia": raspredelenie i rynok v snabzhenii naseleniia v gody industrializatsii, 1927–41.* Moscow, 1999.

Paul, Kathleen. *Whitewashing Britain: Race and Citizenship in the Postwar Era.* Ithaca, N.Y., 1997.

Payne, Matthew. *Stalin's Railroad: Turksib and the Building of Socialism.* Pittsburgh, Penn., 2001.

Peris, Daniel. "Commissars in Red Cassocks: Former Priests in the League of the Militant Godless" *Slavic Review* 54 (1995): 340–365.

———. *Storming the Heavens: The Soviet League of the Militant Godless.* Ithaca, N.Y., 1998.

Petrone, Karen. *Life Has Become More Joyous Comrades: Celebrations in the Time of Stalin.* Bloomington, Ind., 2000.

Peukert, Detlev J.K. *Inside Nazi Germany: Conformity, Opposition, and Racism in Everyday Life.* New Haven, Conn., 1987.

Pinkus, Benjamin. *The Jews of the Soviet Union: The History of a National Minority.* Cambridge, U.K., 1988.

Postanovleniia o rassmotrenii zhalob trudiashchikhsia. Kursk, 1936.

Potapov and Fedorovskii. *Kto lishaet'sia prava.* Perm, 1928.

Pushkin, A.S. "Dubrovskii." *Sobranie sochinenii.* Moscow, 1960.

Pyle, Molly. "Peasant Strategies for Obtaining State Aid: A Study of Their Petitions During World War I." *Russian History/Histoire Russe* 24 (1997): 41–64.

Raleigh, Donald J. "Languages of Power: How the Saratov Bolsheviks Imagined Their Enemies." *Slavic Review* 57 (1998): 320–350.

Ries, Nancy. *Russian Talk: Culture and Conversation During Perestoika.* Ithaca, N.Y., 1997.

Rogovin, Vadim Z. *1937: Stalin's Year of Terror.* Oak Park, Mich., 1998.

Rosenberg, William G., ed. *Bolshevik Visions: First Phase of the Cultural Revolution in Soviet Russia.* Ann Arbor, Mich., 1984.

———, and Lewis H. Siegelbaum. *Social Dimensions of Soviet Industrialization.* Bloomington, Ind., 1993.

Rosenman, Stanlet, and Irving Handelsman. "Identity as Legacy of the Holocaust: Encountering a Survivor's Narrative." *Journal of Psychohistory* 18 (1990): 35–71.

Rossi, Jacques. *The Gulag Handbook.* New York, 1989.

Rossman, Jeffrey J. "The Teikovo Cotton Workers' Strike of April 1932: Class, Gender, and Identity Politics in Stalin's Russia." *Russian Review* 56 (1997): 44–69.

Sahlins, Peter. *Boundaries: The Making of France and Spain in the Pyrenees.* Berkeley, Calif., 1989.

Sbornik zakonopolozhenii po perevyboram v sovety v 1927-28 (Vologda, 1928)

Sandborn, Josh. "Conscription, Correspondence, and Politics in Late Imperial Russia." *Russian History/Histoire Russe* 24 (1997): 27–40.

Scott, James C. *Domination and the Arts of Resistance.* New Haven, Conn., 1990.

Scott, John. *Behind the Urals: An American Worker in Russia's City of Steel.* Bloomington, Ind., 1989.

Seremetakis, Nadia C. *The Last Word: Women, Death, and Divination in Inner Mani.* Chicago, 1991.

Sewell, William H. *Work and Revolution in France: The Language of Labor from the Old Regime to 1848.* Cambridge, U.K., 1980.

Shalamov, Varlam. *Kolyma Tales.* New York, 1994.

Shearer, David R. *Industry, State, and Society in Stalin's Russia, 1926–1934.* Ithaca, N.Y., 1996.

Sheinin, Lev R. *Zapiski sledovatelia; Voennaia taina: Rasskazy, roman.* Kishinev, 1987.

Siegelbaum, Lewis H. "Defining and Ignoring Labor Discipline in the Early Soviet Period: The Comrades-Disciplinary Courts, 1918–1922." *Slavic Review* 51 (1992): 705–731.

——. *Stakhanovism and the Politics of Productivity in the USSR, 1935–1941.* New York, 1988.

Siegelbaum, Lewis H., and Andrei Sokolov. *Stalinism as a Way of Life: A Narrative in Documents.* New Haven, Conn., 2000.

Siegelbaum, Lewis H., and Ron Suny, eds. *Making Workers Soviet: Power, Class, and Identity.* Ithaca, N.Y., 1994.

Slatter, John. "Communes with Communists: The *sel'sovety* in the 1920s." In *Land Commune and Peasant Community in Russia: Communal Forms in Imperial and Early Soviet Society.* Ed. Roger Bartlett, 272–287. London, 1990.

Slavko, T. I., ed. *Sotsial'nyi portret lishentsa (na materialakh Urala), sbornik dokumentov.* Ekaterinburg, 1996.

Slezkine, Yuri. *Arctic Mirrors: Russia and the Small Peoples of the North.* Ithaca, N.Y., 1994.

Sobranie uzakonenii i rasporiazhenii raboche-krest'ianskogo pravitel'stva RSFSR. 1918-RSFSR.

Sobranie zakonov i rasporiazhenii raboche-krest'ianskogo pravitel'stva SSSR. 1923-USSR.

Sokolov, Yuri M. *Russian Folklore.* Trans. Catherine Ruth Smith. Hatboro, Penn., 1966.

Solomon, Jr., Peter H. *Soviet Criminal Justice Under Stalin.* New York, 1996.

Solzhenitsyn, Aleksandr I. *The Gulag Archipelago, 1918–1956: An Experiment in Literary Investigation.* Trans. Thomas O. Whitney. New York, 1975.

Sovetskaia prokuratura: sbornik vazhneishikh dokumentov. Moscow, 1972.

Spravochnik po vyboram v Moskovskii i raionnye sovety (Moscow, 1929).

Spirin, L. M. *Klassy i partii v grazhdanskoi voine v Rossii.* Moscow, 1968.

Steiner, George. *Real Presences.* Chicago, 1989.

Steinmetz, George. "Reflections on the Role of Social Narratives in Working-Class Formation: Narrative Theory in the Social Sciences." *Social Science History* 16 (1992): 489–517.

Stites, Richard. *Revolutionary Dreams: Utopian Vision and Experimental Life in the Russian Revolution.* Oxford, U.K., 1989.

Stoler, Ann Laura. "Sexual Affronts and Racial Frontiers: European Identities and the Cultural Politics of Exclusion in Colonial Southeast Asia." In *Tensions of Empire: Colonial Cultures in a Bourgeois World.* Ed. Frederick Cooper and Ann Laura Stoler. Berkeley, Calif., 1997.

Suny, Ronald Grigor. *The Revenge of the Past: Nationalism, Revolution, and the Collapse of the Soviet Union.* Stanford, Calif., 1993.

Tambiah, Stanley J. "A Performative Approach to Ritual." *Proceedings of the British Academy* 65:113–169.

Tikhonov, V.I., et al. *Lishenie izbiratel'nykh prav v Moskve v 1920–1930–e gody.* Moscow, 1998.

Torpey, John. *The Invention of the Passport: Surveillance, Citizenship, and the State.* Cambridge, U.K., 2000.

Trifonov, I. Ia. *Likvidatsiia ekspluatatorskikh klassov SSSR.* Moscow, 1975.

———. *Ocherki istorii klassovoi bor'by v SSSR, 1921–1937.* Moscow, 1960.

Tucker, Robert, and Stephen Cohen, eds. *The Great Purge Trial.* New York, 1965.

Turner, Victor. *Dramas, Fields, and Metaphors.* Ithaca, N.Y., 1974.

Ukhanov, K. *Perevybory sovetov v Moskovskoi derevne.* Moscow, 1929.

Unger, Jonathan. *Education Under Mao: Class and Competition in Canton Schools, 1960–1980.* New York, 1982.

Van Gennep, Arnold. *The Rites of Passage.* Chicago, 1960.

Verner, Andrew. "Discursive Strategies in the 1905 Revolution: Peasant Petitions from Vladimir Province." *Russian Review* 54, no.1(1995): 65–91.

Viola, Lynne. "The Other Archipelago: Kulak Deportations to the North in 1930." *Slavic Review* 60 (2001): 730–756.

———. *Peasant Rebels Under Stalin.* Oxford, U.K., 1996.

———. "The Second Coming: Class Enemies in the Soviet Countryside, 1927–1935." In *Stalinist Terror: New Perspectives.* Ed. J. Arch Getty and Roberta T. Manning, 65–99. Cambridge, U.K., 1993.

Volodarskii, P.G., and P.V. Terekhov. *Izbiratel'noe pravo i revoliutsionnaia zakonnost'.* Moscow, 1930.

Von Geldern, James, and Richard Stites. *Mass Culture in Soviet Russia: Tales, Poems, Movies, Plays, and Folklore, 1917–1953.* Bloomington, Ind., 1995.

V.I. Lenin i I.V. Stalin o sovetskoi konstitutsii. Moscow, 1936.

Weiner, Amir. *Making Sense of War: The Second World War and the Fate of the Bolshevik Revolution.* Princeton, N.J., 2001.

Werbner, Richard P. "Atonement Ritual and Guardian-Spirit Possession Among Kalanga." *Africa* 34 (1964): 221–222.

White, Hayden. "The Value of Narrativity in the Representation of Reality." In *On Narrative.* Ed. W.T.J. Mitchell. Chicago, 1980.

Wood, Elizabeth A. *The Baba and the Comrade: Gender and Politics in Revolutionary Russia.* Bloomington, Ind., 1997.

Worobec, Christine, "Witchcraft Beliefs and Practices in Prerevolutionary Russian and Ukrainian Villages." *Russian Review* 54 (1995): 165–187.

Zaitsev, P. *Kto i pochemu sovetskaia vlast' lishaet izbiratel'nykh prav.* Moscow, 1931.

234 Selected Bibliography

Zakonodatel'stvo o lishenii i vosstanovlenii v izbiratel'nykh pravakh. Leningrad, 1930.

Zemskov, V. N. "Spetsposelentsy." *Sotsiologicheskie issledovaniia, vol.* 11 (1990).

Zolotarskii, N. *Sel'sovety, gorsovety, s'ezdy sovetov: novaia instruktsiia o vyborakh* (Leningrad, 1926).

Index

235